MICHIGAN

STATE AND NATIONAL PARKS

A COMPLETE GUIDE

FOURTH EDITION

TOM POWERS

Thunder Bay Press

MICHIGAN STATE AND NATIONAL PARKS
A COMPLETE GUIDE
FOURTH EDITION

ALL PHOTOS BY TOM AND BARB POWERS EXCEPT WHERE CREDITED.
BOOK AND COVER DESIGN BY JULIE TAYLOR.

PUBLISHED BY
THUNDER BAY PRESS
HOLT, MICHIGAN

ISBN 10: 1-933272-08-2
ISBN 13: 978-1-933272-08-5

ORIGINALLY PUBLISHED BY FRIEDE PUBLICATIONS:
FIRST EDITION FIRST PRINTING, MARCH 1989
FIRST EDITION SECOND PRINTING, NOVEMBER 1989
FIRST EDITION THIRD PRINTING, DECEMBER 1991
SECOND EDITION FIRST PRINTING, APRIL 1993
SECOND EDITION SECOND PRINTING, JUNE 1994
SECOND EDITION THIRD PRINTING, JULY 1995
THIRD EDITION FIRST PRINTING, MAY 1997
REVISED THIRD EDITION FIRST PRINTING, MAY 2001

PUBLISHED BY THUNDER BAY PRESS:
FOURTH EDITION FIRST PRINTING, APRIL 2007

PRINTED IN THE UNITED STATES OF AMERICA BY MCNAUGHTON & GUNN, INC.

For Barb

Contents

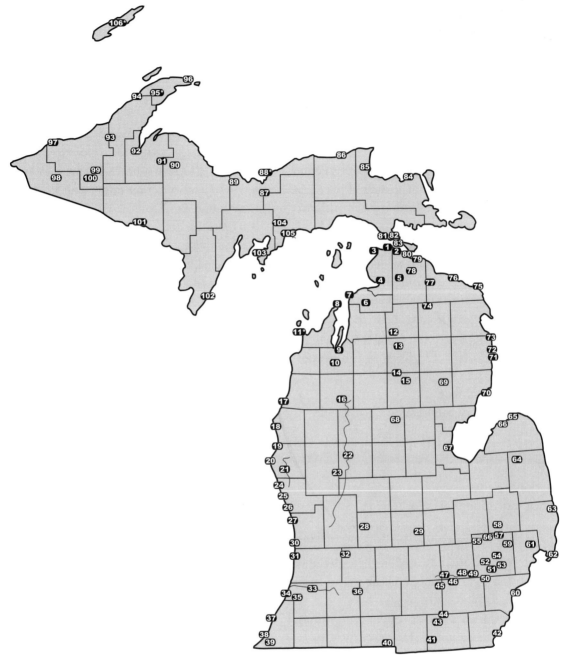

Preface

Fees

State Parks

A motor-vehicle permit is required to enter all state parks. Good for the date of purchase only, a Michigan resident daily permit costs $6, non-resident permit costs $8. A Michigan resident annual vehicle sticker costs $24 and allows the vehicle to which it is affixed and its occupants unlimited entry into any and all state parks during the calendar year it is issued. A senior permit for those people over 65 costs $6. A non-resident annual vehicle sticker costs $29. A towed vehicle permit costs $6.

Campground fees:

Modern campground sites	$16 – $33
Semi modern	$16
Rustic	$10 – $14
Equestrian	$17

National Parks

See individual parks for fees.

Schedule

Except for those indicated in the individual descriptions, parks are open year round from 8 a.m. to 10 p.m. daily.

Campgrounds are also open year round, unless otherwise noted. However, water systems in many parks are turned off from middle or late fall to spring. Dates can vary.

Reservations

The Michigan Department of Resources provides two easy ways to reserve camping sites at state parks. You can call 800-44PARKS (447-2757) or go online to http://www.midnrreservations.com/index.cfm.

If you have access to the Internet reserving online is by far the best method because it enables you to reserve specific sites at any state park campground and also provides you with the approximate size of the campsite, distance to restrooms, whether it is level or uneven, and the maximum length of RV the site can accommodate.

Reservations are only accepted 6 months or less in advance. At one time no more than 80 percent of a park's campsites could be reserved, but that policy has changed, and today, 100 percent of campsites can be reserved in many parks. This, of course, sharply curbs those spur of the moment, "Let's go camping," urges.

A non-refundable $8 reservation fee is charged, and you must secure your reservation with a Mastercard, Visa, American Express or Discover Card. You may cancel your reservation before 3 p.m. on the day of check-in, but you will be charged a $10 cancellation fee in addition to forfeiting the reservation fee.

At many parks you can not make a Friday or Saturday only reservation. The maximum reservation time and site occupancy at all parks is 15 days.

Online reservations can be made 24 hours a day, seven days a week. You can make reservations by phone year round Monday through Friday from 8 a.m. to 8 p.m. and on weekends from 9 a.m. to 5 p.m.

Rent-A-Tent & Tepee

Although the Rent-A-Tent program is all but phased out in favor of mini cabins, there are still a very few state park's where you can rent a wall tent or an Indian-style tepee. The tents and tepees are set up and equipped with bunk beds and sleeping pads. All other camping equipment must be supplied by the camper.

Parks that have tents or tepees are Cheboygan, Interlochen, Wilson, and Warren Dunes. If you are interested in renting one you should call the parks before progressing too far with your travel plans because the status of this service can change rapidly. The rental fee is $30.

PICNIC SHELTERS

If you're planning a group outing and want to insure you're not rained out, you can rent picnic shelters at the parks that have them. The rental fee is approximately $50 – 85 a day. When shelters are not reserved or rented, they're available – first-come, first-served – at no cost to anyone who uses them.

RUSTIC CABINS

For a unique overnight state-park experience, you can rent one of five dozen-plus rustic cabins that are scattered among 17 different parks. In addition to the often rustic and Spartan charm of the cabins is the fact that they nearly always sit in splendid isolation, well away from the park's other facilities.

The cabins vary greatly in sleeping capacity – anywhere from four to 24 – but otherwise are essentially the same: near primitive. Construction is basic – a large single room with finished logs walls and a cement floor. Furnishings are usually Spartan: twin beds or bunk beds with foam rubber pads, a small table with chairs, a broom, a pot-belly stove, and a stack of fire-wood. You have to tote your own water from an outside hand pump, and bathroom facilities consist of vault toilets. That said, furnishings vary greatly from park to park. Cookware, tableware, a coffee pot, an axe and even a mop can be found in the 19 cabins in Porcupine Mountains Wilderness Park while the rustic cabin at Highland Recreation Area reaches the heights of luxury with running water, a stove and refrigerator and, oh yes, a water softener. It's standard practice to call the park and find out what is supplied.

You will have to bring your own linens, cleaning supplies, flashlight, towels, toilet paper, pillows, lantern, portable cooking stove and first-aid kit. Usually you don't have to lug it all on your back. Though most cabins are in quiet, secluded spots (many overlooking water), you can often drive right up to most of them, even in the winter.

Reservations are a must and as far in advance as possible; even more than a year in advance is acceptable. Make reservations directly, preferably by phone, with the park at which you wish to stay. Parks that have rustic cabins are Bald Mountain, Brighton, Cheboygan, Craig Lake, Fort Custer, Hartwick Pines, Highland, Holly, Island Lake, McLain, Porcupine Mountains, Port Crescent, Rifle River, Van Riper, Warren Dunes, Waterloo, Wells, and Wilderness.

The rental fee is $60 – 80 per night. Dogs are not allowed in the cabins.

MINI-CABINS

A step down from the rustic cabins are the 63 mini-cabins found in 37 parks. The small bare-bones structures measure 12 feet square, sleep four (six if you put the kids to bed on the floor), and are equipped with electric lights, one electric outlet, and a small table. Each cabin has a picnic table and a fire ring outside. A few mini-cabins in the Upper Peninsula come equipped with electric heat. All mini-cabins are located on a campsite within the park's campground. Although the mini-cabin has no indoor plumbing, the campground's modern restrooms are never more than a short walk away. You must provide your own bedding, cookware, tableware, cooler and camp stove. No pets are allowed in the cabins, which rent for $45 per night.

MODERN CAMPING HANDICAPPED ACCESSIBLE

Handicapped accessible sites in modern campgrounds usually feature extensive areas of asphalt surrounding the spot where the RV is set-up. They are also often located near modern restroom facilities.

Introduction

The appearance of this Fourth Edition of *Michigan State and National Parks: A Complete Guide* marks the 18th straight year the book has been in publication. During the nearly two decades in which it has guided readers to a wealth of outdoor activities, scenic spots and some of the finest vacation destinations in the Great Lakes Michigan's park system has undergone significant changes and modernization.

When the first edition of this book came out the state park system was just emerging from a long period of stagnation. Worn and ragged facilities and basic services were slowly improving. The passage of Proposal P in 1994 signaled a 17% annual increased in operating funds and the rate of change intensified.

The improvements begun in the mid 1990s continued well into the new century and are evident in most state parks. New restroom facilities have been built throughout the park system, services have been upgraded, interpretive programs have multiplied, and campground layouts have been altered to enhance the camping experience.

Parks have continued to reduce the number of sites in their campgrounds in order to protect threatened habitat, provide space for larger RVs and ease crowding. Pull-through lots have been added to many campgrounds as has 50 amp electrical service. A few state parks even have wireless Internet service areas.

Where there used to be approximately 90 state parks there are now over 100 including two new scenic waterfall sites in the UP and Michigan's first urban state park on the Detroit River only a couple of blocks from the RenCen Center. Three state park campgrounds – Holland, Hartwick Pines and Sterling – offer full hookups (water, sewer and electrical) at most but not all of their campsites.

It's now possible for a camper to choose and reserve a specific camping site in any state park by going online to make reservations. During the reservation process campers are presented with a campsite map of the park that at a glance shows how far any campsite is from the beach or restrooms, where the mini-cabin sits within the campground, and the location of the handicapped accessible sites. When clicking on the campsite number, you will be told if the lot is in sun or shade, its approximate dimensions, whether it's covered with grass or dirt, and if it has a pad. Ten years ago it was pot-luck when reserving a site by mail or phone; today it's like ordering a pizza.

But if much has changed, even more has stayed the same. If you like to do it in the out-of-doors there's a very good chance you can do it in Michigan's state and national parks. Horseback riding, dog sledding, hot-air ballooning, hang gliding, hiking, birdwatching, skiing (downhill and cross-country), hunting, trap shooting, boating, swimming, sliding down an iced tunnel on a luge, fishing, picnicking, walking through a ghost town, archery, snowmobiling, riding a dune buggy over a mountain of sand, exploring living museums, spending the night in a tepee or pedaling a mountain bike over terrain that a donkey would find challenging are only some of the activities regularly pursued in our parks.

As always, laying in wait for park visitors are thousands of unforgettable sights, from the spectacular, overpowering vistas of our inland seas to delicate wildflowers nearly hidden underfoot. It's possible to frame many of the scenes through a vehicle window; others come through binoculars or from under the brim of a sweat-stained hat during a hard day of hiking. Natural beauty is as close at hand as a state park in southern Michigan that serves as an oasis at the fringes of urban sprawl, or as distant as a long drive, followed by a six-hour boat ride to Isle Royale National Park.

Each park is a unique blend of often unmatched scenery and opportunities for solitude or activity. Each presents a different way to relax, renew your body and spirit ... to just plain get away from it all. When you vacation in one of our state or national parks, you'll discover you couldn't spend your travel dollar more wisely.

New Developments

The biggest news in the state park system, since the release of the third edition of this book, is the recent introduction of two new and very different rental units at some parks.

Yurts

As this book goes to press, two state parks – Porcupine Mountains and Pinckney – offer visitors the opportunity to stay the night in a yurt. Based on the traditional Mongolian circular tent with a nose-cone shaped canvas roof, the DNR version is a sixteen-foot diameter tent-like structure with a tight-fitting door and large windows and is snugly weather-resistant. Where the Mongolian yurt was on wheels and highly mobile, the ones found in the state parks are non-nomadic. They come equipped with bunk beds, table and chairs, are heated by wood or propane stoves, and can be rented year round. Yurts can be reserved online, just like campsites or mini cabins. Pets and smoking are not allowed.

The Pinckney yurt can be reached by car, foot or mountain bike and lies close to both Half Moon Lake and the Potawatomi Trail. It sleeps five and offers guests neither electricity nor running water or modern restroom facilities.

Porcupine Mountains boasts three yurts, all of which are accessible by foot trails only. Each sleeps four and is equipped with a wood stove, cook stove, bow saw, cooking and eating utensils, and an outhouse. Water has to be packed in.

Planning is actively underway to introduce the Mongolian equivalent of the covered wagon at numerous parks within the next few years.

Lodges

In a bid to garner at least a small share of the high end tourist trade, the DNR is converting some of their park's former manager residences into lodges they rent to the public by the day or week. The newly remodeled lodges vary from architecturally stunning log or stone homes built by the CCC to a typical house found in a circa 1960s subdivision. But all of them offer visitors the opportunity to vacation with the family surrounded by virtually every modern convenience one usually leaves at home when traveling to a Michigan state park. It is expected more lodges will be added in the future. Each of the new luxury digs currently available for rent are fully described in the chapter on lodges (page 258).

Symbols

Activities and Attractions

Biking

Birdwatching

Boat Ramp

Bridle Trail

Canoe

Cross-country Skiing

Field Trial Area

Fishing

Hiking

Historical Attraction

Hunting

Interpretive Programs

Lighthouse

Metal Detecting Area

Picnic Area

Picnic Shelter

Playground

Scenic Attraction

Shooting Range

Snowmobiling

Swimming

Visitor Center

Waterfall

Wildlife Watching

Overnight Accommodations

Boat Slip

Canoe Camping

Equestrian Camping

Frontier or Rustic Cabins

Mini Cabins

Modern Camping

Modern Camping Handicapped Accessible

Organization Camping

Rent-A-Tent

Rustic Camping

Semi-modern Camping

Tepee / Yurt

Colonial Michilimackinac

Mackinac State Historic Park

OVERNIGHT ACCOMMODATIONS: NONE

ACTIVITIES:

The Straits of Mackinac vibrate, not from the endless line of cars and trucks crossing the Mackinac Bridge, but with history. Centuries ago, Native Americans, explorers, soldiers and fur traders all passed through this crossroads of the Great Lakes. When you stand on the wave-lapped shore today, it isn't hard to imagine Indians pulling fishnets made of twisted-bark rope, French voyageurs paddling by in huge canoes piled high with furs, Father Marquette setting out on one of his explorations, or soldiers standing lonely vigils over the frontier's northernmost outpost.

Fortunately, you don't have to depend entirely on your imagination. A piece of the romantic Straits area is kept very much alive at the tip of the Lower Peninsula inside Colonial Michilimackinac State Historic Park.

The French constructed the fort on this site in 1715 to replace a crude palisade on the north side of the Straits. For the next several decades, explorers set out from the outpost to penetrate the unknown continent, and military expeditions were dispatched to fight in several wars. By 1761, when the British took over, Fort Michilimackinac also controlled a vast Northwest fur trading empire. Two years later Indians nearly wiped out the garrison in one of the most famous massacres in Michigan history. The British returned in 1781, when they moved to a new, more easily defensible installation on Mackinac Island and abandoned Fort Michilimackinac to the shifting sands and creeping vegetation.

When the village of Mackinaw City was laid out in the 1850s, the fort site was designated as a city park, and in 1904 that piece of land became our second state park. During the 1930s workmen discovered the remains of the palisades and rebuilt the fort walls, but it wasn't until 1959 that archaeologists began serious excavations.

Their years of painstaking work have resulted in the fort being rebuilt to look exactly as it did at the height of its power and influence in the 1770s. The reconstruction is so authentic that Fort Michilimackinac has been designated a National Historic Landmark. Inside the wood gates, the Church of St. Anne, row houses, the blacksmith shop, officer's quarters and other reproductions all stand on the exact location of the originals. Several of the larger structures enclose displays and exhibits of some of the more than one million artifacts archaeologists have discovered in the half of the fort area they have unearthed to date. If you visit from early June to late August you can watch archaeological digs in progress.

This is truly living history. When you look into many of the buildings, you get the eerie feeling that the original inhabitants must have left just minutes before. In others people in authentic period-dress practice crafts of the 1770s, or are cooking meals as they

Courtesy of Mackinac State Historic Parks

were prepared over two centuries ago. Booms from cannons, the crack of muskets, a re-enactment of the arrival of Voyageurs and a French Colonial Wedding and Dance and special events such as the re-enactment of the 1763 massacre add more realism and color. This is a place for the ages, and all ages.

The entrance is directly under the south ramp of the Mackinac Bridge and through as good a themed gift shop as you'll find in Michigan.

COUNTY: EMMET
CAMPING SITES: NONE
SCHEDULE: OPEN MAY 4 TO OCTOBER 9.
ADMISSION: ADULTS, $10.00; CHILDREN 6-17, $6.00; CHILDREN 5 AND UNDER, FREE.
DIRECTIONS: TAKE THE LAST EXIT FROM I-75 BEFORE THE MACKINAC BRIDGE AND FOLLOW THE SIGNS.
FURTHER INFORMATION:
COLONIAL MICHILIMACKINAC, P.O. BOX 873, MACKINAW CITY, MI 49701; 231-436-4100; WWW.MACKINACPARKS.COM

Map Key:
1. Native American Encampment
2. Water Gate
3. Cannon Firing Demonstration
4. King's Storehouse
5. Commanding Officer's House
6. Parade Ground
    Musket Demonstration
7. Military Latrine
8. Northwest Rowhouse
    Entrance, Archaeology Exhibit
9. Guardhouse
10. Blacksmith Shop
11. Priest's House
12. Church of Ste. Anne
    French Colonial Wedding
13. Soldier's Barracks: Exhibit
14. Southwest Rowhouse
    Cooking Demonstration
    Trader's Store
15. French Fireplace
16. Solomon/Levy and British Officer's Houses
17. Powder Magazine, original remains
18. Chevalier House
19. Land Gate
20. Barnyard and Corrals
21. Restrooms
22. Archaeology in Progress

Old Mackinac
POINT LIGHTHOUSE

OVERNIGHT ACCOMMODATIONS: NONE

ACTIVITIES:

Old Mackinac Point Lighthouse sits at the northern tip of the Lower Peninsula and has a commanding view of the narrow waters it guarded in the past century. Invariably visitors' eyes are drawn to the grand vista of the Straits while overlooking the lighthouse itself, but the light station is worth a second look. If the tower wasn't capped by a light it could almost be mistaken for a medieval castle keep. The house itself looks like a cross between a 19th century light keepers quarters and the summer retreat of a wealthy Victorian family, except, that is, for the Late Middle Ages castle wall that springs from the north face of the house and overlooks the Straits. The place begs to be explored, and finally that's possible.

The Old Mackinac Point Lighthouse may be well over a hundred years old but it's still the newest attraction in the family of Mackinac State Historic Parks. Beginning in 1892 the lighthouse guided sailors through the Straits of Mackinac until 1957 when the Mackinac Bridge was completed and shipping started using the bridge lights to traverse the crossroads of the Great Lakes (the lighthouse sits just to the east of Big Mac).

COURTESY OF MACKINAC STATE HISTORIC PARKS

The lighthouse was acquired by the Mackinac Island State Park Commission in 1960 and served as the centerpiece of the Mackinac Maritime Park from 1972 until it closed in 1989. Restoration of the station began in 1999 and opened to the public in 2004 as a work in progress. When completed, the light station and its various buildings will look as it did in 1910.

The entrance to the complex is through the 1907 Fog Signal Building that now serves as the entry gate and Lighthouse Museum Store. The lighthouse contains a variety of hands-on exhibits and the restored light keeper's living quarters. Costumed interpreters lead regularly scheduled tours and give

Courtesy of Mackinac State Historic Parks

visitors a real sense of what life must have been like for light keepers and their families, the first of which was a wounded Civil War veteran.

For many, the high point of the tour – literally – is a climb to the top of the light tower. Reaching that pinnacle involves a climb of four stories via 51 steps and a final 11-rung, 8-foot vertical ladder. If you have a fear of heights, or tight places, or you're just not physically up to the climb a new video presentation takes you to the top of the tower without leaving your chair.

County: Cheboygan
Camping Sites: None
Schedule: May 14 – June 8, 9 a.m. to 4 p.m.; June 9 – August 25, 9 a.m. to 5 p.m.; August 26 – October 7, 9 a.m. to 4 p.m.
Admission: Adults $6, Youths (6 – 17) $3.50.
Directions: Take the last exit from I-75 before the Mackinac Bridge (339) and follow the signs to Colonial Michilimackinac Visitors Center. The lighthouse is just to the east of bridge and visitors center.
Further Information: Mackinac State Historic Parks, P.O. Box 873, Mackinaw City, MI 49701; 231-436-4100; www.MackinacParks.com.

Map Key:
A. Fog Signal Building
        Entrance and Tickets
        Lighthouse Museum Store
B. Old Mackinac Point Lighthouse
C. Barn
D. Restrooms
E. Parking

Wilderness State Park

OVERNIGHT ACCOMMODATIONS:	
ACTIVITIES:	

More than 26 miles of coastline shapes Wilderness State Park, a finger of land that points into Lake Michigan at the western end of the Straits of Mackinac. Most of the shore is a broad band of blinding white sand that stretches away to distant headlands. You can wander nearly deserted beaches for days without crossing the same sand twice, or you can wear a single path to and from the water at a favorite spot. Along the string of uninhabited islands that form the finger's tip, picturesque rock outcroppings, not sand, mark the transition from land to lake.

Away from the water, dense forest blankets one the Lower Peninsula's largest tracts of wilderness. The area shelters deer, black bear, bobcats, beaver, coyotes and small game. The park's bird checklist numbers more than 100. Loons and bald eagles nest in the park, the coastline abounds with gulls, terns and waterfowl while the area's dense woods shelter numerous songbirds. A similar guide to wildflowers, with bloom dates, includes several rare and endangered species. Park personnel present programs and hikes throughout the summer that explore the area's natural heritage.

At Wilderness State Park you also have the opportunity for a real change of pace in overnight accommodations; rustic rental cabins. Six of the one-room trail-side cabins, which sleep four to eight, are set in private, exceptionally scenic surroundings. All but one are on their own stretch of beach. The log cabins are furnished with only the bare necessities: a wood stove, bunks with mattresses, a table and chairs, outdoor vault toilets, a hand water pump and unsplit firewood. You have to bring cooking utensils, a cooler, lanterns, an

axe, bedding and other comforts. Three larger, bunkhouse-style cabins, which sleep up to 24, are grouped together near the campgrounds.

All cabins rent for around $70 a night, for up to a 15-night maximum stay, year round. Snowmobilers – although not allowed in the bunkhouse cabins or Nebo Trail area – do, along with cross-country skiers, make heavy use of the trail-side cabins. They usually rent approximately a year and a half in advance, so reservations are a must.

Most overnighters stay at one of two modern campgrounds, both of which receive heavy use throughout the summer. It's best to make a reservation, but park personnel note that, because of a high daily turnover, you have a good chance at finding a vacancy if you arrive before noon except on summer weekends.

A total of 250 sites are split into two areas by the park entrance road. Inland on a wooded bluff, lots 151-250 make up the Pines Campground, which features asphalt pads, good shade, plenty of space and a thick carpet of grass. It's only a short walk to the camper's

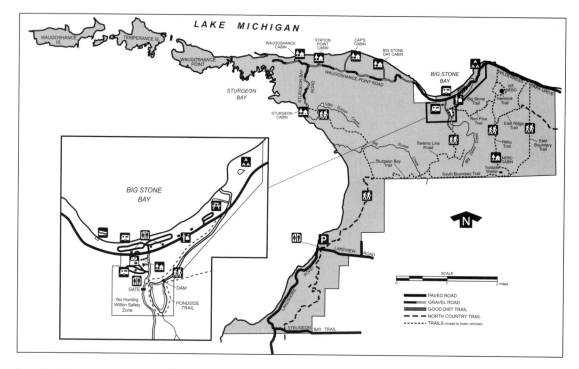

beach plus great views of the Straits from the fine, soft sand edging Big Stone Bay.

Some of the best lakeside camping on the Great Lakes attracts vacationers to the park's 150 sites in the Lakeshore Campground. Campers there give up the grass and spaciousness of the Pines for the sandy, well-worn, shady and often smaller campsites that line the shore four rows deep. Roughly a quarter of the sites are directly on the beach and they are in high demand.

About halfway between the campgrounds and the park entrance, the day-use picnic area lines Big Stone Bay. Tables and grills are nestled among pines and cedars, and you can usually claim a large, private parcel of the wide, sandy beach that extends on both sides of the picnic area. To the east you have

a couple of miles of beach to comb before running into the park's east boundary.

West of the campground, and a small parcel of private land, Waugoshance Point Road burrows a green tunnel through a cedar/pine forest. The scenic, gravel drive is popular with mountain bikers and gives access to four cabins and miles of near-deserted Lake Michigan shoreline. For those looking for a Robinson Crusoe experience, a parking lot on Lakeshore Drive (on the southwestern edge of the park) provides access to miles of seldom-trod beach on Sturgeon Bay. On a good day, the farther north you walk, the further removed is civilization.

Turning inland there are more than 16 miles of trails that range from a leisurely stroll to a day-long tramp through wild, re-

mote backcountry. The park's shortest path, the Pondside Trail, circles a small pond created by the damming of Big Stone Creek. On the north side of the dam Big Stone Trail follows the meandering creek for less than a mile to where it empties into Lake Michigan. Just a few yards south of the dam, the Red Pine Trail cuts east and connects with the Hemlock Trail for a 3.5-mile round-trip nature tour guided by a brochure available at park headquarters. If you really want to do some serious hiking, or simply enjoy being alone in beautiful wilderness, take one of the well-marked 8-, 10- or 11-mile routes that loop from the park road into the vastness of the park's wild backcountry. Mountain bikes are permitted on all trails except Big Stone, Pondside and Red Pine. In the winter cross-country skiers and snowmobilers use the extensive trail system.

Day sailors, fishermen, and pleasure boaters make heavy use of the boat launching ramp west of the campground. The sheltered waters of Big Stone Bay are a summer playground for water skiers and sailboarders, and in June

and July the area surrounding Waugoshance Point is ripe with smallmouth bass.

Much of the park is open to hunting in season. Deer are plentiful, but park rangers say it's a hard area to hunt. Bear, rabbits, woodcock and partridge are also taken. Metal detectors are permitted in certain areas of the park.

Should one's thoughts turn from enjoying the out-of-doors to more touristy pursuits, Mackinaw City's many attractions are 20 minutes away by car and Mackinac Island but an additional short ferry ride away.

County: Emmet
Camping Sites: 250, all modern, plus 6 trailside log cabins and three large bunkhouse style cabins.
Directions: Drive 12 miles west of Mackinaw City on Wilderness Park Drive.
Further Information: Wilderness State Park, Carp Lake, MI 49718; 231-436-5381.

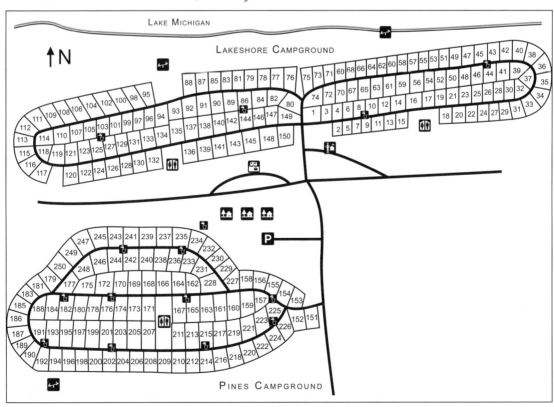

etoskey

State Park

Overnight Accommodations:

Activities:

You can have the best of two world's at Petoskey State Park. If you want to recharge your batteries in a setting of great natural beauty, you can relax on glistening sand that edges the blue waters of Little Traverse Bay or climb soaring, heavily wooded dunes. On the other hand, if and when relaxation flirts with boredom or you want to temper your dune walks with a stroll through two of northern Michigan's most attractive and popular tourist communities, you can make the short drive to Petoskey or Harbor Springs.

The park's shoreline, which punctuates the east end of Little Traverse Bay, certainly holds its own when compared to the many other great beaches along Lake Michigan. The broad expanse of blinding white sand gently arcs for nearly a mile around both sides of the U-shaped bay. There's plenty of room for solitary sunbathing or beachcombing in sand so fine and soft you'll sink up to your ankles. The ends of the park beach point west to distant views of Harbor Springs, on the north side of the bay, and Petoskey on the south. Just a step away from the sand, between the two wings of the day-use parking lot, is a large, modern bathhouse.

Nestled in a low hollow a short distance back from the beach parking lots is a picnic area sheltered by a line of low dunes and canopied by large pines. Be prepared, however, to share your table and maybe your lunch with inquisitive chipmunks and begging gulls.

The park's two campgrounds are among the finest in the Lower Peninsula. All 170 lots have electrical hookups and access to modern restrooms and, all things considered, there isn't a bad site among them. Not surprisingly,

the campgrounds are heavily used, but park officials say that you can occasionally find a vacancy on summer weekdays.

The original 70-site unit, over the dunes behind the beach, is especially appealing because of the natural privacy afforded by some sites. Several of the original sites have been lost to the dunes, while others, still in use are wedged between the between mountains of sand. Retaining walls around other lots keep the dunes from completely engulfing them. Away from the foot of the dunes, trees and shrubs divide sites into secluded, wooded enclaves. Only rarely do any of these sites back up to others. It's a sharp climb over the dunes, or a half-mile drive or bike ride to the beach/day-use area.

Farther south, 100 lots (71-170), divided into four short loops make up the park's newest campground. Nestled in a stand of mature pines and hardwoods, the grass-covered sites (including two with mini-cabins) are fairly private, well shaded, and generally larger than those in the older unit. Paved slips at each lot make for easy setup of trailers and RVs, and nearly two dozen sites are equipped with 50-amp electrical hookups. From anywhere in the unit it's just a short walk to a section of beautiful beach well away from the often crowded day-use area.

Inland, a palisade of high dunes along the east border cuts the 305-acre park off from the sights and sounds of busy M-119. You can get to the top of one of the mountains of sand by taking the Old Baldy Trail. The short route, which starts directly opposite the campers-registration station, is a climb up a series of stairs and steep paths that will literally leave you breathless as you take in the panoramic view of the bay through the trees. Other marked routes skirt the base of the dunes – their height and steepness hidden under a blanket of trees – and swing close to the beach. In the winter, two and a half of the park's three miles of trails, although not groomed, are regularly used by cross-country skiers.

Only minutes away by car, almost equal distances from the park along the north and south shore of the bay are fine restaurants, expensive boutiques, unique gift shops, art galleries, and streets lined with Victorian summer cottages in the small resort towns of Harbor Springs and Petoskey. Both have served as summer playgrounds for the rich and famous for more than a century, and you can easily spend a day and a month's salary in either. Better yet, people-watching is just as much fun in either place and costs nothing. Even better yet, a paved bike trail runs from Petoskey to Harbor Springs and passes the entrance of the park.

Metal detectors can be used in specific areas of the park

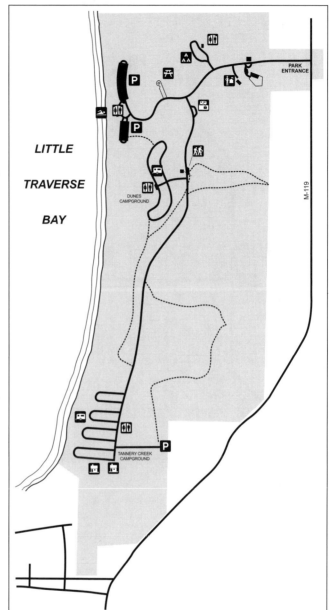

County: Emmet
Camping Sites: 168, all modern, plus two mini-cabins.
Directions: Drive north from Petoskey on US-31 approximately three miles to M-119. Turn north (left) onto M-199 and drive about 1.5 miles to the park entrance.
Further Information: Petoskey State Park, 2475 Harbor Petoskey Road, Petoskey, MI 49770; 231-347-2311.

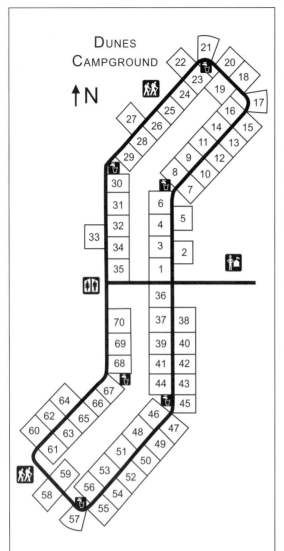

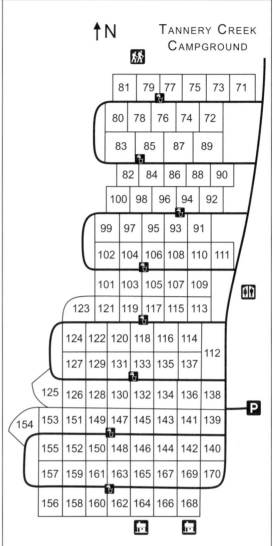

Burt Lake State Park

5

OVERNIGHT ACCOMMODATIONS:

ACTIVITIES:

Burt Lake State Park is a perfect example of why Michigan is called a "water wonderland." The park spreads back from the southeast shore of Michigan's fourth-largest lake, a lake that is a magnet for both pleasure boaters and fisherman. Only minutes away by car are scores of inland lakes, gentle serpentine rivers popular with canoeists and innertube riders and boisterous trout streams. An easy half-hour drive in any of three directions leads to the special character, mood, and beauty of the waters of Lake Huron, Lake Michigan, and the Straits of Mackinac.

But most importantly, Burt Lake is one in a chain of lakes and rivers that make up the Inland Waterway, a 40-mile route across the northern tip of the Lower Peninsula that many claim is one of the most beautiful boat trips anywhere in the country. Boaters can travel any or all of the waterway, which connects Lake Huron at Cheboygan – inland through Mullet, Burt, and Crooked lakes and the Indian, Cheboygan, and Crooked rivers – to Conway, only three air miles from Lake Michigan.

At Burt Lake State Park, which just about marks the halfway point of the route, you can launch your boat or canoe, and then head out on the unique water highway in either direction. If you don't own your own craft, you can rent nearly anything ranging from a rowboat or canoe to a small houseboat from marinas along the Inland Waterway. For a detailed guide to the entire Inland Waterway that includes pictures and maps go to www.fishweb.com/maps/inlandwater on the Internet.

You don't have to go any farther than Burt Lake's 17,000 acres of water for fine fishing, however. The popular, heavily fished lake rates as one of the best in the Midwest for walleyes, and it consistently yields impressive catches of large and smallmouth bass, plus rock bass, plenty of perch, brown and rainbow trout and some northern pike.

The park campground offers both a refuge and respite from a busy day afloat or afield. The grounds are large, and in recent years the number of campsites were reduced from 375 to 306 to ease crowding and allow campers room to sprawl. Most sites provide plenty of shade and some grass, and are large enough to comfortably hold big rigs. The campground contains one mini-cabin. Reservations are almost mandatory to ensure a space on a July or August weekend, but you can usually find a vacancy in midweek if you arrive early in the day. About 10% of the sites cannot be reserved and are filled on a first-come, first-served basis.

North of the campground, tables and grills mix with widely spaced, mature hardwoods and cedars on the large, grassy picnic grounds overlooking the lake. Conveniently located less than a mile from I-75, this picnic

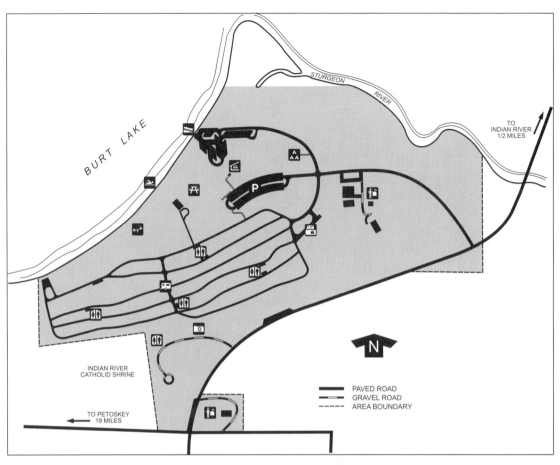

STURGEON RIVER

BURT LAKE

TO
INDIAN RIVER
1/2 MILES

P

N

INDIAN RIVER
CATHOLID SHRINE

TO PETOSKEY
19 MILES

PAVED ROAD
GRAVEL ROAD
AREA BOUNDARY

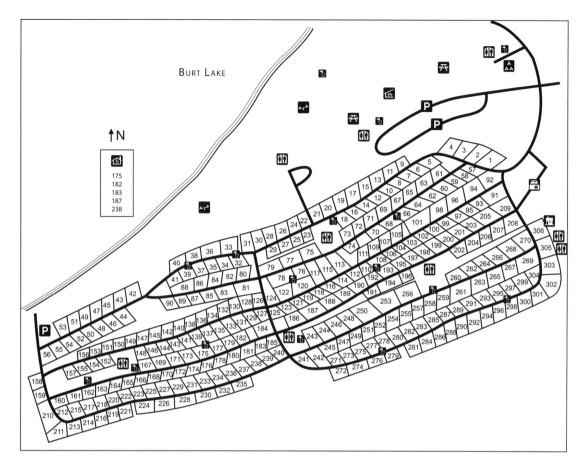

area makes a pleasant break from expressway travel.

An excellent swimming beach with a bathhouse rests near the middle of the park's 2,000 feet of lakefront. There's enough sand to satisfy the most ambitious castle builder, lots of shallow water for wading, and plenty of room for sunbathing or just sitting and enjoying the view. The boat launch ramp lies up the beach to the left.

Park personnel present nature programs throughout the summer or you can seek out your own personal nature adventure on the park's 1-mile hiking trail.

COUNTY: CHEBOYGAN

CAMPING SITES: 306, ALL MODERN, PLUS 1 MINI-CABIN.

SCHEDULE: THE PARK CLOSES (DEPENDING ON SNOWFALL) FROM ABOUT DECEMBER 1 TO MID-APRIL. CALL FOR EXACT DATES.

DIRECTIONS: FROM I-75 TAKE THE INDIAN RIVER EXIT (310) AND GO WEST 0.5 MILES ON M-68 TO OLD US-27. TURN LEFT (SOUTH) AND DRIVE ABOUT A HALF MILE TO THE PARK ENTRANCE.

FURTHER INFORMATION: BURT LAKE STATE PARK, 6635 STATE PARK DRIVE, INDIAN RIVER, MI 49749; 231-238-9392.

OVERNIGHT ACCOMMODATIONS:

ACTIVITIES:

A pleasing mixture of the unexpected and the presumed, Young State Park is easy to love. For instance, with a mile-plus shoreline on Lake Charlevoix, Michigan's fourth-largest inland lake, you would expect a beautiful beach. But after entering the park, you begin to wonder if you will ever see any water. You wind through almost a mile of thick, lush woods just to get to the contact station, where the forested landscape still hides any sight of the lake. Not until you reach one of three campgrounds or the day-use area do you catch a glimpse of the water through the trees.

Then finally, at the picnic area your presumption is verified – you get a close-up look at the beach readers of a northern Michigan newspaper named as their favorite, and one of the finest inland beaches in the state. The wide, sandy strip approaches the water at such a slight angle the lake appears undecided as to just where it leaves off and the land begins. The long expanse of sand often holds shallow pools, left after an overconfident encroachment by waves or from rain that couldn't find its way to the lake without the help of a more-precipitous slope. A beach house allows day-use visitors a place to change into swimsuits. Additionally, unlike most parks where you have to lug cooler and basket seemingly forever before arriving at a table, the parking lot here is conveniently close. Metal detector use is restricted to the campgrounds, beach and picnic areas of the park.

Overnighters are spread among 240 sites in three modern campgrounds that receive very heavy use throughout the summer. Considering the entire park can be reserved in advance, only the hopelessly optimistic should show up here in mid-summer without a reservation and expect to find a vacant campsite.

The best sites – with shade, some privacy, and views of the water from most – are in two adjoining campgrounds, Oak and Terrace, located south of the picnic area. These two campgrounds offer the only lakeside camping in the park. The 147 grass-covered lots at the Spruce Campground, north of the picnic area, are spread in four loops over an open meadow and provide some shade and privacy. Though there are no lakeside lots, it's just a short walk to the beach. Spruce and Terrace Campgrounds each have a mini-cabin.

Extending inland from the rear of the campgrounds are acres of forest that are overlooked or just plain forgotten by most visitors, who focus on the beautiful beach and lake. Casual hikers or those with a purpose such as mushroom hunting, birdwatching or wildflower gazing have their choice of

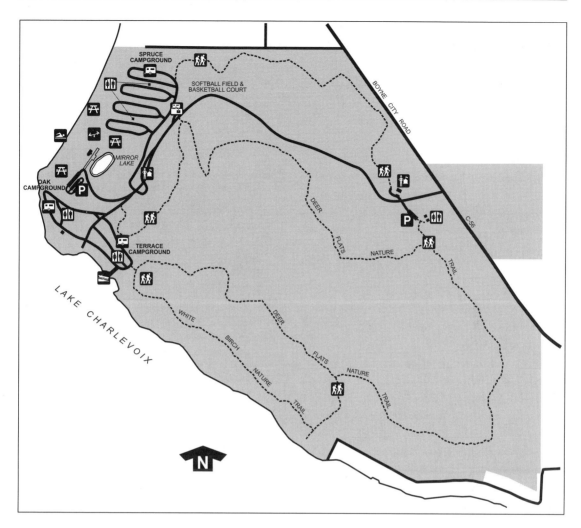

the short White Birch or longer Deer Flats nature trails, which loop through deep, quiet woods. Nature programs that highlight the park's flora, fauna, and natural heritage are offered by park rangers. Cross-country skiers crease the same five miles of trails when the snow flies.

Lake Charlevoix is a playground for sailboats, water-skiers, powerboats, and fishermen. The park's boat launch ramp can handle craft under 16 feet and there are several

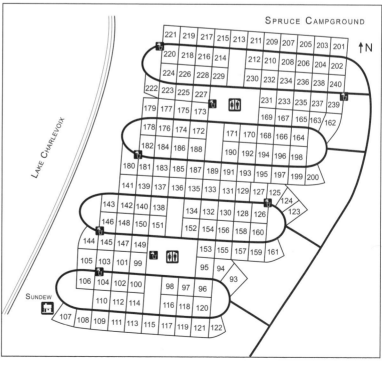

nearby marinas that can launch bigger boats. Fishing is rated good for smallmouth bass, perch and other panfish. Rainbow, brown and lake trout are stocked annually. Mirror Lake, behind the park store, offers good fishing for children and is stocked with sunfish and rock bass.

The resort communities of Charlevoix, Boyne City, and East Jordan, and their many attractions, are all short drives from the park. The nearby village of Horton's Bay is rich in Ernest Hemingway history and hosts the most unusual July 4th Parade in the Midwest.

COUNTY: CHARLEVOIX
CAMPING SITES: 240, ALL MODERN, PLUS TWO MINI-CABINS.
SCHEDULE: OPEN MID-APRIL THROUGH OCTOBER 30TH.
DIRECTIONS: DRIVE 2.5 MILES NORTHWEST OF BOYNE CITY ON BOYNE CITY ROAD.
FURTHER INFORMATION: YOUNG STATE PARK, 02280 BOYNE CITY ROAD, BOYNE CITY, MI 49712; 231-582-7523.

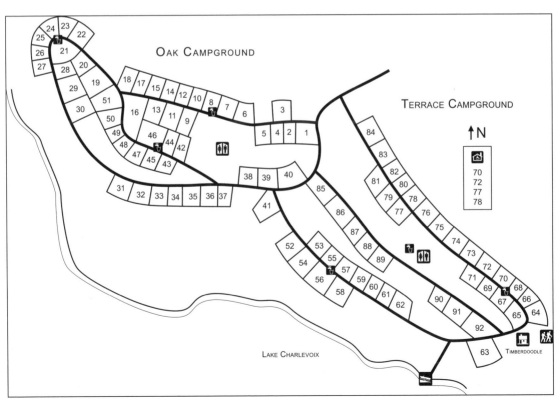

Fisherman's Island
State Park

Overnight Accommodations:

Activities:

Shhh! Don't tell anyone else, but if you'd like to have miles of superb Lake Michigan shoreline and over 2,000 acres of unspoiled wilderness virtually to yourself, go to Fisherman's Island State Park. Compared to other nearby state parks this undiscovered gem is all but ignored by vacationers. Its beautiful 81-site campground is lightly used, even during peak summer months.

It's not hard to figure out why attendance is so low – services and facilities are minimal. The southern half of the park isn't developed at all, and facilities in the northern section are rustic, approaching primitive.

The park's main, partially paved road closely parallels Lake Michigan for almost 3 miles through the northern parcel. A few tables at the southern end of the road make up the park's only picnic area. You can park in a small lot at either end of the road and wander down to the beach.

The shoreline alternates between sand and piles of gravel created by centuries-long pounding of waves on low, exposed outcroppings of soft sedimentary rock. In other places huge boulders poke out of the lake near shore or rest right at the water's edge. The miles of shoreline promise hours of beach combing and plenty of solitude.

The scenic, partially paved road also connects the two widely separated loops of the park's rustic (pit toilets and potable water spigots) campground. Most of the 81 spacious, secluded sites are set on the inland side of the road in the shade of heavy woods. The half dozen widely spaced lots that do line the shore are among the most-scenic camping

spots in the Lower Peninsula. At any of the other lots, though, you're never more than a short walk from the beach as well as hundreds of acres of seldom-trod woods.

The only posted trail slips into the quiet woods near the park entrance and parallels the park road for three miles before emerging from the woods at the southern end of the road. If you're not up to walking the entire distance, you can take either of two short spurs – which cut the trail into three loops of about equal length – back out from the park road. Cross-country skiers can work the trail in winter. Several other unmapped and unmarked paths also penetrate the pine-, cedar-, and hardwood-blanketed terrain. Most of the park is open to hunting, with deer, grouse, and rabbits the game most often pursued.

The park's nearly six miles of Lake Michigan coastline is neatly split at its mid-point by a mile of private property. In the park land south of that partition you will find no restrooms, picnic tables, campgrounds, and rarely a sign; nothing except unsurpassed beauty few people take the trouble to discover. It's not easy, but it sure is worth the effort. The only way into the area – other than your own two feet – is via a rutted, pot-hole

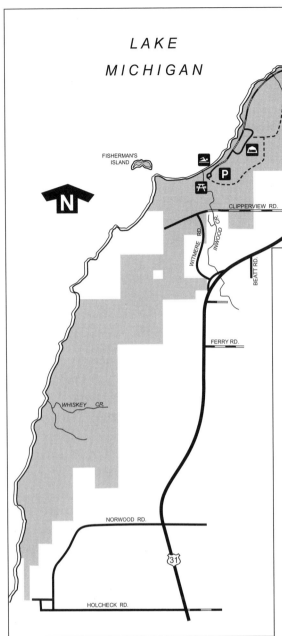

LAKE MICHIGAN

FISHERMAN'S ISLAND

WHISKEY CR.

WITMERE RD.

INWOOD CR.

BEAT RD.

CLIPPERVIEW RD.

FERRY RD.

NORWOOD RD.

HOLCHECK RD.

BELL'S BAY RD.

TO CHARLEVOIX 1.5 MILES

HIKING TRAIL

31

31

N

Part or all of any day walking the mile or so beach on either side of Whiskey Creek will be among the most memorable experiences to be had in northern Michigan. Looking west on a cloudless day, blue meets blue on the distant horizon. On either side, cords of randomly scattered driftwood and occasional treasure troves of Petoskey stones mark wide expanses of white sand that arch out of sight. At your back are thick, cool stands of pine and cedar, probed by unmarked but well-worn paths. Be sure to pack food, water and anything else you consider a necessity, because once here, you'll find it difficult to leave.

When you want to knock the hard edges off of roughing it, fine restaurants, fast food grub, flush toilets, art galleries, fudge shops, gift shops to match any budget, and a drawbridge are all 10 minutes away in the busy little tourist town of Charlevoix.

infested two-track that begins behind the Norwood Township Park in the village of Norwood, then leads north along the shore. First, check on the condition of the road at park headquarters. Then, if you're adventurous or have a four-wheel-drive vehicle, make your way 2.3 miles north along the road until it ends at Whiskey Creek. The more prudent and cautious can drive up the road until ruts and potholes force you into a turnoff, then hike the rest of the way.

No matter how you get there, get there.

COUNTY: CHARLEVOIX
CAMPING SITES: 81, ALL RUSTIC.
SCHEDULE: OPEN EARLY APRIL (WEATHER PERMITTING) TO DECEMBER 1.
DIRECTIONS: FROM CHARLEVOIX, DRIVE 5 MILES SOUTH ON US-31 TO BELL'S BAY ROAD. TURN RIGHT ON BELL'S BAY AND GO 2.5 MILES.
FURTHER INFORMATION: FISHERMAN'S ISLAND STATE PARK, P.O. BOX 456, BELLS BAY ROAD, CHARLEVOIX, MI 49720; 231-547-6641.

Leelanau State Park

OVERNIGHT ACCOMMODATIONS:

ACTIVITIES:

Perched like a crown on top of the peninsula from which it takes its name, Leelanau State Park royally welcomes you with scenic views of Grand Traverse Bay and Lake Michigan, rugged shoreline, untouched woods, a picturesque lighthouse, a grassy picnic area, and a small, secluded campground.

The "crown" is the smaller of the park's two parcels, which total 1,253 acres and are separated by a section of private land. Almost all of the park's facilities have been developed around an historic lighthouse that stands at the edge of that 250-acre tip's rocky shore. The solid, white two-story structure, currently being restored by the Grand Traverse Lighthouse Museum, was built in 1858 as the last in a series of beacons that guided ships into Grand Traverse Bay from the site since 1852. Tours of the lighthouse are given during the summer.

A few hundred feet away, well back from and out of sight of the water, picnic tables, grills and playground equipment are scattered across a large, open, grassy meadow.

In a dense grove of pine and cedar just east of the lighthouse, a 52-site rustic campground, including two mini-cabins, lines one of the few rocky stretches of shoreline along the entire eastern Lake Michigan coast. Amenities here include potable water and pit toilets. Campers do not have access to electricity nor does the park have a dump station where RVers can empty their black and gray water. But, the combination of few sites, great beauty and seclusion add up to

a full campground on most summer weekends, so reservations are a must if you plan to stay here.

All sites are large, deeply shaded and private, and great views of the lake come from most, even those not right on the beach. No matter which site, you won't have far to drag your lawn chair to the rock strewn beach to sit and gaze at the water, soak up some sun, or read in the exceptionally quiet, peaceful surroundings. Because of the rocks, however, it's a less-than-desirable spot to swim but a good place for hunting Petoskey Stones.

A long stretch of wide, sandy beach lines the shore where the park's larger, south section, presses against Lake Michigan. But to get to it you have to hike almost a half mile from the parking area at the end of Densmore Road that intersects with County Road 629 about four miles south of the campground entrance.

From the beach, the 1,000-acre-plus tract sprawls inland and in one area comes close to bridging the narrow strip referred to as the Lower Peninsula's "little finger." Eight miles of hiking and cross-country ski trails loop through the dunes, marsh areas, interdunal wetlands, and deep, cool woods. Branch-

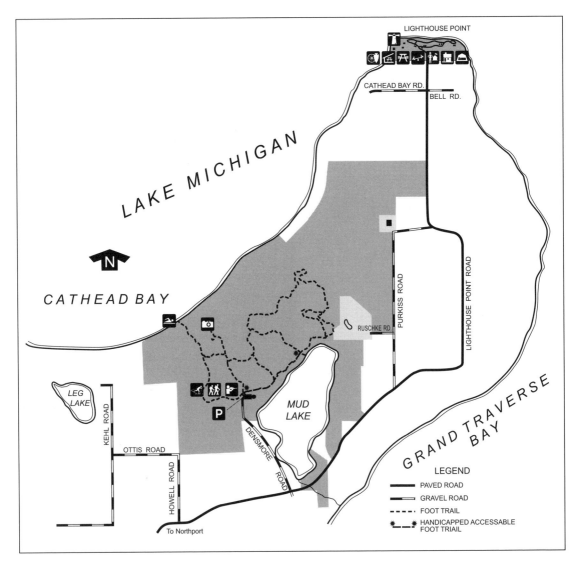

ing from the loops are three short spurs that lead to the beach, a magnificent overlook of Lake Michigan from atop a dune, and to the shoreline of Mud Lake. You probably won't bump into hikers, but you may have to share the path with deer, raccoons, rabbits, fox, porcupine, and other small mammals that are sheltered and fed by the diverse habitat. This section of the park is open to hunting and trapping in season.

Because of its location, Leelanau State Park is excellent for birding. Migrating raptors and songbirds resist crossing open water as long as possible. In spring, as the migrants move north along the Lake Michigan shoreline, the peninsula acts like a giant funnel, and its tip becomes a natural resting place.

Raptors begin moving through the area in early spring and songbird migration usually hits its peak in the first two weeks of May. The dense woods and varied habitat of the park's southern section also attract many summer nesting species.

COUNTY: LEELANAU

CAMPING SITES: 52, ALL RUSTIC, AND TWO MINI-CABINS.

DIRECTIONS: APPROXIMATELY 8 MILES NORTH OF NORTHPORT ON COUNTY ROAD 629.

FURTHER INFORMATION: LEELANAU STATE PARK, 15310 NORTH LIGHTHOUSE POINT ROAD, NORTHPORT, MI 49670; 231-386-5422.

Traverse City

State Park

OVERNIGHT ACCOMMODATIONS:

ACTIVITIES:

You don't go to Traverse City State Park to get away from it all; you go there to be right in the middle of it all. The 47-acre parcel borders busy US-31 and lies near the center of one of the most-expensive zones of commercial real estate in northern Michigan. Restaurants, condominiums, million-dollar homes, a shopping center, expensive gift shops, luxury motels, and at least three elaborate miniature golf courses all share a 2- to 3-mile stretch of highway with the park.

A quarter-million-plus annual visitors have discovered that the park's 343-site campground is one of the least expensive places from which to enjoy one of Michigan's most-attractive vacation areas. To most campers it's a very reasonably priced outdoor resort in the middle of a good time.

Downtown Traverse City, just a few minutes west of the park, offers great shopping, fine dining, a zoo, a museum, and countless other attractions and activities. Ringing the urban area are vineyards, cherry or-

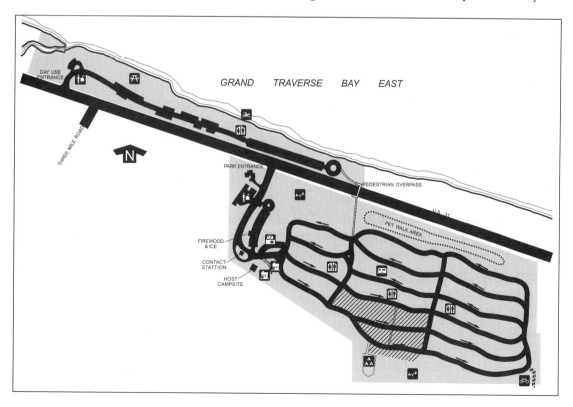

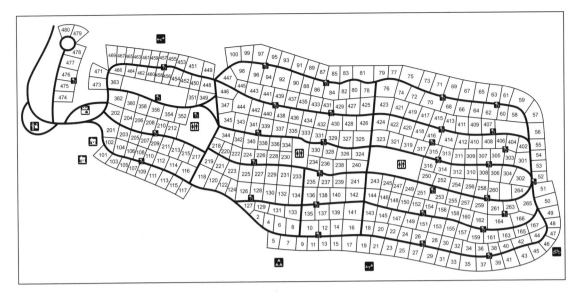

chards, and ubiquitous roadside stands that sell mouth-watering fresh fruit, vegetables and homemade baked goods. Both arms of Grand Traverse Bay and other beautiful scenery are almost always in view, and M-37 – which branches off US-31 less than a mile from the park and runs up to the tip of Old Mission Peninsula – is one of the prettiest drives in the state.

Farther afield, Sleeping Bear Dunes National Lakeshore is less than an hour's drive, and the quaint and scenic vistas of the Leelanau Peninsula add up to a memorable day trip. Anglers can wet a line on any number of inland lakes as well as the bay and several classic trout streams.

Naturally, the campground is always full, with a daily lineup of inquirers hoping for rare vacancies. The only sure way to get a camping spot at any time during the summer is to reserve one well in advance. The campsites have been shoe-horned into nearly every available inch of park property, including an old parking lot. Generally the sites are well worn, heavily shaded and surprisingly large. A section of the campground has been designated pet free. The campground contains three modern restroom buildings (with showers). Two mini-cabins sit near the campground office.

The park is not without its own attractions other than camping. Just across the highway from the campground, via a pedestrian overpass, is a long strip of land along the east arm of Grand Traverse Bay that makes up a day-use area. A fine, sandy swimming beach, with a modern bathhouse, edges the bay at the east end, and picnic tables and grills overlook the blue-green water at the west end.

Immediately south of the camper's playground the Reffitt Nature Trail winds through nearly a mile of mixed hardwoods and pines and presents hikers with views of most northern Michigan ecosystems. If you want to stretch your legs on a longer hike or bike trip, the Traverse Area Recreation Trail is accessible from the southeast corner of the campground. That paved trail generally parallels the railroad tracks and allows bikers to pedal the three miles to downtown Traverse City without having to ride on any major highways. Metal detectors are permitted in certain areas of the park.

County: Grand Traverse
Camping Sites: 342, all modern, and two mini cabins.
Directions: Approximately a mile east of Traverse City limits on US-31.
Further Information: Traverse City State Park, 1132 US-31 North, Traverse City, MI 49686; 231-922-5270.

Interlochen

State Park

OVERNIGHT ACCOMMODATIONS:

ACTIVITIES:

A stay at Interlochen State Park has the feeling of being at a Victorian-era summer encampment where vacationing families were entertained by fine music and educational lectures. Most of the park's quarter-million annual visitor's set up tents or RVs at the state park system's largest campground, then flock to soak up some culture directly across the highway. There, among the pines in this rural, off-the-beaten-track corner of Michigan is the world-renowned Interlochen Center for the Arts. You can tour the complex, which includes the National Music Camp and year-round Arts Academy, and attend daily plays, exhibitions and, under the curving amphitheater of the sky, public concerts performed by both students and visiting guest artists. A schedule of performances is available online at http://www.interlochen.org/arts_festival/festival_calendar or by phone 231-276-9221.

Strains of music also drift on the wind through the parks three campgrounds, which opened in 1917 as the first in the Michigan state park system. They may be old, but they've kept pace, Four hundred twenty-eight of the 490 sites are completely modern, with electrical hookups and access to modern restrooms with showers.

The modern sites are divided into two wings that extent along the west shore of Duck Lake. The spots are generally small, grassy, and deeply shaded by stately, old trees, but most lack privacy. Both wings are laid out like large subdivisions, and it's easy for small children to get lost in the bewildering number of loops that cut through the deep woods. Older youngsters, on the other hand, dodge cars as they whiz along the paved, ready-made race tracks on their bikes.

The south wing has three pull-through sites, two rent-a-tents, tepee, mini-cabin and eleven handicapped accessible sites. The north wing also has a mini-cabin and two

rent-a-tents in addition to five pull-through sites.

Sandwiched between the two wings is a wide, sandy swimming beach backed by a broad meadow. Picnic tables and grills dot the grassy area and also hide in the surrounding woods. Other facilities in the day-use area include a playground, picnic shelter, bathhouse, store/restaurant, and boat rentals. All park users are welcome at a variety of natural programs and hikes presented by rangers throughout the summer.

Across M-137 and slightly south of the modern campground/day-use area is a small, rustic (no flush toilets, showers, or electricity) campground. Sixty spacious, fairly private sites there are widely spaced in the shade of heavy woods on a low bluff overlooking Green Lake.

All 490 sites (more than in any other state park) at the three camping areas fill on most weekends in July and August. Spots usually open in the middle of the week, but driving

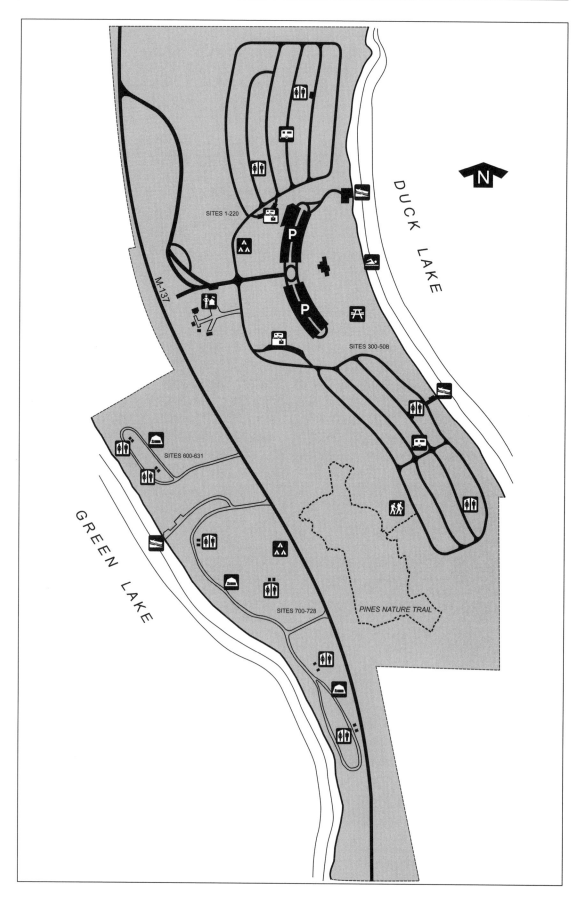

DUCK LAKE

N

SITES 1-220

P

P

SITES 300-508

M-137

GREEN LAKE

SITES 600-631

SITES 700-728

PINES NATURE TRAIL

there without reservations can spoil a vacation.

Though most visitors won't rate the scenery or outdoor activities as their number-one reason for camping at Interlochen, there are natural attractions to fill time between concerts. Several short

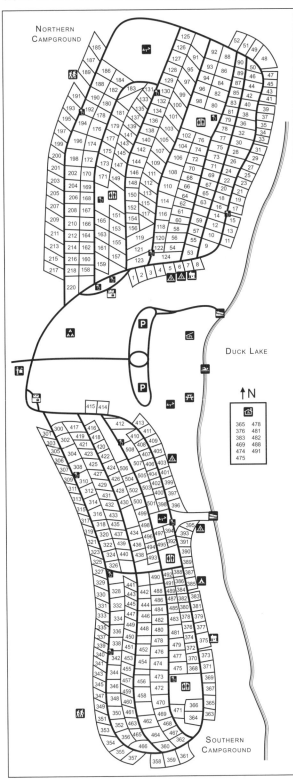

paths, including a self-guided nature trail, wind through a few of the park's 187 acres that aren't developed. The most awe-inspiring are walks in the shadow of 300-year-old virgin white pines that make up one of the last remaining stands in the state. You can also burn off enough calories on a walk to Interlochen, about a mile north of the park on M-137, to indulge in an almost guilt-free ice cream cone at a roadside stand in the small village. Farther afield are more natural attractions at Sleeping Bear Dunes National Lakeshore and the beautiful scenery of the Leelanau Peninsula, or the zoo, museum, tourist attractions, and heavy-duty shopping to be found in Traverse City.

Fishermen wet lines in both Green and Duck lakes, which sandwich the park. Good catches of large and small-mouth bass, panfish, splake, cisco, walleyes, northern pike, and brook, brown, rainbow and lake trout are pulled from both lakes and surrounding rivers and streams.

Boat access comes from a pair of launch sites on Duck Lake and one on Green Lake.

County: Grand Traverse

Camping Sites: 488 (428 modern, 60 rustic), including four rent-a-tents, one tepee and two mini-cabins.

Schedule: The park is open April to November.

Directions: Drive approximately 14 miles southwest of Traverse City on US-131 to M-137. Turn south onto M-137 and go about 1.5 miles.

Further Information: Interlochen State Park, M-137, Interlochen, MI 231-276-9511.

Sleeping Bear Dunes
National Lakeshore

OVERNIGHT ACCOMMODATIONS: 🚐 ⛺ 🏠 ⛺

ACTIVITIES: 🚲 🛶 🎿 🎣 🥾 ☸ 🔫 🚶 🧍 🏕️ 🛷 📷 🚤 🏊 Ⓥ

The beautiful sand-swept beach – often backed by striking dunes and always flanked by the glorious blue-green waters of Lake Michigan – that runs nearly uninterrupted from the Michigan/Indiana border to the Straits of Mackinac is a unique state treasure.

* Numbers in parentheses correspond to numbered hiking trailheads on map.

The 40 miles between Platte Bay and Good Harbor Bay, where the coastline reaches its high point of dramatic natural beauty, has been declared a keepsake of the entire country as the Sleeping Bear Dunes National Lakeshore. There, massive headlands, some that rear up more than 400 feet, shoulder their way out into the lake. Frozen waves of sand top the towering bluffs and, below, march away from the glistening Lake Michigan beaches. Offshore, two beautiful wilderness island retreats stand guard, and inland, sand mixes with forest to form white-and-green necklaces around some of the world's most beautiful small lakes.

There's so much scenery, so much space, and so much to do that you can't possibly take in all of this vast natural area in just one day. The best way to enjoy the sprawling park is a section at a time. Conveniently, both nature and man have divided the national lakeshore land into four distinct parcels, separated either by private property or the waters of Lake Michigan.

CRYSTAL LAKE TO EMPIRE

Most of the action and scenery in this southern section of park land, which drops from high bluffs near Empire to low coastal plains around the mouth of the Platte River, comes on foot. The Empire Bluff Trail (3*), for instance, heads west from a park road just south of the Village of Empire to a breathtaking overlook of Lake Michigan from a bluff that's a popular hang-gliding spot. Farther south, between Otter Creek and the Platte River, a network of old logging roads and the abandoned grade of a narrow-gauge railroad make up most of the 15 miles of hiking and backpacking paths of the Platte Plains Trail (2). The system winds to several scenic overlooks of Lake Michigan, past a ghost town, and along the crests of ancient dunal ridges created during much-higher water levels shortly after the retreat of glaciers. In the heart of the Platte Plains Trail system, near the shore of Platte Bay, and reached only on foot, are a number of rustic backcountry sites at the White Pine Campground.

Just a mile south White Pine, and connected by the trail (2) system, is the park's largest camping area, the Platte River Campground. The 179 sites have access to a building with flush toilets and token-operated hot showers. Walk-in tent sites, group camping spots, pull-through and regular sites for RVs are widely spaced on tree-covered, low, rolling dunes just north, across a road, from the river. The 96 sites with electrical hookups make the Platte River unit the only campground in the park offering this service. Other than group sites it's also the only campground in the park that allows you to reserve any of the sites in advance. Overnighters at this busy area are only about two miles by car and four miles by river from Lake Michigan.

The Platte River dominates the southern quarter of the park as it flows out of Platte Lake and makes its way in lazy S's to Lake Michigan. The stream is popular with tube rafters, canoeists, and especially anglers when king and coho salmon cause a fishing frenzy here in the fall. Boat access to Lake Michigan comes from a ramp at the river-mouth, but the outlet can run very shallow across shifting sand bars.

Near the southern tip of the park, two 2.2-mile loops of the Old Indian Hiking Trail (1) both lead to a scenic overlook of Lake Michigan and the Platte River Dunes. As you can guess from the name, the paths follow parts of an old Indian route.

EMPIRE TO GLEN ARBOR

The park's most strenuous (and rewarding) walks, one of the state's most beautiful picnic areas, one of the nation's most scenic drives, and the world's most famous sand dune complex are packed into this, the heart of the national lakeshore area.

The starting point for all the activity is the Philip A. Hart Visitor Center, in Empire, where you can pick up self-guiding brochures, detailed maps of the trail system, and loads of other information about the park. The Visitor Center presents a variety of programs from campfire talks and nature hikes to historical presentations. Interpretive programs are also offered at the Platte River and D.H. Day campgrounds.

About three miles north of the Center, Pierce Stocking Scenic Drive, one of the most beautiful paved roads in the country, leaves M-109 to loop for 7.6 miles around the top of forested dunes. (If you want to mix beauty with strenuous exercise, pedal the bordering bike path.) Panoramic views along the one-way route come from four observation platforms, one constructed at the very edge of the cliffs, where sand and gravel fall sharply to the shore below. The view from the 450-foot-high crest of the park's largest dune rates as one of the top scenic sights in the state.

Tucked into a shaded, sheltered, grassy area 400 feet atop another area of the gigantic dune is one of the Midwest's most picturesque picnic areas. You can explore on foot from any of the stops, and you may be tempted to skid down the bluff face to the narrow strip of beach. Though it looks inviting, remember, it's a long, tough climb back to the top and highly discouraged by park rangers.

At its northernmost point, the road rises to skirt the edge of the world's most famous sand dune, from which the park takes its name – Sleeping Bear (so named by Indians who thought the then tree-covered bluff looked like a sleeping bear). North of Pierce Stocking Scenic Drive, from a parking lot off M-109, you can climb what looks like a football-field-tall wall of sand and enjoy the fine views of the surrounding countryside including Glen Lake and the Manitou Islands. From the top of the climb a 3.5-mile round-trip trail (7) leads across the broad plateau of sun-baked sand to Lake Michigan. Trail conditions here are hot and dry, and if you leave the trail it's easy to get lost in this Sahara of sand. It is for these reasons the park service advises that you stay on the trail, carry plenty of water and wear a hat, shoes and suntan lotion. A much easier, handicapped

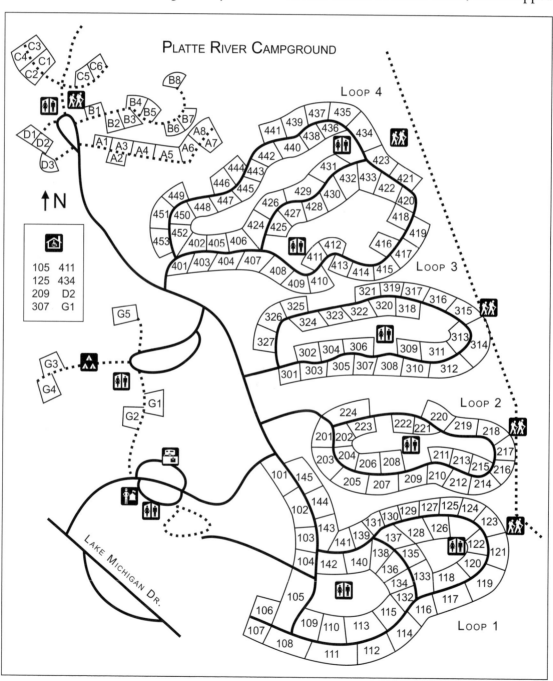

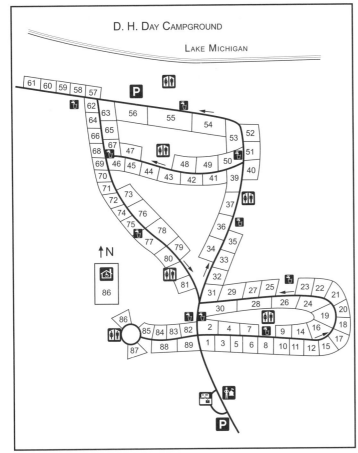

D. H. Day Campground

Lake Michigan

↑N

86

East of Glen Haven, nestled in low, wooded dunes along Sleeping Bear Bay, you will find 88 large, shaded lots at the D. H. Day Campground. The rustic sites (no electricity or modern restrooms) have lots of privacy and lie within a short walk of Lake Michigan. There is a dump station for RVs and generator use is permitted in sites 1 – 31 from 9 a.m. to 6 p.m. Campground use is heavy throughout the summer, but since only the four group sites can be reserved, you can often find a vacancy, especially in midweek.

Glen Arbor to Good Harbor Bay

The restored Olsen farmhouse on Port Oneida Road is one of eighteen farms listed on the National Register of Historic Places in the Lakeshore's Port Oneida Rural Historic District. The Olsen house uses displays, exhibits and maps to tell the story of how farming developed in the area. This is also the site of the annual Port Oneida Fair that recreates the farming experience and pioneer life of the late 1800s.

In this northernmost mainland unit, you can enjoy the same striking scenery as in the rest of the park but without the crowds. Basch and Port Oneida roads both lead to the head of massive Pyramid Point and the start of several hiking trails. A quarter-mile-long branch from one, the 2.5-mile Pyramid Point Trail (12), climbs steeply up the back of the bluff that marks the end of the blunt peninsula. From atop the bluff come spectacular views

accessible, self-guided nature trail edges the base of the dune and passes through open fields and moist woods in its 1.9 mile circuit.

An antidote for the strenuous Dune Climb and hikes lies just across the highway where you can cool off by jumping into Glen Lake at a shallow, sandy swimming beach backed by a few picnic tables. From the highway just up from the beach, side roads lead to the start of several long trails (10) that lope through the landscape north of Glen Lake.

From M-109 farther north, Michigan's shortest highway, M-209, leads to Glen Haven and the Sleeping Bear Point Coast Guard Station and Maritime Museum. U.S. Life Saving Service displays there include a fully restored rescue-boat house, a crew bunkhouse, and a ship pilot house. Trails (9) that begin at the end of the road circle south into a sandy wasteland, with the longest loop measuring 2.8 miles. And while in Glen Haven do not pass up the historic Glen Haven General Store. The small emporium has been restored to its 1920s appearance and carries merchandise typical of a general store of that time period in addition to items related to the history of the area.

of the Manitou Islands, Lake Michigan and on a clear day the Fox Islands, more than 25 miles to the north. You might be in the company of hang gilders who launch from the spot, but you can walk along the crest of the bluff in either direction with little chance of meeting the crowds found in other areas of the park.

From M-22 farther east, County Road 699 ends at miles of beautiful beach that edge Good Harbor Bay. A sand road leads east a few hundred yards to a picnic area and the start of another 2.8 miles of hiking trails (13).

Manitou Islands

Least-accessible, yet near-irresistible, are North and South Manitou islands, the cubs, according to Indian legend, of the sleeping bear on the mainland. You can cross the seven miles to South Manitou on a walk-on ferry, which makes one daily trip from Leland. Trouble is, the boat returns after only five hours, but there's more than a day's worth of things to see and do. The only sure way to take in everything in that short time – albeit, cursorily – is to ride the motor tour.

To see less, but at a more leisurely pace, hike the many old roads that crisscross the island. And be sure to pack a lunch; there are no restaurants or stores on the island.

If you want to fully experience South Manitou, stay the night at one of three primitive campgrounds scattered over its 5,000 acres. You have to backpack in (the closest is a few hundred yards from the boat dock) and low-impact camping methods are a must. You have access to pit toilets and potable water, but no supplies are available.

The island is packed with both natural and man-made attractions. You can walk through a lighthouse, rebuilt in 1871, and the island post office, that now serves as a museum. Old deserted farms dot the interior, and off the southern shore the wreck of the Francisco Morazan, a freighter that ran aground in 1961, juts from the water as mute testimony

to the dangers of the coast. Tucked away in the southwest corner is the Valley of the Giants, a grove of towering virgin white cedar that includes the world's largest specimen.

While South Manitou has minimal facilities, North Manitou has none – no supplies and, away from the reception area, no toilets or potable water. It is 15,000 acres of wilderness about as remote as you can find in the Lower Peninsula. The only way to the island is on a walk-on ferry from Leland. Once there, you can wilderness camp at the single designated campground, near the ranger station, or anywhere else on the heavily wooded island as long as it's more than 300 feet from water and trails.

The ferry also takes hunters to North Manitou in season to thin the deer herd that was introduced on the island in 1927 and managed for a time as a private hunting-preserve herd. The rest of the park is open to hunting, with deer, rabbit, squirrel, ruffed grouse and waterfowl all successfully taken.

During the winter, many trails are open to cross-country skiers. Although the ski trails are not groomed, they are usually well tracked by previous skiers. Many of the trails are marked by color-coded triangular signs. Green, blue and black respectively stand for easy, intermediate and advanced and are based on the steepness of the slopes.

Counties: Benzie and Leelanau
Camping Sites: 251 (179 modern, 88 rustic). Call 1-800-365-2267 for reservations.
Directions: Highways M-22 and M-109 run through the park from Frankfort to Leland.
Further Information: Sleeping Bear Dunes National Lakeshore, 9922 Front Street, Empire, MI 49630; 231-326-5134.
Entrance Fees: Park pass (per vehicle) $10 valid for 7 days; Annual pass $20; Gold Age Passport $10 valid for lifetime.

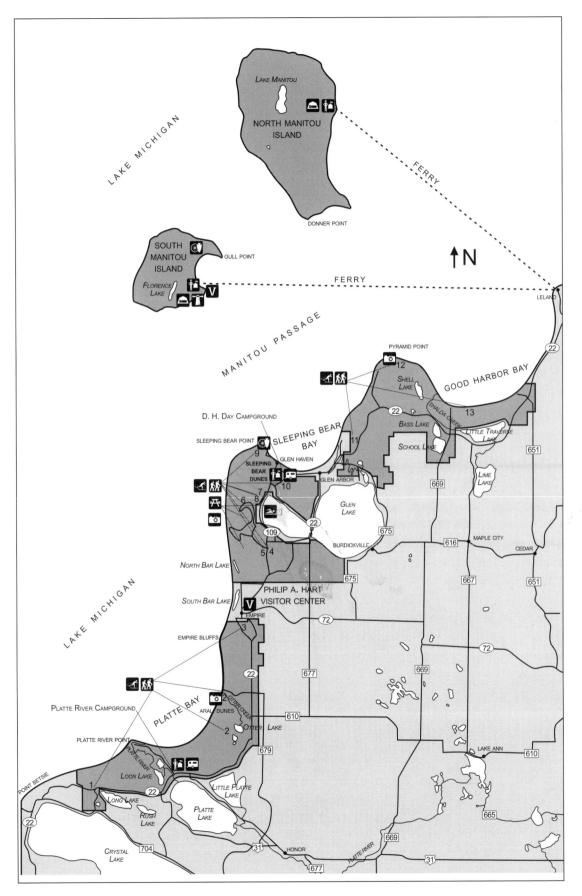

LAKE MICHIGAN

Lake Manitou

NORTH MANITOU
ISLAND

DONNER POINT

FERRY

SOUTH
MANITOU
ISLAND

GULL POINT

Florence
Lake

V

FERRY

LELAND

↑N

MANITOU PASSAGE

PYRAMID POINT

12

Shell
Lake

GOOD HARBOR BAY

22

Shalda Creek

13

Bass Lake

Little Traverse
Lake

D. H. Day Campground

SLEEPING BEAR
BAY

School Lake

651

SLEEPING BEAR POINT

9

SLEEPING
BEAR
DUNES

GLEN HAVEN

11

Lime
Lake

669

10

GLEN ARBOR

7

8

109

6

GLEN
LAKE

675

BURDICKVILLE

616

MAPLE CITY

CEDAR

651

5 4

North Bar Lake

675

667

PHILIP A. HART
VISITOR CENTER

South Bar Lake

V

EMPIRE

72

72

EMPIRE BLUFFS

3

22

677

669

Platte River Campground

PLATTE BAY

2

OTTER CREEK

ARAU DUNES

Otter Lake

610

LAKE ANN

610

PLATTE RIVER POINT

679

LAKE MICHIGAN

1

PLATTE RIVER

Loon Lake

Little Platte
Lake

POINT BETSIE

Long Lake

665

22

Rush
Lake

Platte
Lake

704

31

HONOR

PLATTE RIVER

669

31

CRYSTAL
LAKE

677

31

Otsego Lake
State Park

Overnight Accommodations:

Activities:

If your idea of a great vacation is to set up camp in quiet surroundings, then do little more than park your backsides in a comfortable chair and tend a campfire within view of a beautiful lake, then Otsego Lake State Park may well be your nirvana.

There are no hiking trails and few distractions in this 62-acre park, one of the smallest in northern Michigan. If you do get the urge to move, a first-rate beach, fishing or boating are close at hand. Farther afield, Gaylord and its many golf courses lie a half-dozen miles to the north, with Traverse City, Petoskey, and Mackinaw City all within an hour's drive.

The park's half-mile-plus of Otsego shoreline includes a large, triangular peninsula that noses out into the water near the center. There, nearly surrounded by water and sand, picnickers have their choice of widely spaced tables and grills right at the water's edge or nestled in a quiet, secluded stand of mature red and white pine just a few yards inland. A convenient parking area rests at the base of the peninsula and on the landward side of the lot is a more-open, grassy picnic area with a large adjacent playground. On the northern side of the peninsula, a wide sandy beach and large swimming area front a park store (primarily ice cream and snack foods) and picnic shelter. A second swimming area and playground lie farther up the beach near the park's northern border.

The nearly 5-mile-long, narrow lake is popular with both pleasure boaters and fishermen, who go after perch, pike and tiger muskies. Otsego Lake also rates among the best in the area for smallmouth bass and has a reputation for great walleye fishing. The park's boat ramp is located on the south edge of the peninsula. A fishing pier pokes out into the lake only a few steps to the west of the ramp.

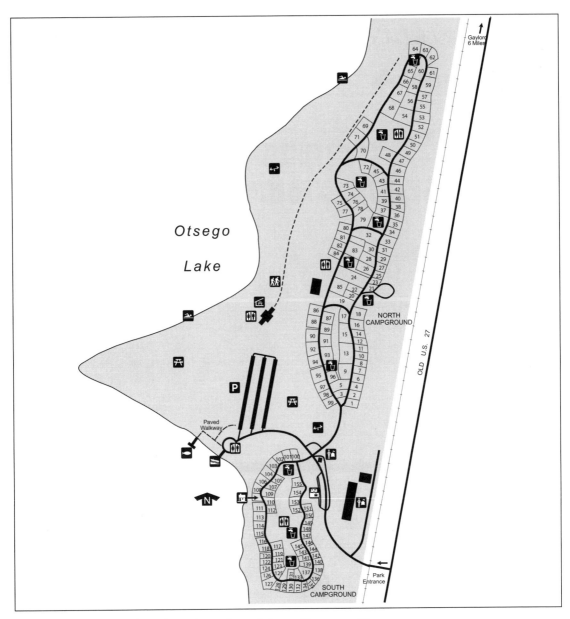

Strung out behind and to the sides of the peninsula is the park's modern campground, with mostly shaded, generously sized, well-worn and level sites divided into north and south loops. The northern camping ring sits on a tree-covered bluff with several scattered sets of stairs leading from the unit down to the water's edge. The smaller southern loop is closer to the water but numerous sites in both loops offer pleasing views of the lake.

Although there is some room to wander and a few informal pathways, the park contains no designated hiking trails. Metal detectors are permitted in some areas.

COUNTY: OTSEGO

CAMPING SITES: 155, ALL MODERN WITH 4 HANDICAPPED ACCESSIBLE, PLUS ONE MINI-CABIN.

SCHEDULE: OPEN YEAR-ROUND, BUT CAMPING IS ONLY AVAILABLE FROM LATE APRIL TO NOVEMBER 1.

DIRECTIONS: FROM I-75 TAKE EXIT 270 (WATERS) AND GO WEST LESS THAN HALF A MILE TO OLD US-27. TURN RIGHT (NORTH) AND DRIVE ABOUT 3 MILES.

FURTHER INFORMATION: OTSEGO LAKE STATE PARK, 7136 OLD US-27 SOUTH, GAYLORD, MI 49735; 989-732-5485.

Hartwick Pines
STATE PARK

13

OVERNIGHT ACCOMMODATIONS:

ACTIVITIES:

A hundred fifty years ago, you could have walked just about anywhere and everywhere in the northern regions of our state through magnificent white-pine forests. But by the turn of the 20th century, 160 billion board feet of the timber had been harvested, a near clear-cutting that yielded more wealth than all the gold mined in California but left us with little more than the lore and legends of lumberjacks and logging camps. That colorful, bygone way of life, plus an awesome glimpse at what northern Michigan looked like before it fell to axes and saws are both preserved at Hartwick Pines State Park.

Be sure to begin your visit at the Michigan Forest Visitor Center, a 1,500-square-foot exhibit hall filled with hands-on exhibits, dioramas, and even a talking tree. Together they tell the story of the natural origin of Michigan's once magnificent forests, recount the colorful history of the state's lumbering era, and explain the development of modern forest management. A 14-minute, nine-projector, multi-image slide program continuously showing in a 105-seat auditorium complements and expands on the lessons learned in the exhibit hall.

From the rear door of the Center a paved trail winds through the spiritual heart of the park; a 49-acre tract of old growth white pine and an adjacent lumbering museum. The path, named the Old Growth Forest Foot Trail, is one of the most memorable short walks in the state. In the shadows of the towering old pines, voices are hushed and no one rushes. You can't help but pause – often to contemplate, almost in spiritual awe, the beauty, grace, and noble bearing of these relics of Michigan's past, some of which are well over 300 years old and approach 150 feet in

height. The Center and trail are handicapped accessible.

From the pines the route gently winds to a logging museum that includes replicas of a bunkhouse, mess hall, camp-store, and blacksmith shop, which re-create the atmosphere of an authentic old-time logging camp. You don't have to spend much time at the complex to get the feeling that cutting timber from sunup to sundown, six months a year, for a dollar a day plus room and board wasn't a glamorous job. Scattered around the grounds near the museum are some large tools of the trade, such as a steam-powered sawmill and 10-foot-high logging wheels used to drag huge logs out of the woods.

To fully enjoy and appreciate the Old Growth Forest Foot Trail, join one of the regularly scheduled tours led by park interpreters or pick up a detailed, self-guiding pamphlet at the visitor center.

Three other pamphlet-guided trails loop through areas near the pine tract. South of the grove is the 2-mile-long Mertz Grade Trail, an hour route along the roadbed of a narrow-gauge railroad that once hauled logs

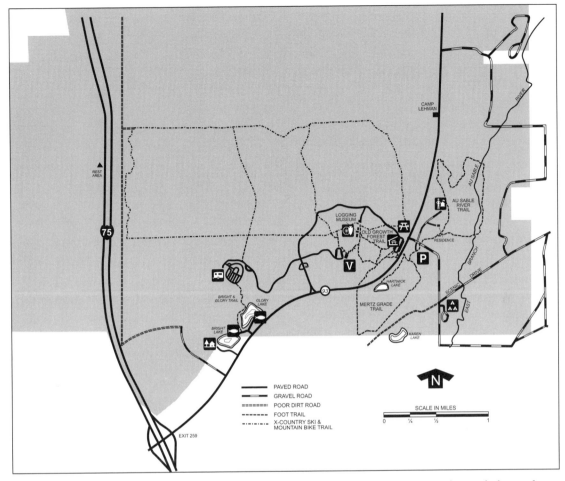

	PAVED ROAD
	GRAVEL ROAD
	POOR DIRT ROAD
	FOOT TRAIL
	X-COUNTRY SKI & MOUNTAIN BIKE TRAIL

SCALE IN MILES

0   ¼   ½   1

out of the area. The 3-mile Au Sable Trail swings north over high, rolling hills blanketed with a variety of forest types, and makes two crossings of the East Branch of the Au Sable River. Both trails begin at the day-use parking lot.

Bright and Glory Nature Trail, the shortest of the self-guided trails, departs from the park's campground and gives a lesson in botany and natural history as it leads to the two lakes bearing the trail's name. Weary Legs, Deer Run, and Aspen trails cut 7.5-, 5- and 3-mile-long loops through the park's vast backcountry. According to the season the trails are open to either cross-country skiers or mountain bikes. The various trails reward the adventurous with solitude and excellent views of cedar swamps, a stand of old growth hemlock, several pocket-sized lakes and vast pine plantations. Depending on the season and the locale, a variety wildflowers,

berries, and mushrooms abound throughout the park. Lastly, a new paved bike path, that borders M-93, runs for two miles from the park entrance to the I-75 overpass.

Deer, bear, grouse, rabbits, woodcock, and other wildlife are rife, and hunting, in season, is allowed in the park's backcountry. The area is popular with deer hunters, some of whom use the campground as their base.

Fishermen can break out fly rods and test their skill and luck on two designated trout lakes, Bright and Glory, as well as nearly three miles of river. Bright and Glory lakes each have handicapped accessible fishing piers.

The park's open and sunny campground is ringed by low, wooded hills. All sites sport a thick carpet of grass, paved slips and electrical hookups. Thirty-six sites in the center of the campground come with water, sewer, and electrical hookups and are all pull-throughs.

Those seeking shade and some privacy will want to camp on the outer ring. Six of the sites are handicapped accessible and within easy distance of the modern toilet/shower building. If the campground is far removed from the traffic of the day-use area it's just a short walk to the trout fishing at Bright and Glory lakes, and a trailhead for the cross-country skiing/mountain bike trails lies just outside the campground entrance. Demand is high from Memorial to Labor Day and reservations are highly recommended. Another option for overnighters is a rustic cabin (it sleeps six) located near the shore of Bright Lake.

It's a mile-long scenic drive from the park entrance on M-93 to the day-use parking lot. Only steps away from your car picnic tables, grills and a picnic shelter rest in the shade of mature pines. Later, hamburgers and potato salad can be walked off on the Old Growth Forest Trail which is immediately accessible from the picnic grounds.

COUNTY: CRAWFORD

CAMPING SITES: 100, ALL MODERN, INCLUDING 36 WITH FULL HOOKUPS; AND ONE RUSTIC CABIN.

SCHEDULE: THE PARK IS OPEN 8 A.M. TO 10 P.M. YEAR ROUND.

THE MICHIGAN FOREST CENTER IS OPEN DAILY MEMORIAL DAY WEEKEND THROUGH LABOR DAY, 9 A.M. TO 7 P.M. ALL OTHER TIMES THE HOURS ARE 9 A.M. TO 4 P.M. THE CENTER IS CLOSED MONDAYS AFTER LABOR DAY THROUGH MID-NOVEMBER AND FROM MID-NOVEMBER THROUGH MID-APRIL THE CENTER IS OPEN ONLY ON SATURDAYS AND SUNDAYS.

THE LOGGING MUSEUM IS OPEN 9 A.M. TO 4 P.M. IN MAY, SEPTEMBER, AND OCTOBER AND 9 A.M. TO 7 P.M. FROM MEMORIAL DAY TO LABOR DAY. THE MUSEUM IS CLOSED DURING THE WINTER.

DIRECTIONS: FROM I-75 TAKE EXIT 259 AND DRIVE EAST ON M-93 TWO MILES.

FURTHER INFORMATION: HARTWICK PINES STATE PARK, 4216 RANGER ROAD, GRAYLING, MI 49738; 989-348-7068.

Northern Higgins Lake
State Park

14

OVERNIGHT ACCOMMODATIONS:

ACTIVITIES:

Fifteen hundred feet of frontage on the distinctive blue-green waters of Higgins Lake, a beautiful campground, outstanding beach and picnic areas, and miles of trails past lakes and through seemingly boundless woods make North Higgins Lake State Park a near-perfect vacation spot.

It wasn't always that way.

A hundred-plus years ago, if you had visited here or nearly anyplace else in northern Michigan, you would have faced a scarred, barren land. Lumbermen had ravaged the forest that once blanketed the state and the fires and erosion that followed the axes left a bleak and sorry landscape.

In 1903, as a first step in reforesting the wind-swept plains, Michigan created its first nursery on land that is now part of the park. During the Great Depression – thirty-some years later – young men who couldn't find work elsewhere came to northern Michigan and planted more than 400 million trees, built 504 bridges, 222 buildings, improved wildlife habitat, and built campgrounds, picnic areas and hiking trails while working with the Civilian Conservation Corp. One of the state's largest CCC camps shared space with the nursery.

Today, many restored nursery buildings, (including Michigan's first iron fire tower), a 1.5-mile self-guided nature trail through the nursery grounds, and a one-of-a-kind museum modeled after a 1930s CCC barracks all bring to life the story of the people who restored the state's grandeur and turned it into an immense outdoor playground. At the former Cone Barn, for instance, you can learn how 20-22 million seedlings were grown and shipped annually. Daily interpretive programs add more details to the story of forest fires, reforestation and forest management past and present.

For a close-at-hand look at the results of the great reforestation undertaking, take the 3.8-mile Bosom Pine Trail, the 6.5-mile Beaver Creek Trail, or other long paths that penetrate the 429-acre park's backcountry from the old nursery area. A 1.5-mile fitness loop, with 20 exercise stations, also begins and finishes at the parking lot next to the nursery. The trails are open to biking, and cross-country skiers can glide over the backcountry routes in the winter.

Across North Higgins Lake Drive from the nursery/museum area, the focus is on the crystal-clear waters of Higgins Lake and the park's 1,500 feet of sandy shoreline. The lake bottom slopes so gently that you have to wade out 50-100 feet just to get waist deep.

Close to the water on either side of a bathhouse and small picnic shelter, tables and grills dot the grass under a canopy of mature red pines and the occasional hardwood.

Water skiers, fishermen, sail boaters and powerboats all make waves after putting in

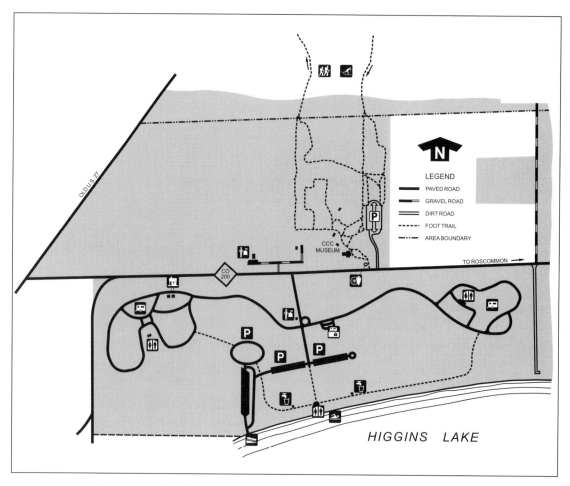

at a ramp at the west end of the beach/pic-
nic area. And scuba divers love to take the
plunge into the deep, clear water of Higgins
Lake.

Short trails from the day-use area connect
inland to each of the modern campground's
two widely spaced wings. Many of the 175
lots are well worn, and most are roomy,
shaded and fairly private. Generally the lots
on the east wing are smaller and offer less
privacy. The west wing contains two mini-
cabins. The campground fills every weekend from Memorial through Labor Day and
experiences heavy use throughout the week
making reservations a must.

During the warm-weather months the
entire park is almost always busy. But even
when full it doesn't seem particularly crowded and is a nice alternative to its sister park
on the south side of the lake.

Counties: Crawford and Roscommon
Camping Sites: 175, all modern, and
two mini-cabins.
Directions: From US-27 just south of
its junction with I-75, take County
Road 200 a half mile east.
Further Information: North Higgins
Lake State Park, 11747 North Higgins
Lake Drive, Roscommon, MI 48653; 989-
821-6125.

South Higgins Lake
State Park

15

OVERNIGHT ACCOMMODATIONS:

ACTIVITIES:

Since its creation in 1924, South Higgins Lake State Park has been one of the most-popular vacation destinations in northern Michigan, and for good reason. Higgins is one of the most-beautiful inland lakes in Michigan. Its unusually blue, clear, spring-fed water is a magnet that draws nearly 350,000 outdoors lovers each year to its sandy south shore.

That's a lot of people, but there's a lot of beach and water. The 10,000-acre lake laps up against almost a mile of sandy park shoreline, half of which fronts the day-use area. The gently sloping lake bottom there makes for very shallow water far out into the lake, and tree-shaded grills, picnic tables and playground equipment creep right to the water's edge. Just a few steps away is a bathhouse and camp store, where you can buy ice cream, pop, snacks, some camping-grocery needs, and a plethora of typical "up-north" souvenirs.

West of the day-use beach, power boaters and fishermen can launch into a large protected basin, troll out to the lake entrance, and then weave past sail-boarders into the open waters. Most fishermen go after perch. But lake and brown trout, which were introduced in the early 1970s, as well as smallmouth bass also provide good action. Rental rowboats, pontoons, sailboats, canoes and pedal-boats are available at the store. Fishermen also have great success going after perch, smallmouth bass and northern pike on Marl Lake. A light rowboat or canoe that can be carried to the water and take anglers into middle of the lake pays dividends.

The boat basin and trailer parking lot behind it cut off the day-use area from the second-largest campground in the state park system. Four hundred modern, heavily shaded sites are arranged in a series of long, narrow loops that point to the lake. None of the lots are especially small, but nearly all are cheek by jowl with each other and you'll see (and be seen by) dozens of your neighbors. Most campsites are heavily shaded and dirt surfaced; however, sites closer to the water receive more sunlight and have some grass. There are several pull-throughs and four different boat trailer parking lots within the campground attest to the popularity of boating here. The campground also has one mini-cabin. None of the sites directly edge the water, so overnighters can swim and sunbathe on a long, uninterrupted stretch of beach directly in front of the campground.

This is not only one of Michigan's largest campgrounds, but one of the busiest. Reservations can be made up to six months in advance and all campsites are reservable, which means there's still ice on the lake when the park is fully booked for the July 4th weekend. You may be lucky enough to find a vacant site mid-week but park officials warn

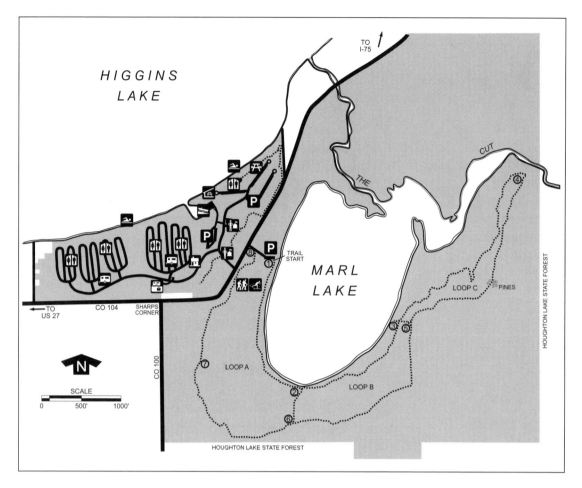

that the chances of camping for extended periods of time here without a reservation are not good.

If you want to get away from all the people and hubbub, cross County Road 100 and hike all or part of 5.5 miles of trails that cut through a 700-acre tract of undeveloped land. You can choose between 2.0-, 3.5- and 5.5-mile-long loops, the inner parts of which follow the shoreline of Marl Lake. The far end of the longest circuit, which nearly circles the small lake, reaches The Cut, a channel dug during the logging era to connect Higgins and Houghton lakes.

The trails are used by cross-country skiers in the winter, and both lakes are popular with ice-fishermen. Hunting is permitted in the Marl Lake area with ducks, squirrels, rabbit and deer all successfully taken. The area also yields bear and turkey during their respective seasons.

Throughout the summer park personnel offer a variety of nature programs and hikes that explore the natural history and resources of the area. Hobbyists are allowed to use metal detectors in specific areas of the park.

COUNTY: ROSCOMMON

CAMPING SITES: 400, ALL MODERN, PLUS A MINI-CABIN.

DIRECTIONS: GO 6 MILES EAST OF US-27 ON HIGGINS LAKE ROAD.

FURTHER INFORMATION: SOUTH HIGGINS LAKE STATE PARK, 106 STATE PARK ROAD, ROSCOMMON, MI 48653; 989-821-6374.

Mitchell State Park

16

OVERNIGHT ACCOMMODATIONS:

ACTIVITIES:

If you like water or water sports, Mitchell State Park is an ideal vacation destination. The heart of the park covers a narrow isthmus that is nearly surrounded by water. Lake Cadillac laps at the park's east border and Lake Mitchell at the west. Connecting them along the north edge of the day-use and camping areas is a navigable 60-foot-wide canal, dug during the 1870s to move logs between the two lakes. A few campers, at sites that border the canal, have the rare opportunity in a Michigan state park to dock their boats practically next to their RVs.

From the dock of a heavily-used, campers-only boat ramp on Lake Cadillac, or a day-use ramp on Lake Mitchell it's a short ride to fishing, water skiing, or just cruising on either of the two lakes. On Lake Cadillac, for instance, you can motor past fine old homes that line the shore on your way right to downtown Cadillac at the east end of the lake. And on Lake Mitchell, which stretches several miles to the north and west, you can water ski in a straight line until your arms fall off.

Mitchell's large 221-site campground spreads south from the channel in four elongated loops whose eastern tips point to a campers-only beach and playground on Lake Cadillac. The modern campground is usually filled to capacity during the summer, so reservations are a must to ensure a spot. Almost all sites are roomy and well shaded. There are eight handicapped accessible campsites and the lone mini-cabin sits just steps away from the campers' beach. All campers have access to modern restroom buildings with showers. If you have a watercraft, you'll want to try

for the lots that edge the canal so you can literally step from your tent or RV right into your boat.

The canal is also popular with shore fishermen, who go after pike, perch, walleyes, bluegills and bass. Walleyes are the number-one game fish in Lake Cadillac, and good catches of northern pike, perch and bluegill are also reported. Lake Mitchell is best known for its largemouth bass but also walleyes and perch. Both lakes sprout ice-fishing shanty towns in the winter.

Across M-115 from the campground a day-use area takes up a few hundred yards of Lake Mitchell's shoreline. Within a few feet of the parking lot (and only yards from the sight and sound of busy M-115) huge, old pines stand like sentinels over scattered tables and grills. Sweeping views of the lake come from a narrow, sandy swimming beach that skirts the waterline in front of the small grassy picnic grounds. Day-use boaters can launch their craft in Lake Mitchell from a ramp on the south side of the swimming beach. Metal detector use is restricted to the swimming

beach in the day-use area and the campers-only swimming beach on Lake Cadillac.

On park property north of the canal is the Hunting and Fishing Visitor Center and Heritage Nature Study Area. Inside the center, dioramas, an aquarium, and other displays feature live and mounted Michigan wildlife plus a variety of interactive exhibits. A store offers nature guides, T-shirts, wildlife art and other items.

A trail from the Center leads to the Heritage Fisheries and Wildlife Study Area, a 70-acre marsh encircled by a 2.5-mile-long path atop a dike. From the encircling dike, you have the option of cutting through the heart of the marsh via an extensive system of boardwalks and bridges, or taking a short bridge to an observation tower offering a panoramic view of the area. All the trails pass through a profusion of wildflowers, and there are plenty of opportunities to spot waterfowl, marsh birds, turkey, white-tailed deer and beaver. You can walk through the area on your own or join a guided hike that leaves from the center. Cross-country skiers

replace hikers here in the winter.

Snowmobiles can operate in parts of the park when snow cover has reached four inches.

COUNTY: WEXFORD

CAMPING SITES: 221, ALL MODERN WITH 8 HANDICAPPED ACCESSIBLE, PLUS 1 MINI-CABIN.

SCHEDULE: THE VISITOR CENTER IS OPEN 10 A.M. – 6 P.M. DAILY FROM MAY – NO-VEMBER. DECEMBER – APRIL THE CENTER IS OPEN FRIDAYS AND SUNDAYS 12 NOON – 5 P.M. AND SATURDAYS 10 A.M. – 5 P.M.

DIRECTIONS: THE PARK IS LOCATED ON M-115, ON THE WEST SIDE OF CADILLAC.

FURTHER INFORMATION: MITCHELL STATE PARK, 6093 EAST M-115, CADILLAC, MI 49601; 231-775-7911.

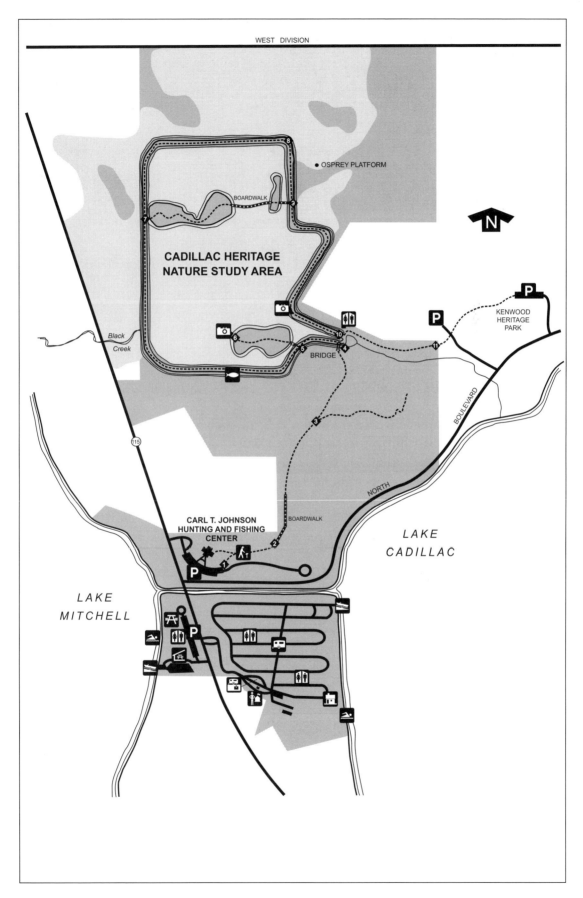

OSPREY PLATFORM

BOARDWALK

CADILLAC HERITAGE
NATURE STUDY AREA

Black
Creek

BRIDGE

N

KENWOOD
HERITAGE
PARK

NORTH

BOULEVARD

BOARDWALK

CARL T. JOHNSON
HUNTING AND FISHING
CENTER

LAKE
CADILLAC

LAKE
MITCHELL

115

Orchard Beach

State Park

17

Overnight Accommodations:

Activities:

Orchard Beach State Park perches on a high bluff overlooking Lake Michigan, and the crow's-nest view from the edge is hard to beat. Beneath the arch of sky, distant freighters plow faint V's through the constantly shifting hues of blue and green. Closer to shore, smaller boats, often too numerous to count, bob in the waves that sweep one of Michigan's favorite fishing spots.

Just behind the crest of the bluff, somewhat protected from strong offshore breezes, lies the park's 167-site modern campground. Mature hardwoods and remnants of an old orchard shelter and shade the large level, grassy lots. Privacy, however, is minimal. The park's sole mini-cabin sits on the southern edge of the campground. This especially fine campground is extremely busy throughout the summer making reservations a must from July through Labor Day. A long flight of stairs at the south end of the campground drops from the bluff to the swimming beach. The strip of sand, though not very wide, edges the water for nearly 3,000 feet.

North of the beach and campground, picnic tables and grills decorate a large, grassy meadow atop the bluff. Hobbyists may use metal detectors in the campground, beach and day-use area only. Check with park officials for any changes.

Across M-110 from the picnic grounds, a half-mile self-guided nature trail and two additional miles of hiking trails, divided into three loops, wind through the 201-acre park's deer-rich backcountry. A trail guide, available from the contact station, describes the natural and geological history of the area traversed by the trails. Cross-country skiers rule the trails in the winter.

Though there is no boat access or good shore fishing within the park, prime angling beckons from several ramps, charter boats and two piers in Manistee, just two miles south. Action on the big lake, Manistee Lake, and from two piers is good year-round but in August and September when coho and chinook salmon make their spawning runs wetting a hook in the above waters can be the high point of any fisherman's year.

The quaint lumbering village of Manistee is rich in Victorian homes and buildings. The restored downtown, listed as a National and State Historic District, contains antiques and gift shops, bakeries, and restaurants. Other attractions include a 1.5-mile river walk and an historic trolley tour that connects the town with the state park.

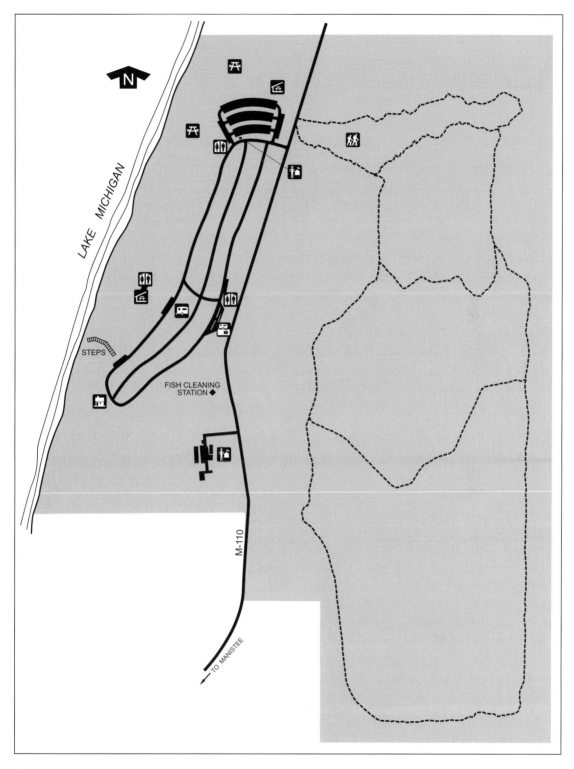

STEPS

LAKE MICHIGAN

FISH CLEANING STATION ◆

M-110

TO MANISTEE

County: Manistee

Camping Sites: 167, all modern plus a mini-cabin.

Directions: Go 2 miles north of Manistee on M-110.

Further Information: Orchard Beach State Park, 2064 Lakeshore Road, Manistee, MI 49660: 231-723-7422.

Ludington State Park

18

OVERNIGHT ACCOMMODATIONS:

ACTIVITIES:

Don't be in a hurry to get to the heart of Ludington State Park. Drive slowly up M-116, which hugs Lake Michigan the last two miles to the entrance, to catch as many glimpses of the water and beach as you can through the breaks in the curtain of low dunes. Or take advantage of the numerous opportunities to pull off the road, scramble over the dunes, and join campers from the park, locals and others who have lugged coolers, beach chairs and umbrellas to the magnificent beach. On summer weekends, you may have to parallel park in a line of vehicles at the edge of the highway, but even so, you'll find that the vast stretch of sand appears only lightly salt and peppered with people.

The park embraces one of Michigan's finest outdoor playgrounds: 5,308 acres of beautiful beaches, dunes, and forests that wrap around picnic areas, hiking trails, three campgrounds, and the Great Lakes Visitor Center, and fishing, hunting, canoeing, and river-tubing opportunities. It's all spread over a wide strip of land between Lake Michigan and Big Hamlin Lake (Michigan's largest man-made lake), with the main facilities lining the Sable River, which connects them. Tube riders and canoeists float the stream, and cyclists pedal along a paved, picturesque path that borders the river. Next to the river at close to the halfway point between the two lakes are pleasant picnic grounds.

Near the Hamlin Lake end of the river, a shaded picnic area closely borders a small, sandy beach. South of the beach parking lot a historical plaque marks the site where the logging village of Hamlin stood before an earlier version of the present Hamlin Dam burst and swept the village's forty homes, sawmill and a million board feet of lumber

into Lake Michigan. The lake water there is warm, shallow, and only a step away from a concession stand and bathhouse. The Hamlin Lake beach also marks the starting point of a short canoe trail that edges the southeastern shore of the lake. At the opposite, west end of the stream, a large bathhouse and a concession stand overlook a broad expanse of sand that gently slips under the crystal-blue waters of Lake Michigan. This beach – the park's most popular – and its small parking lot are often crowded.

Three heavily used, reservations recommended, modern campgrounds totaling 344 sites cut long loops into the country north of the Big Sable River. Three-hundred-yards east of Lake Michigan are the rather small, shaded lots (1-97) and one mini-cabin that make up Pine Campground. Five of the sites are handicapped accessible. Open, sunny lots (101-205) at Cedar Campground are about halfway between lakes Michigan and Hamlin. Most of the sites there, including a mini-cabin, are roomy and grass covered and you're

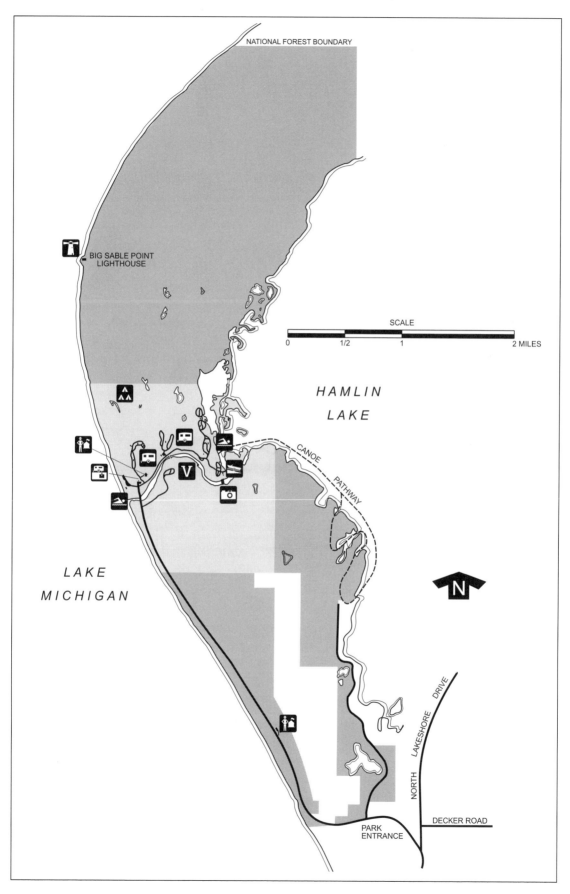

NATIONAL FOREST BOUNDARY

BIG SABLE POINT
LIGHTHOUSE

SCALE

0   1/2   1   2 MILES

HAMLIN

LAKE

CANOE

PATHWAY

V

LAKE

MICHIGAN

N

NORTH   LAKESHORE   DRIVE

DECKER ROAD

PARK
ENTRANCE

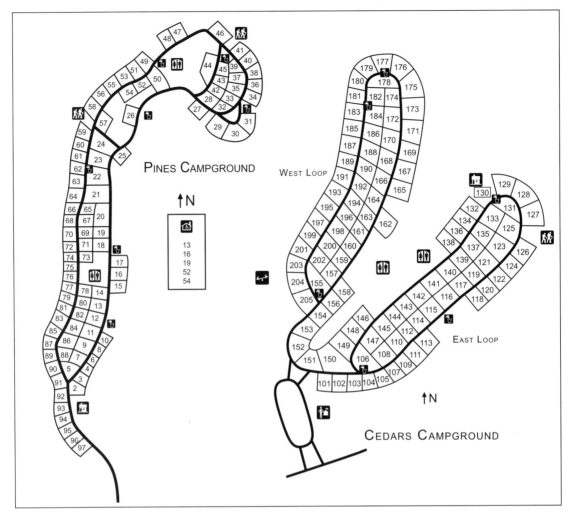

PINES CAMPGROUND

WEST LOOP

EAST LOOP

CEDARS CAMPGROUND

only a few steps from the park store. Farthest east, the generally large, old, well-worn lots (210-354) in Beechwood Campground rest under a canopy of stately hardwoods, and a few line the shores of Hamlin and Lost lakes. Four handicapped accessible sites and a mini-cabin are included in the campground. All three campgrounds have modern restroom buildings with showers.

The eleven trails that lace the park's interior number among the finest foot paths in the Lower Peninsula. You can take a half-hour walk or an all-day outing on the 18-mile system, with loops and branches that reach far north to the historic Point Sable Lighthouse, follow the jigsaw-puzzle-shaped shore of Hamlin Lake, climb forested dunes, and lead to the Lake Michigan shoreline. Three shelters are scattered along the remote sec-

tions of the trail. The lighthouse is open to the public and maintained by the Big Sable Lighthouse Keepers Association. The sand and gravel surfaced Lighthouse Trail is the only hiking trail in the park that is also open to mountain bikes. Nature lovers will find plenty of wildflowers and an array of striking habitats that attract a wide variety birds, especially waterfowl.

One short and especially scenic route, the Skyline Trail, forms a large loop around the Great Lakes Visitor Center on the south side of the Big Sable River. The trail climbs a long flight of stairs, and then follows the crest of a towering, wooded dune with sweeping views of both Lake Michigan and the low dunes that range inland. Inside the Center you can get a good overall picture of the Great Lakes' ecology, geology, history and wildlife from live exhibits, slide shows, special programs and other displays. The Center can be reached by car from M-116 or on footpaths from the campgrounds.

Summer anglers can launch their boats on Hamlin Lake from a ramp south of Beechwood Campground and test their luck and skill against northern pike, large- and smallmouth bass, tiger musky and panfish on the 5,000-acre inland lake. Lots of visitors enjoy fishing the Big Sable River, especially in the spring and fall when salmon, lake trout, steelhead and brown trout come off Lake Michigan and swim upriver until they hit the dam. Ice fishermen pull fine catches of pike and bluegill from Lake Hamlin after freeze up.

Cross-country skiers have 16 miles of trails to work, and much of the park is open to hunting. Metal detectors can be used in certain areas of the park and wireless Internet access is available from within a radius of 150 feet of the main office headquarters.

COUNTY: MASON

CAMPING SITES: 344, ALL MODERN, PLUS THREE MINI-CABINS AND SEVERAL HANDICAPPED ACCESSIBLE CAMPING SITES.

DIRECTIONS: SEVEN MILES NORTH OF LUDINGTON ON M-116.

FURTHER INFORMATION: LUDINGTON STATE PARK, 8800 WEST M-166, BOX 709, LUDINGTON, MI 49341; 231-843-2423 OR 231-843-8671.

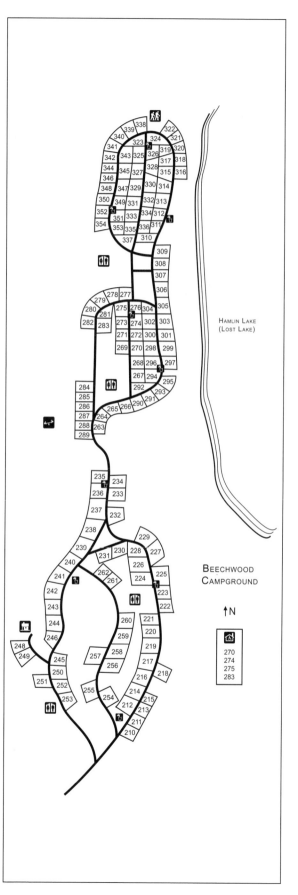

HAMLIN LAKE (LOST LAKE)

BEECHWOOD CAMPGROUND

↑N

270
274
275
283

19

Charles Mears
State Park

OVERNIGHT ACCOMMODATIONS:

ACTIVITIES:

If your definition of a fine park is, "a great beach," then Charles Mears State Park will qualify as one of your favorites. More than 300,000 visitors a year leave footprints in the feather-soft sand that covers almost all of the park's 50 acres, including the main attraction: a several-hundred-yard-long, over-50-yard-wide stretch along Lake Michigan.

Changing courts, restrooms and a concession stand separate that swimming area from a large day-use parking lot. A few picnic tables are widely scattered throughout the concession/parking area.

Most visitors also walk a dozen yards south to a pier to watch pleasure and fishing boats parade between Pentwater Lake and Lake Michigan. (The park has no launch facilities, but there are several ramps on Pentwater Lake in the nearby village of Pentwater.) Fishermen also line the pier and in season pull salmon, steelhead, perch, lake trout and smelt from the channel.

If you're thinking about staying at the park's campground on any weekend during the warm-weather months, make a reservation well in advance because your chances of finding an empty campsite without one are only slightly better than hitting the Daily Three lottery game. The 175 relatively small sites are arranged very close together in several loops behind a low dune that separates and partially shelters the area

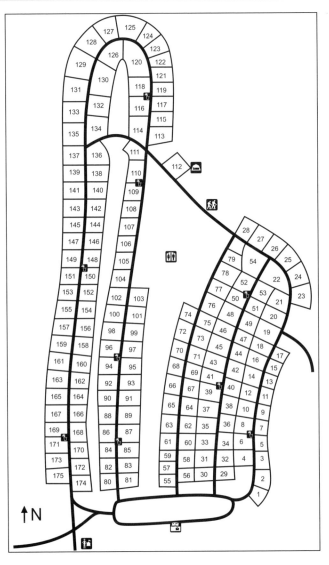

N

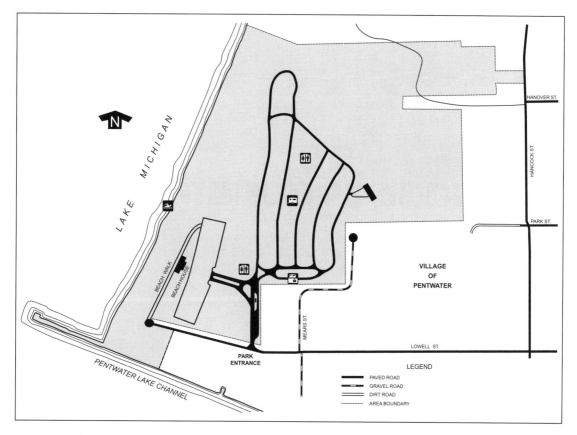

from Lake Michigan. Each lot has an asphalt slip on which to park vehicles or set up trailers, as well as an electrical hookup and access to modern restroom facilities. Recently planted trees on many of the lots are just beginning to cast some shade. Most campers can be found on the beach, fishing, or exploring the small resort town of Pentwater and use their tents and RVs just for sleeping or grabbing a bite to eat. To date, the park is one of the few in the state with wireless Internet access.

Park rangers offer interpretive programs and nature walks throughout the summer. A one-mile-long nature trail leading to the top of a barrier dune rewards climbers with a grand view of the surrounding area. Metal detectors are allowed in certain areas of the park.

COUNTY: OCEANA

CAMPING SITES: 175, ALL MODERN.

SCHEDULE: OPEN FROM APRIL 15 – NOVEMBER 1.

DIRECTIONS: GO 4 BLOCKS WEST OF DOWNTOWN PENTWATER ON LOWELL STREET

FURTHER INFORMATION: CHARLES MEARS STATE PARK, P.O. BOX 370, WEST LOWELL STREET, PENTWATER, MI 49449; 231-869-2051.

Silver Lake
State Park

20

Overnight Accommodations:

Activities:

> Don't come to Silver Lake State Park looking for rest and relaxation or expecting peace and quiet. Do come here if you'd like to spend time on an enormous, fun-filled sand pile that is surrounded by a virtual amusement park.

At Silver Lake you really can't separate the outside attractions from the park itself – the entire area is a huge playground. Within walking distance from the park are bumper boats and cars, arcades, one of the state's two commercial dune buggy rides, sailboat and sailboard rentals, and slightly farther afield, riding stables and canoe rentals.

The main attraction within the park and covering half its 2,675 acres is sand, enormous mounds that separate Lake Michigan from Silver Lake. Except for the water, the treeless, wind-swept dunes are remindful of the Sahara Desert, and it isn't hard to imagine a camel caravan appearing over the nearest crest.

Instead, what you're likely to see and hear are dune buggies and other off-road vehicles (ORVs). The northern quarter of the dune area has been set aside as a 450-acre Off Road Vehicle Area, the only such parcel in a Michigan state park. On summer weekends the park and surrounding area buzzes with dune-buggy traffic to and from the ORV dunes. The parking lot there is usually jammed full, and riders often wait a half hour or more just to get on the sand. If you want to give it a try but don't own your own ORV, you can rent one from a private concession-

aire nearby. Special vehicle regulations and requirements must be met before an ORV is permitted on the course.

If you'd rather hit the sand with both feet instead of four wheels you can hike and climb 740 acres of the dunes that are reserved for pedestrians. Access comes from a parking area just south of the ORV lot. If you like to combine a large expanse of sand with sun and water, head to the opposite (southern) edge of the park where a sand road leads to a small parking lot and access to a stretch of Lake Michigan beach guarded by the historic Little Sable Point Lighthouse.

Most of the park's developed facilities are compressed into a small parcel on the east shore of Silver Lake, out of sight and sound of the ORV hills. A small, sandy swimming beach there borders the warm shallow waters of the lake, and a few picnic tables and trees ring a bathhouse and picnic shelter. The view across the lake is like no other in the state. Looking completely out of place, a wall of sand rises out of, towers over, and is the lake's west shore.

Just a short walk from the day-use area is the older of the park's two camping areas. Lots (1-84) in that unit are heavily shaded, well worn, and so tightly packed they offer

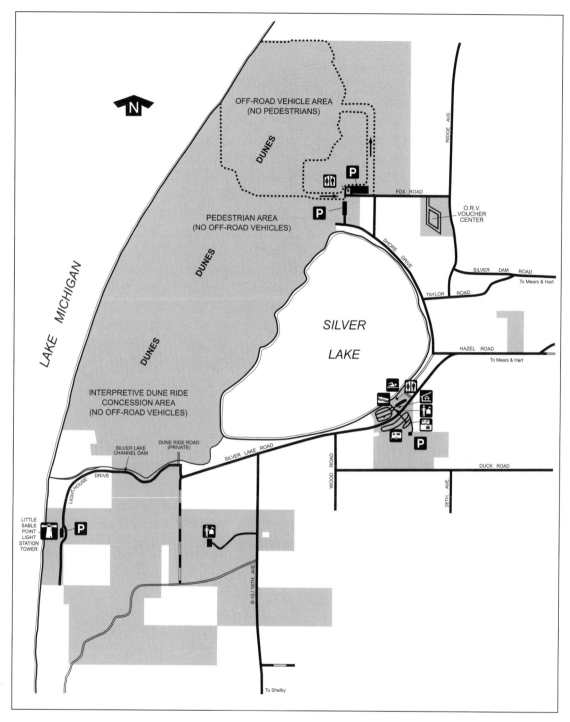

little room or privacy. The crowding is further aggravated by the shoehorning of boats and ORVs into almost every campsite. Across the road from the lake, the newer campground (lots 102 and up) offers the same deep shade, but sites with some elbow room and privacy. Both campgrounds have electrical hookups and modern restrooms. The choice of sites doesn't matter much to most campers, who only return to eat, sleep or rest between activities. A dozen campsites have been made handicapped accessible. The campground is busy, filling to capacity every summer weekend, so reservations are a must.

Boaters can put in at a launch ramp on Silver Lake in the day-use area. Fishermen, who

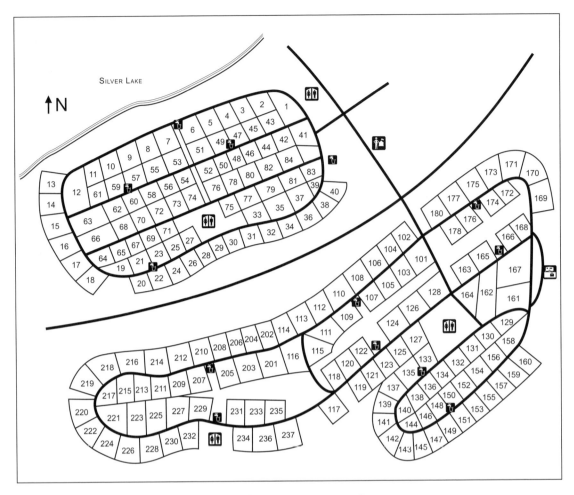

wet lines in Silver Lake go after walleyes, perch, brown trout, large and smallmouth bass, crappies and other panfish. Ice fishing is popular in the winter.

Park rangers lead a variety of educational tours and natural history programs throughout the summer. In the less-developed sections of the park – including a good chunk of the dunes area – hunters bag deer, rabbits, raccoon, squirrels and grouse in season. Hobbyists are allowed to use metal detectors in certain areas.

Alcoholic beverages are prohibited throughout the park from May 15 to June 10.

COUNTY: OCEANA

CAMPING SITES: 200, ALL MODERN WITH SOME HANDICAPPED ACCESSIBLE.

SCHEDULE: THE PARK IS OPEN ALL YEAR AND THE CAMPGROUNDS ARE OPEN APRIL-NOVEMBER, BUT MODERN RESTROOMS ARE CLOSED FROM OCTOBER 15 TO APRIL 15.

DIRECTIONS: FROM US-131 ABOUT 35 MILES NORTH OF MUSKEGON EXIT ONTO SHELBY ROAD AND DRIVE WEST 6 MILES TO SCENIC DRIVE. TURN RIGHT (NORTH) ONTO SCENIC DRIVE AND FOLLOW THE ROAD (WHICH CHANGES NAMES SEVERAL TIMES) 4.5 MILES.

FURTHER INFORMATION: SILVER LAKE STATE PARK, 9679 WEST STATE PARK ROAD, MEARS, MI 49436; 231-873-3083.

Hart-Montague Trail
State Park

21

OVERNIGHT ACCOMMODATIONS: NONE

ACTIVITIES:

The Hart-Montague Trail was the first "rail-to-trail" state park in Michigan. A 10-foot-wide strip of asphalt that winds from Montague to Hart has replaced tracks that carried Chesapeake and Ohio trains along the route for nearly a hundred years.

The pathway is intended for use primarily by bicyclists, but hikers, cross-country skiers and snowmobiles are also welcome. The trail, which parallels US-31, passes through some of the finest landscape in western Michigan.

Although trail users encounter several small villages, most of the trail's 22 miles traverse open and uninhabited land. Woodlots, wetlands, open fields, picturesque streams, a few scattered picnic areas and scenic overlooks contribute to an ever changing panorama. The northern section passes over rolling terrain while the southern part belies its railroad heritage and is straight and level. Mile markers are posted the entire length of the trail.

A detailed trail guide, available from the address below, lists all access points, private campgrounds adjacent to the trail, and restaurants and grocery stores found along its length.

A planned 10-mile-long extension will reach from Montague to Dalton, north of Muskegon.

COUNTIES: MUSKEGON AND OCEANA

CAMPING SITES: NONE

DIRECTIONS: THE HART TRAILHEAD IS IN JOHN GURNEY PARK, ON THE SOUTH SHORE OF HART LAKE. THE MONTAGUE TRAILHEAD IS ON STANTON BOULEVARD JUST OFF BUSINESS ROUTE US-31 ON THE NORTHEAST SIDE OF TOWN.

FURTHER INFORMATION: HART-MONTAGUE TRAIL STATE PARK, 9679 WEST STATE PARK ROAD, MEARS, MI 49436; 231-873-3038

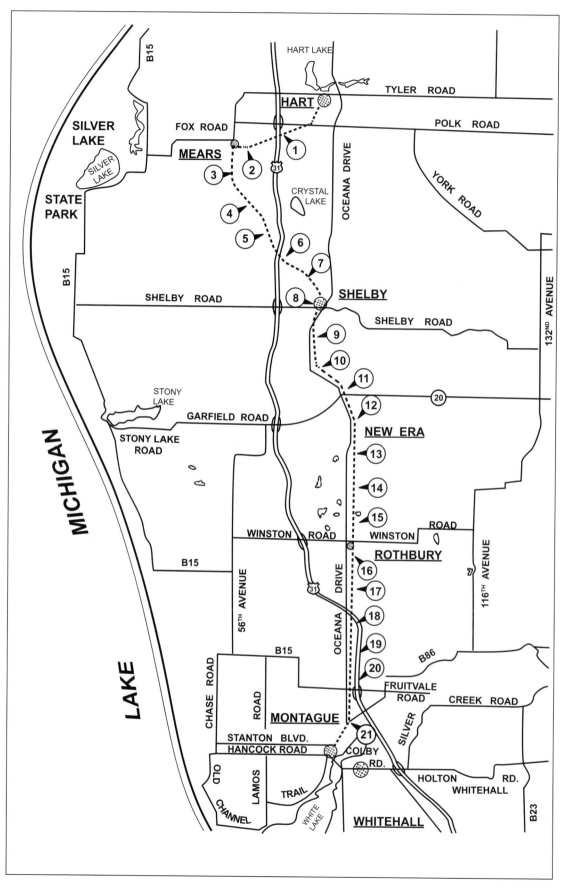

White Pine Trail

STATE PARK

22

OVERNIGHT ACCOMMODATIONS: NONE

ACTIVITIES:

The White Pine Trail State Park is not only one of the newest in Michigan's system, but on completion will also be, by far, the longest. The gravel-surfaced ballast route will eventually stretch from Cadillac to Grand Rapids, 92 miles to the south.

To date, 88 miles of the route – from Cadillac to Belmont, just north of Grand Rapids – is open, offering opportunity for some serious depletion of shoe leather or bicycle tire tread.

This "rails-to-trails" route follows the roadbed of the Michigan Northern Railroad and generally parallels US-131. Some 20 rivers and streams cross the trail, which parallels the Muskegon, Grand and Rouge rivers, each for significant distances. Some of the crossings offer attractive views, and plans call for the addition of boardwalks and viewing platforms. The trail may be long but it's also generally flat as it cuts through wetlands, woods, and farmland. Two sections – the 14 miles from Reed City to Big Rapids, and another 7 miles from Belmont to Rockford – have been paved.

In Mecosta County, 8 miles north of Big Rapids, the trail borders Paris County Park and its 70-site campground. Other campsites are available within a mile of the route in or near Morley, Sand Lake and Reed City. Motels are also within walking distance of the trail.

Cross-country skiers set their own tracks in the winter and snowmobiles are allowed when snow depth reaches 4 or more inches.

COUNTIES: MECOSTA, OSCEOLA, WEXFORD, MONTCALM AND KENT.

CAMPING SITES: NONE ON THE TRAIL ITSELF BUT CAMPING IS AVAILABLE IN CITIES ALONG THE ROUTE.

DIRECTIONS: PLANS CALL FOR A NUMBER OF PARKING/STAGING AREAS, BUT CURRENTLY ONLY THREE ARE OPEN. TO REACH THE CADILLAC TRAILHEAD, FROM THE JUNCTION OF M-115 AND US-131 DRIVE NORTHWEST ON M-115 FOR A HALF MILE TO NORTH 41 ROAD. TURN RIGHT ONTO 41 ROAD AND DRIVE ONE MILE TO NORTH 44 ROAD. TURN LEFT ONTO 44 ROAD AND DRIVE ABOUT A HALF MILE TO THE TRAILHEAD.

TO REACH THE BIG RAPIDS TRAILHEAD, FROM US-131 EXIT (139) ONTO M-20 AND DRIVE EAST ABOUT 3 MILES TO MAPLE STREET. CONTINUE EAST ON MAPLE FOR TWO BLOCKS TO A DEPOT BUILDING ON THE RIGHT.

TO REACH THE SAND LAKE staging AREA, FROM US-131 TAKE EXIT 110 AND GO EAST ON LAKE STREET FOR ABOUT 1.25 MILES.

FURTHER INFORMATION: WHITE PINE TRAIL STATE PARK, 6093 M-115, CADILLAC, MI 49601; 231-775-7911.

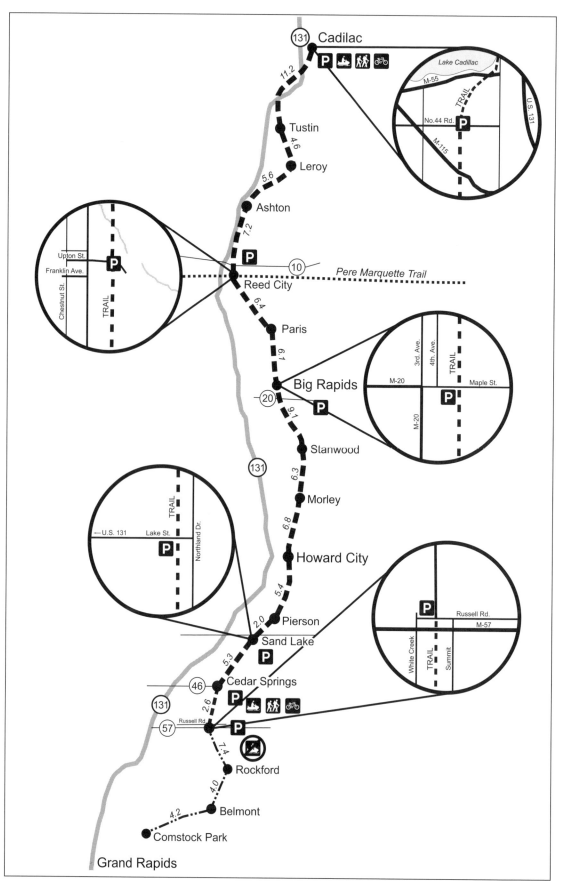

131 Cadilac

Lake Cadillac
M-55
TRAIL
No.44 Rd. P
M-115
U.S. 131

11.2

Tustin

4.6

Leroy

5.6

Ashton

7.2

P

10 Pere Marquette Trail

Upton St.
Franklin Ave.
Chestnut St.
TRAIL
P

Reed City

6.4

Paris

6.1

3rd. Ave.
4th. Ave.
TRAIL
M-20
Maple St.
Big Rapids
20 M-20
P

9.1

Stanwood

131

6.3

Morley

TRAIL
U.S. 131 Lake St.
Northland Dr.
P

6.8

Howard City

5.4

P Russell Rd.
M-57
White Creek
TRAIL
Summit

2.0

Pierson

Sand Lake
P

5.3

46 Cedar Springs
P

131

2.6

57 Russell Rd. P

7.4

Rockford

4.0

4.2 Belmont

Comstock Park

Grand Rapids

Newaygo

State Park

23

Overnight Accommodations:

Activities:

Newaygo State Park is not the Club Med of Michigan state parks. Camping conditions are rustic, there's only a small swimming beach and picnic area, and there are no hiking trails and no fancy facilities. So why come here? Well, if you're looking for a naturally beautiful place to get away from it all while staying at a campground where you're not crammed in cheek by jowl, this park rates four stars.

The park's 257 acres embrace a high bluff on the south side of a large impoundment of the Muskegon River called Hardy Dam Pond. "Pond," however, hardly seems the proper name for a body of water over a mile wide and six miles long. Canoeing is rated good along its wooded shore, and anglers go mainly after walleye, but also smallmouth bass, perch and pike. Other fishing options and opportunities are available within a few miles of the park. The large impoundment is also popular with water skiers and those with pleasure boats. Watercraft have easy access from a launch ramp (with a large boat-trailer parking lot) situated in a small inlet that breaches the line of bluffs and separates the campground's two wings.

The campground is rustic – meaning pit toilets and no electricity – although RV freshwater tanks can be filled and holding tanks emptied at a sanitation station near the park entrance. The overnight area is exceptionally quiet and peaceful but is only moderately used because of the lack of facilities. You can generally find a vacant space even on summer weekends.

Ninety-nine sites in two double-looped wings spread across the top of the bluff, with good views of the lake coming from some lots. The campsites are little more than small clearings carved out of the thick woods that blanket the entire area, so you get lots of privacy and deep shade. Each wing has a playground for children.

A small picnic area flanks either side of the inlet holding the boat ramp and the west side of the inlet sports a small swimming beach. No marked hiking trails crease the thick forest of oak, large-tooth aspen, and white pine, but it's easy to wander the woods and lakeshore in search of the many wildflowers and mushrooms that poke up in season. Park officials say that birdwatching can be excellent, especially for numerous waterfowl and shorebirds on the pond and warblers, thrushes and other songbirds in the woods.

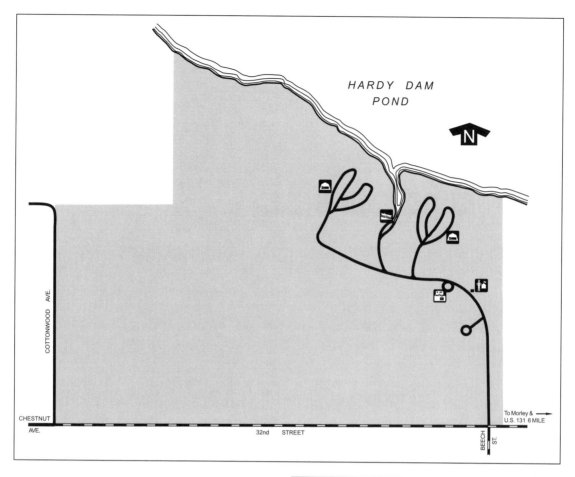

COUNTY: NEWAYGO

CAMPING SITES: 99, ALL RUSTIC.

SCHEDULE: THE CAMPGROUND IS OPEN
APRIL 15 – OCTOBER 23.

DIRECTIONS: APPROXIMATELY 43 MILES
NORTH OF GRAND RAPIDS ON US-131, TAKE
THE MORLEY EXIT AND GO WEST 7 MILES ON
USFS-5104 (JEFFERSON ROAD) TO BEECH
STREET. TURN RIGHT (NORTH) ONTO BEECH
AND GO A HALF MILE.

FURTHER INFORMATION: NEWAYGO STATE
PARK, 2793 BEECH STREET, NEWAYGO, MI
49337; 231-856-4452.

Duck Lake

State Park

24

OVERNIGHT ACCOMMODATIONS: NONE

ACTIVITIES: [icons]

Duck Lake State Park, with its half mile of dramatically beautiful Lake Michigan shoreline and quiet waters of the inland lake from which it takes its name, has been discovered. This used to be the place to go to get away from people, but numerous changes in 2005 improved facilities as well as access to the park and one of its prime attractions. All of which will undoubtedly increase attendance.

A new entrance road off Scenic Drive leads to a larger parking lot with overflow sites and two new vault toilets. A barrier-free sidewalk used to run from the parking lot to Scenic Drive which had to be crossed, by foot, to reach Lake Michigan. A new boardwalk takes beach goers under the road and Duck Lake Channel Bridge, and safely onto park's most heavily used and popular area – the Lake Michigan beach and the small channel that empties into the big lake.

Duck Lake Channel reaches bathwater temperatures and snakes through the sand on the Lake Michigan side of the road. Families with small children can swim in either Lake Michigan or the warmer waters of the channel, and test their sand castle building skills on a broad expanse of beach. The magnificent view begs you to spread a blanket, unpack a picnic lunch, and while away an afternoon.

Back at Duck Lake fishermen and boaters can gain access to the smaller lake from a boat ramp just east of the parking lot. Bass, crappie, northern pike and panfish will keep anglers busy. Although the lake empties into Lake Michigan, a dam under the bridge blocks boater access to the big lake. Farther east along the Duck Lake shoreline lies a sheltered swimming beach ringed by a wooded picnic area, a small bathhouse and a picnic shelter. A half-mile, paved foot path slips through the trees and parallels the lakeshore in its run from the picnic/beach parking lot to the larger lot near the entrance.

A mixed hardwood/pine forest blankets the entire park. There are no formal hiking trails, but the park's 704 acres give bushwhackers plenty of opportunity to try not to get lost. The only manmade break in the woods is the old entrance road that inscribes a north/south, asphalt crease through the heart of the park. The road ends short of the old entrance in a turnaround. Deer and squirrel hunting here is rated excellent and very good for woodcock and waterfowl. Turkeys are also hunted.

Metal detectors can be used in certain areas of the park.

COUNTY: MUSKEGON
CAMPING SITES: NONE
DIRECTIONS: FROM US-31 ABOUT 15 MILES NORTH OF MUSKEGON TAKE LAKEWOOD

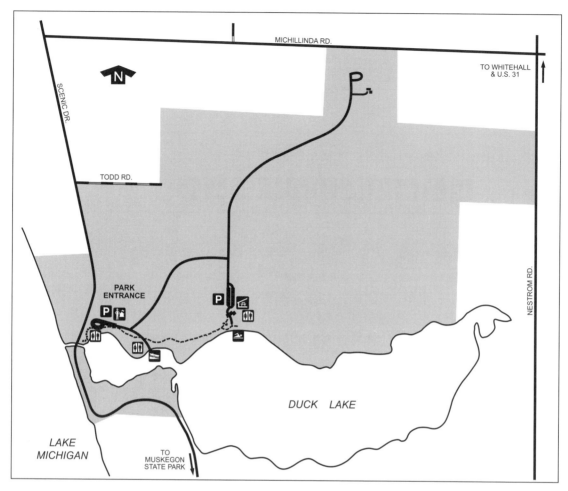

Club exit and drive west on White Lake Road to the first stoplight. Turn left (south) onto Whitehall Road and go 2 miles to Michillinda Road. Turn right (west) onto Michillinda and go 7 miles to Scenic Drive, turn left (south) onto Scenic and drive 2 miles to the park entrance. The route is well signed.

Further Information: Duck Lake State Park, c/o Muskegon State Park, 3560 Memorial Drive, North Muskegon, MI 49445; 231-744-3480.

Muskegon State Park

25

OVERNIGHT ACCOMMODATIONS:

ACTIVITIES:

You would expect Muskegon State Park – with a half million swimmers, beachcombers, surfers, fishermen, boaters, cross-country skiers, luge enthusiasts, campers, snowshoers, and picnickers and other visitors descending upon it each year – to be crowded. Surprisingly, in most areas it isn't.

In the summer a seemingly endless expanse of Lake Michigan sand, a connecting channel to a bay of Muskegon Lake, and the dunes and forest that back all the shoreline soak up the heavy crowds and leave room for more. The many developed facilities are so spread out over the 1,357 acres that it's easy to get the feeling you're really visiting several parks. You can spend a day at any one and have a great time without ever seeing the rest.

Campers who like to fish, or fishermen who like to camp, for instance, find themselves drawn to the Channel Campground's two loops overlooking the southern edge of the park where Muskegon Lake flows through a channel to Lake Michigan. Campers can drop fishing lines from two small piers that nudge out into the channel or a walkway that borders the narrow strip of water. (Day fishermen, who park in a convenient, specially designated lot, also use the boardwalk as do non-fishermen, who come to watch the parade of fishing and pleasure boats that pass through the channel to the Great Lake.)

Channel Campground's 140 sites have paved slips, electrical hookups and access to modern restrooms and showers. Lots 105 and up in the eastern loop, are generally larger and offer more privacy. This campground has

COURTESY OF GARY BARFKNECHT

no camper's beach, but the park's huge day-use area beach on Lake Michigan is only a short hike, drive or bike ride away.

If you want to camp only a short walk from a seemingly endless beach, stay at the north edge of the park at one of the 106 modern sites, including 2 mini-cabins, that make up the Lake Michigan Campground. The shaded, well-worn lots are spread under a stand of lofty old hardwoods, and less than a football field away from a wide swath of sand that stretches south along Lake Michigan for more than two miles. Both campgrounds have designated 50 amp hookup sites.

All campgrounds are heavily used throughout the summer and usually fill on weekends. In addition, the campgrounds are 100% reservable making reservations a must from June through August.

Day-trippers, too, can choose from several spots, but the overwhelming favorite is a huge, unshaded beach/picnic area along Lake Michigan at the south end of the park. It's only a few feet from the large bathhouse to superb swimming, but because of the relatively few picnic tables and large crowds, you may have to eat from a blanket on the sand. For a cozier, less-crowded lunch, but without a beach, try the grassy, tree-sheltered grounds (including the park's two picnic shelters) alongside Muskegon Lake's Snug Harbor.

A fishing pier pokes out into Snug Harbor and boaters can launch from a ramp bordering the picnic area. This is the closest ramp to the Muskegon Lake Channel and the great fishing for salmon and lake trout out on the big lake. Anglers will also find the channel and Lake Muskegon provides plenty of action from a variety of fish. The park has added a fish cleaning station near the ramp at Snug Harbor. Fishermen can dress their catch there from early spring to late fall.

No matter where you camp or visit, be sure to take one of the prettiest short drives in the state along the road that follows the park's Lake Michigan coastline. About two-thirds of the way up the route, a trail from a small parking lot leads to a sweeping view of the surrounding countryside and Lake Michigan from a replica rustic log blockhouse.

From the parking lot adjacent to the blockhouse, or for that matter virtually any parking lot or campground, you can access 12 miles of well-marked hiking trails that honeycomb the park's backcountry. And when you drag your eyes away from the many scenic overlooks you'll find an abundance of wildflowers poking from the forest floor in season, plus more than 200 species of birds to search for – including

LAKE MICHIGAN CAMPGROUND

N

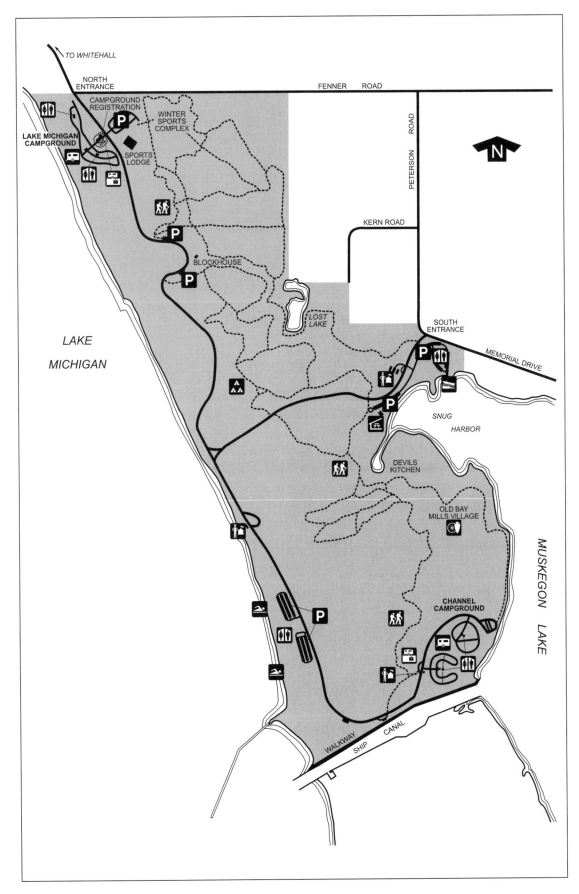

waterfowl, hawks, shorebirds and impressive numbers of warblers – which have been documented within the park. The staff offers a variety of programs and hikes that reflect the area's natural heritage. Metal detectors are permitted within certain areas of the park.

Unlike many state parks that, with the exception of a few snowmobiles or cross-country skiers, hibernate in winter, Muskegon State Park hums with activity. When the snow flies a beautiful lodge – complete with fireplace, concession area and restrooms – on the park's northern edge is headquarters for the Winter Sports Complex, which includes one of three luge runs in the country. There are regularly scheduled races and leagues and the public is welcome. No, not just welcome to watch, but to throw your self down the icy serpentine chute on what looks like a "go cart" version of a bobsled. Luge clinics are scheduled on Saturdays and Sundays throughout the winter and anyone who completes the two-and-a-half-hour course is welcome to race. The luge participant checklist includes, among other things, a proof of insurance form. Since the clinics have become very popular, reservations are highly recommended. Call 231-744-9629 to secure a spot.

Cross-country skiers can "shush" over five miles of lighted and groomed trails and an additional 2.5 miles of advanced natural trails. Cross-country ski equipment can be rented at the lodge, as well as ice skates and snowshoes. Ice skaters can cut a figure 8 or chase a hockey puck on two natural outdoor ice rinks. Each has a hockey and a family skating area.

COUNTY: MUSKEGON
CAMPING SITES: 246, ALL MODERN, PLUS 2 MINI-CABINS.
SCHEDULE: THE PARK IS OPEN YEAR ROUND, BUT THE CAMPGROUNDS' OPENING AND CLOSING DATES DEPEND ON WEATHER AND SAND BUILDUP.
DIRECTIONS: FROM US-31 NORTH OF MUSKEGON EXIT ONTO M-120 AND GO SOUTHWEST APPROXIMATELY 1.5 MILES TO GILES ROAD. TURN RIGHT (WEST) ONTO GILES AND GO 6 MILES TO SCENIC DRIVE. TURN LEFT (SOUTH) ONTO SCENIC DRIVE AND DRIVE A MILE TO THE PARK.
FURTHER INFORMATION: MUSKEGON STATE PARK, 3560 MEMORIAL DRIVE, NORTH MUSKEGON, MI 49445; 231-744-3480.

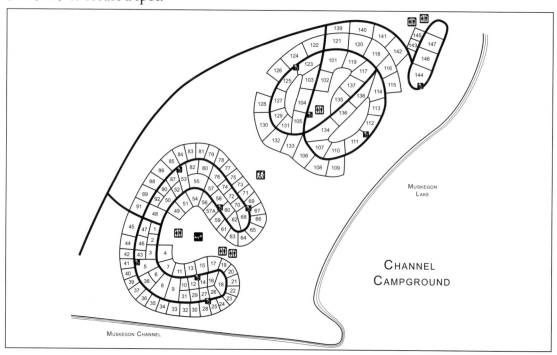

MUSKEGON LAKE

CHANNEL CAMPGROUND

MUSKEGON CHANNEL

PJ *Hoffmaster*
STATE PARK

26

OVERNIGHT ACCOMMODATIONS:

ACTIVITIES:

> The majestic mountains of sand that line the eastern shore of Lake Michigan are the longest stretch of dunes along fresh water anywhere in the world. Some of the finest views of this beautifully unique natural phenomenon come from the more than three miles of shoreline that edges P.J. Hoffmaster State Park. Towering dunes there stand guard over sandy beach, scenic picnic areas, deep forest, interdunal valleys, miles of hiking trails, and one of Lower Michigan's premier campgrounds.

It's hard not to head right for the beach or the top of one of the dunes on your arrival. But to better understand and appreciate what you are about to experience, try to first spend some time at the Gillette Visitor Center, near the geographic center of the park. Inside, slide shows in an 82-seat theater, plus dozens of colorful displays and dioramas combine to give you a basic education in the natural forces that created the dunes and the fragile dune ecology. Lectures, special programs and guided hikes are offered throughout the year.

But even the visitor center hardly prepares one for the emotional impact of that first stirring sight of the giant ramparts of sand that rise skyward only yards inland from the crystalline-blue waters of Lake Michigan. You can't make even a short visit and leave without a lasting memory of the scene. One of the most striking views comes from a platform less than a quarter mile from the nature center. It's only a 10-minute walk, but the climb to the sweeping vista of Lake Michigan and surrounding dunes takes at least another 10 minutes up what seems to be an interminable flight of stairs.

You can get other excellent views and more walking from the 10 miles of hiking trails that network the 1,150-acre park. Several routes follow breaks in the high dunes down to remote stretches of beach. Other longer trails climb over the dunes, weave through steep-sided interdunal valleys, and cut through the park's forested backcountry.

Local birdwatchers have spotted a variety of species of waterfowl, shorebirds, and upland birds in the diverse habitat. The park is also a prime area for warblers, and you can often see hawks soaring on the updrafts created by the dunes.

The easiest and shortest route to the shoreline is from a large day-use parking lot. A short walk from there past changing courts ends at a sandy swimming beach that stretches away in either direction for nearly a mile.

A small, open picnic area next to the beach parking lot is the closest in the park to water, but there's little privacy. For more seclusion, plenty of shade, and much less traffic try one of three picnic grounds strung along the road that leads to the visitor center. Hobbyists can operate their metal detectors in certain areas of the park which includes the picnic grounds, parking lots, campground, and very short sections of the beach.

Tucked into a wooded valley on the extreme north edge of the park well away from the picnic areas, visitor center and beach is one of the finest campgrounds in southern Michigan. From the seclusion of any of the 293 spacious, shaded lots that are nestled in a stand of mature red pine or scattered amid towering hardwoods, you'll rarely see or hear any of the day-users who run the park's visitor count up to nearly half a million a year. All lots have electrical hookups, and it's a short walk from any of the sites to restrooms with flush toilets and showers. There are eight pull-through campsites for those who don't like to back up their rigs. In addition, a quarter-mile walk through the woods leads to a campers swimming beach. Alcoholic beverages are banned in the campground from April 15 through Labor Day.

The popular campground is heavily used throughout the summer, filing almost every weekend, and you can't always count on finding a vacant lot even in midweek. Weekend use during fall color season can also be heavy. It pays to make reservations.

When snow blankets the dunes, three miles of cross-country ski trails, rated as intermediate, lace the south end of the park. Sledding down the face of the dunes and snowshoeing through the backcountry are also popular winter exercises.

COUNTY: MUSKEGON
CAMPING SITES: 293, ALL MODERN.
SCHEDULE: THE PARK IS OPEN YEAR ROUND. CAMPING IS PERMITTED FROM MID APRIL TO LATE OCTOBER.
THE GILLETTE VISITOR CENTER AND ITS ART GALLERY, BOOKSTORE, AND NATURAL-SCIENCE ROOM IS CLOSED FOR THE MONTH OF DECEMBER AND ON MONDAYS YEAR ROUND.
DIRECTIONS: FROM US-31 ABOUT 6 MILES SOUTH OF MUSKEGON TAKE PONTALUNA ROAD WEST ABOUT 2 MILES.
FURTHER INFORMATION: P.J. HOFFMASTER STATE PARK, 6585 LAKE HARBOR ROAD, MUSKEGON, MI 49441; 231-789-3711.

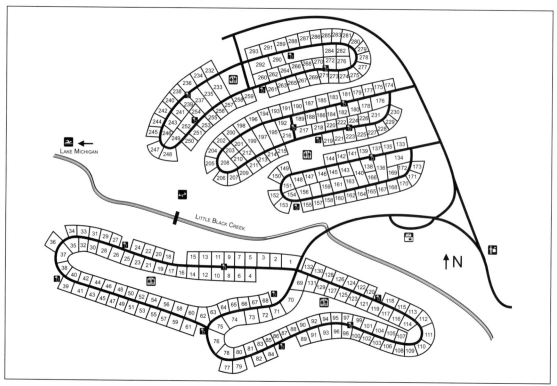

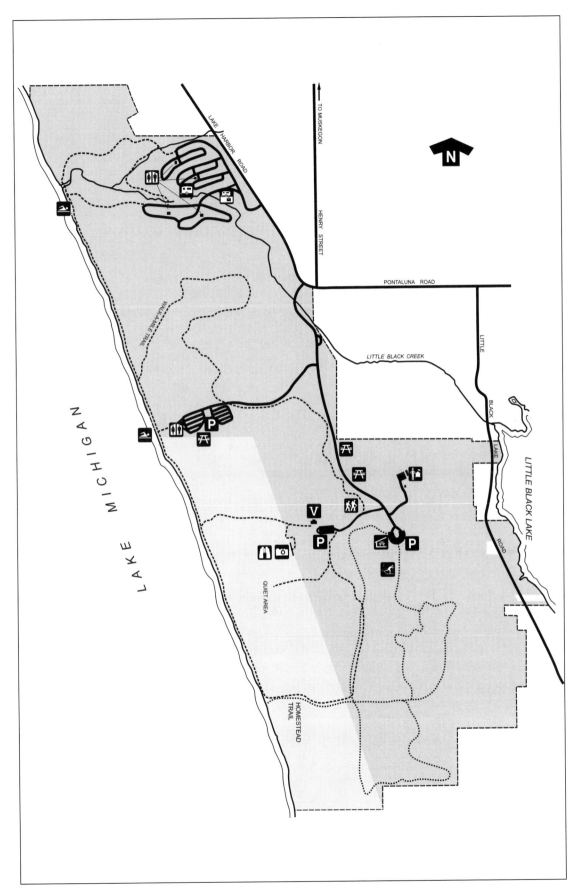

Grand Haven State Park

27

OVERNIGHT ACCOMMODATIONS: 🚐 ♿

ACTIVITIES: 🎿 🎣 🥾 🗼 🔦 🧺 🏕️ 🛟 📷 🏊

At Grand Haven State Park, what you see is what you get: a magnificent view and a fine, white sand that stretches for a half mile along Lake Michigan. Essentially, the park is the beach; only a slab of asphalt and a few buildings interrupt the wide, nearly flat expanse. And, to use another adage, the early bird here doesn't get the worm; he or she gets to play in the giant sandbox.

For its size (48 acres), Grand Haven may be the busiest state park in Michigan (a million visitors each year). Demand for campsites during prime summer weekends is so great reservations must be made months in advance. On those same weekends, if you're planning to just have a picnic or spend a day at the beach, you'd better arrive right after breakfast, not brunch, to get a parking spot.

The large, open, sand-covered picnic area and modern bathhouse and concession stand are within a few steps of the parking lot. It's only a few yards farther to the glistening strip of beach and sparkling Lake Michigan waters. Picnickers, swimmers, and most everyone in the park have full views of passing freighters and pleasure boats, windsurfers, a picturesque lighthouse that punctuates the tip of a long pier, and spectacular sunsets.

North of the day-use area lies one of the most unique campgrounds in the state. The 174 modern sites are nothing more than lines painted on an open asphalt slab completely surrounded by sand, which stretches north to the Grand River and west to Lake Michigan. There is no shade from the sun, little privacy, and no shelter from potentially strong on-shore winds or heavy rain. Setting up motorhomes and trailers on the blacktop is a snap, but staking down a tent in the soft sand can be like trying to anchor it in meringue. For those who love beach living, this is the place. Several camping sites are handicapped accessible and a recent upgrade made 50 amp service available to many campers. All sites are reservable.

Just north of the campground, a pier that juts out into Lake Michigan is curtained by monofilament when fish are biting. Day anglers who use the breakwater have their own special parking lot. Perch, salmon, steelhead, and brown and lake trout are caught from the pier and in surrounding waters. A nearby launch ramp gives access to both the Grand River and Lake Michigan.

If you don't fish and find yourself in need of a break from the sand, downtown Grand Haven is only a couple of long blocks away, and a trolley can take you farther afield. The world's largest musical fountain, only a short walk away, offers nightly performances throughout the summer.

No alcoholic beverages are allowed within the park at anytime without the written permission of the park ranger. Metal detectors are permitted in certain areas.

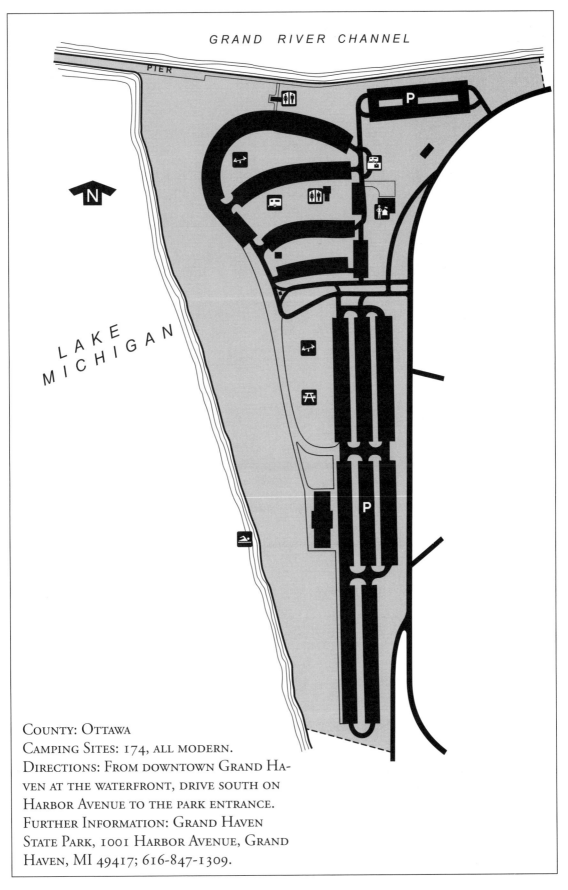

GRAND RIVER CHANNEL

PIER

N

LAKE
MICHIGAN

P

P

County: Ottawa
Camping Sites: 174, all modern.
Directions: From downtown Grand Ha-
ven at the waterfront, drive south on
Harbor Avenue to the park entrance.
Further Information: Grand Haven
State Park, 1001 Harbor Avenue, Grand
Haven, MI 49417; 616-847-1309.

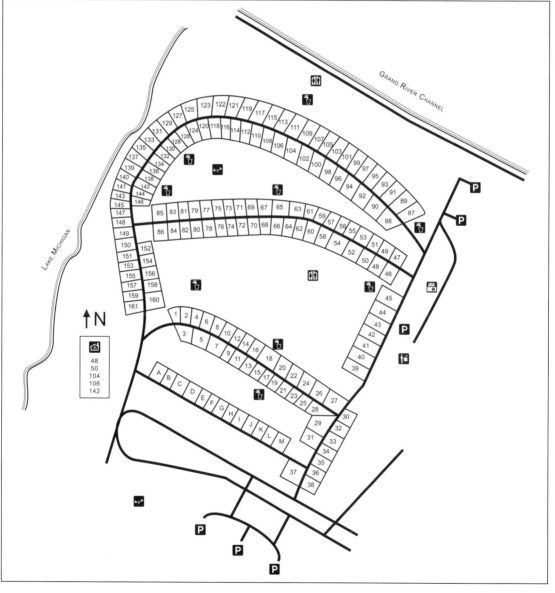

GRAND RIVER CHANNEL

LAKE MICHIGAN

↑N

48
50
104
106
142

125 123 122 121 119 117 115 113 111 109 107 105 103 101 99 97 95 93 91 89 87
127 129 131 133 135 137 139 141 143 145 147 148 149 150 151 153 155 157 159 161
124 120 118 116 114 112 110 108 106 104 102 100 98 96 94 92 90 88
128 126 130 132 134 136 138 142 144 146
152 154 156 158 160

85 83 81 79 77 75 73 71 69 67 65 63 61 59 57 56 55 53 51 49 47
86 84 82 80 78 76 74 72 70 68 66 64 62 60 58 54 52 50 48 46
45 44 43 42 41 40 39

1 2 4 6 8 10 12 14 16 18 20 22 24 26 27
3 5 7 9 11 13 15 17 19 21 23 25 28 30 32 34 35 36 38
A B C D E F G H I J K L M
29 31 33 37

P P P P P P P

Ionia
RECREATION AREA

28

OVERNIGHT ACCOMMODATIONS:

ACTIVITIES:

More than three miles of frontage on Grand River, some of the best bass fishing in the state, very good birdwatching, a 140-acre man-made lake flanked by a large swimming beach and beautiful picnic areas are only some of the features that draw 300,000 annually to the Ionia Recreation Area.

Most of the day-use activities revolve around the small but scenic Sessions Lake. The damming of Sessions Creek created numerous little bays and thin peninsulas that jut far out into the water. One willow-thin, tree-clad finger of land is not only the park's most scenic, but includes a specially designed table, built out to the water's edge, next to a fishing pier, for the wheelchair bound. You can cart coolers to tables and picnic shelters at two other areas: among towering hardwoods on the west shore of the lake and near the Grand River on the park's northern edge.

A sprawling swimming beach hugs the north side of Sessions Lake. The open, shadeless area, with excellent views across the water, is the only stretch of shoreline not crowded by trees and or marshes.

About a half-mile east of the lake and well away from most day-use facilities lies the park's 100-site modern campground. Just to the north of it is a 49-site rustic equestrian campground (no electricity, pit toilets only) with hitching posts at each lot.

Horsemen have 15 miles of bridle paths to ride that loop through the southern half of the 4,500-acre park. Hikers also use those routes, in addition to a 3.5-mile hiking trail

that circles the lake. Mountain bikers will find nine miles of designated bike paths winding through marsh, meadow and woods near the Grand River.

In the winter the entire park is open to cross-country skiers in addition to the three marked ski trails ranging from beginner to expert and running in length from one to six miles. Snowmobilers are welcome when four or more inches of snow blanket the park but they must stay off designated ski trails and the campground.

The park's diverse habitat – from riverine to lakeshore and open meadows to deep woods – shelters numerous wildflowers and attracts a surprisingly wide variety of birds. The local Audubon Society lists 199 bird species that have been spotted here.

Perhaps the biggest surprise is the DNR rates the Grand River as one of the two or three best bodies of water, lakes included, in the state for bass fishing. The section near the park is especially productive, and the stretch of river from Ionia west to Grand Rapids may well be the best smallmouth bass hole in Michigan.

The park's single access point onto the river accommodates canoes or car-toppers only,

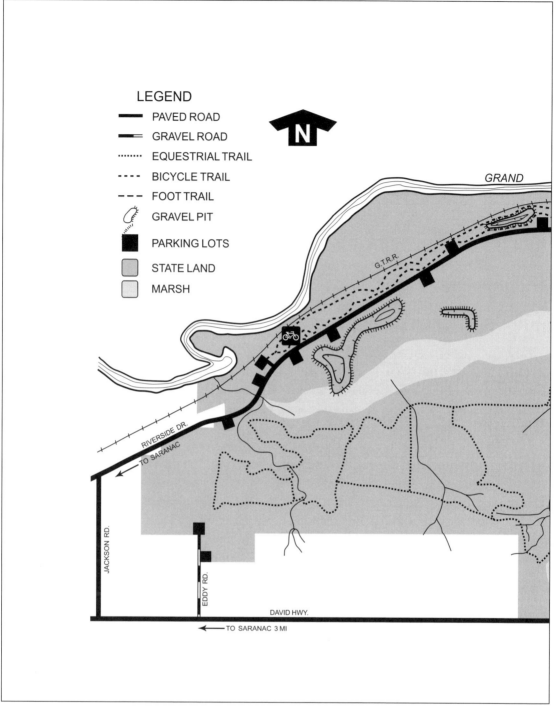

LEGEND

— PAVED ROAD
— GRAVEL ROAD
······· EQUESTRIAL TRAIL
----- BICYCLE TRAIL
- - - FOOT TRAIL
⌒ GRAVEL PIT
■ PARKING LOTS
▨ STATE LAND
▨ MARSH

N

GRAND

G.T.R.R.

RIVERSIDE DR.

TO SARANAC

JACKSON RD.

EDDY RD.

DAVID HWY.

← TO SARANAC 3 MI

but you can launch larger craft from a ramp just off M-66 on the south side of the city of Ionia or in Saranac, to the west.

There is a launch ramp on the west side of Sessions Lake. A no-wake speed is in effect. Fishing – including from shore on peninsulas that nearly enclose weed-filled bays – is good for large and smallmouth bass, walleye, catfish and panfish.

Except for a few posted areas, the park allows hunting with rabbits and deer the most plentiful game. Grouse, waterfowl, pheasants, squirrels, turkey and woodcock are also taken. Hunters can keep their dogs sharp at a field-trial area.

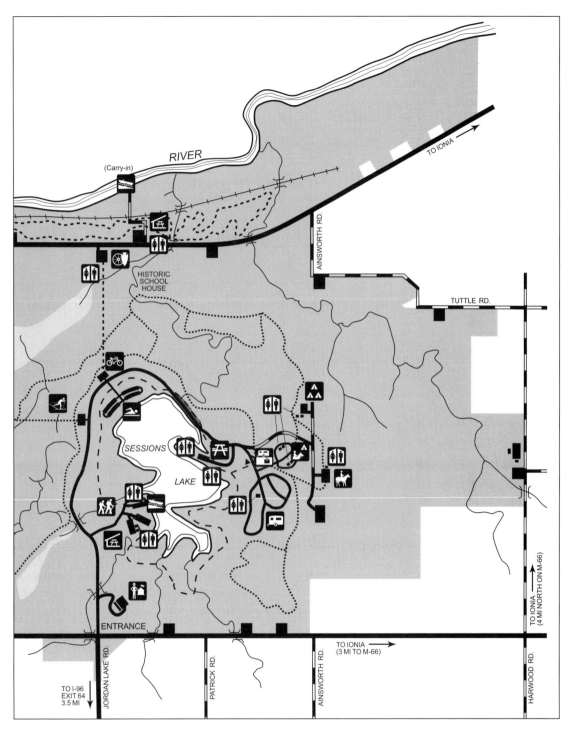

County: Ionia

Camping Sites: 149 (100 modern – some handicapped accessible, 49 rustic equestrian) plus 2 mini-cabins.

Directions: From exit 64 on I-96 drive 3 miles north to the park.

Further Information: Ionia Recreation Area, 2880 West David Highway, Ionia, MI 48846; 616-527-3750.

Sleepy Hollow
STATE PARK

29

OVERNIGHT ACCOMMODATIONS:

ACTIVITIES:

The centerpiece of Sleepy Hollow State Park is Lake Ovid, a large, island-dotted lake that was created by damming the Little Maple River. You can see the lake from nearly anywhere in the 2,600-acre park, and most facilities hug its shore. At the north end is a small swimming beach. The narrow strip of sand separates the water from a treeless lawn big enough for spreading a blanket or playing catch. Facilities there include a modern bathhouse and a few widely scattered grills and picnic tables. Other large, grass-carpeted picnic grounds ring the lake. One on the west shore features a bridge leading to the lake's largest island. All picnic areas provide plenty of room to claim a spot and a view for the day.

Striking views of the lake also come from a couple of sites in the modern campground a quarter mile from the lake on the east side of the park. The line of sight to the water from most of the 181 lots, however, is obstructed, but there is enough variety among the many pleasant sites that you won't have trouble finding a camping spot to your liking.

Many of the sites are in full sun, old hardwoods shelter others, and a few are almost completely screened by shrubs and low trees. All lots are flat and level, with asphalt slips for easy parking and setup of trailers and RVs. A minimum 100-foot power cord is required. Reservations are recommended from May 15 to September 30.

Walking is easy on 16 miles of foot trails, which are also open to mountain bikers. The paths cross over open, gently rolling land and occasionally probe into stands of hardwoods that fringe the park's boundaries and completely circle Lake Ovid. Cross-country skiers use the trails during the winter, and snowmobilers have a section of the park marked off for their use when snowfall reaches four or more inches.

Sleepy Hollow has nine miles of bridle trails open to horsemen who trailer their mounts in for the day. Mountain bikers are not allowed on bridle trails and likewise horses are not allowed on the hiking/biking trails.

The park is also an excellent birdwatching area. More than 200 species of birds have been recorded in the park, including significant numbers of waterfowl, which use the lake as a spring stopover.

The lake itself is popular with canoeists, who enjoy paddling along the winding shoreline, across small bays and around several islands. Fishermen can access the lake from a boat launch on the west shore or cast a line from either of two floating fishing piers. Anglers report regular catches of bluegills, bass, northern pike, and channel catfish. Fishing and canoeing is made even more pleasant because Lake Ovid is a no wake lake.

Hunting is allowed, with turkeys, deer, rabbits, ducks, and squirrels the game most often taken. Metal detectors are also permitted within certain areas of the park. Nature

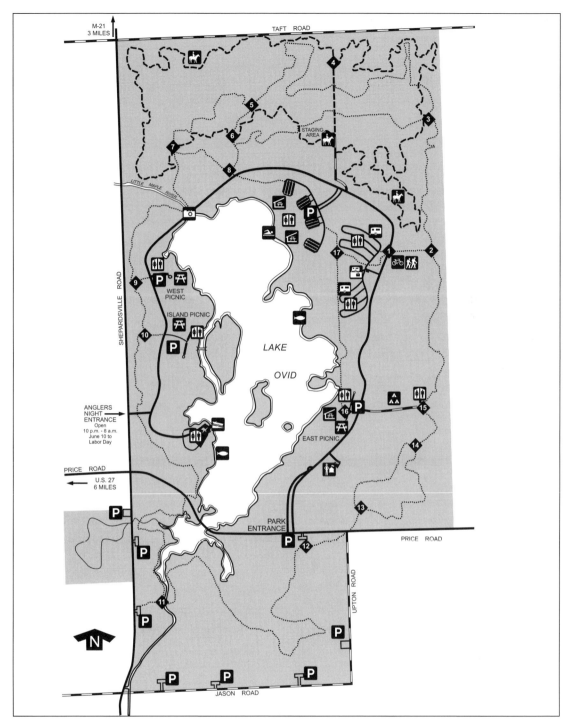

walks and informal programs that highlight the park's natural history are offered throughout the summer.

COUNTY: CLINTON
CAMPING SITES: 181, ALL MODERN.
SCHEDULE: THE PARK IS OPEN YEAR ROUND. THE CAMPGROUND IS GENERALLY OPEN

FROM EARLY APRIL TO LATE OCTOBER BUT DATES VARY EVERY YEAR.
DIRECTIONS: FROM US-27 APPROXIMATELY 5 MILES SOUTH OF ST. JOHNS, TAKE PRICE ROAD EAST 5.5 MILES.
FURTHER INFORMATION: SLEEPY HOLLOW STATE PARK, 7835 EAST PRICE ROAD, LAINGSBURG, MI 48848; 517-651-6217.

olland
STATE PARK

30

OVERNIGHT ACCOMMODATIONS:

ACTIVITIES:

Each year a million and a half visitors take advantage of the fact that the long, broad beach that edges Lake Michigan northwest of Holland is one of the most accessible and beautiful along the Lower Peninsula's west shore. Though this is one the heaviest-used parks in Michigan, there's always plenty of room on the acres of pillow-soft sand to stroll or spread blankets and towels.

The beach is just a few steps west from the large day-use area, which is front-and-centered by a large, modern bathhouse and concession stand. Lining the sand behind the bathhouse are a dozen or so well-used beach volleyball courts. You can picnic at a few tables that edge the parking lot and bathhouse, but you'll feel like you're eating in a department store window. For a little more privacy and, in some spots, even a hint of shade, carry your basket and cooler south from the parking lot to a picnic area that borders Lake Macatawa and the channel connecting it to Lake Michigan. Tables there are also front-row seats for watching the boat traffic on the busy channel.

In the summer park personnel present a variety of natural history programs and hikes that highlight the park's natural features and resources. The programs are open to both campers and day-users.

Across the road from the day-use parking area is one of the park's two widely separated and markedly different modern campgrounds. The recently upgraded Beach Campground features two modern restroom buildings and 98 sites, all of which can accommodate 50-

foot rigs. Thirty-one of those sites have sewer, water, and 50-amp hookups, making it one of only three campgrounds in the state park system to offer full hookups.

The camping spots are nothing more than lines painted on an asphalt island surrounded by sand, but if you love beach camping and don't mind a lack of privacy or shade, it doesn't get much better than this. Eight of the sites meet ADA accessibility standards. You can build sand castles next to your lot, walk just a few dozen steps to a magnificent beach, and bask in the glow of beautiful Lake Michigan sunsets. The campground also has a new sanitary dump station.

Sitting about a half mile inland and separated from the rest of the park by private property lies the Lake Macatawa Campground. The campground's 211 grassy sites – with some privacy, especially those nestled in a stand of red pine – are strung together in eight loops along the park road. This unit contains a number of 50-amp hookups, 10 handicapped accessible sites and two pull-throughs. Across Ottawa Beach Road from the campground is a camper's beach

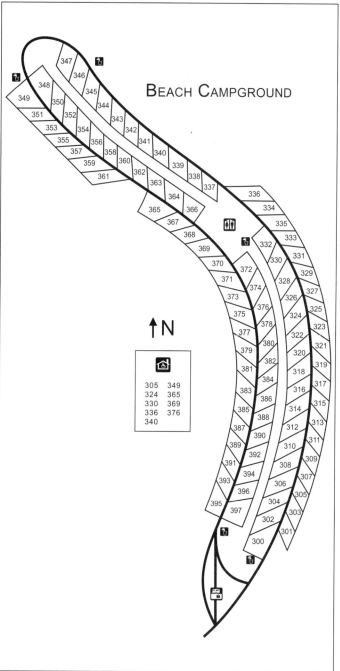

BEACH CAMPGROUND

↑N

305	349
324	365
330	369
336	376
340	

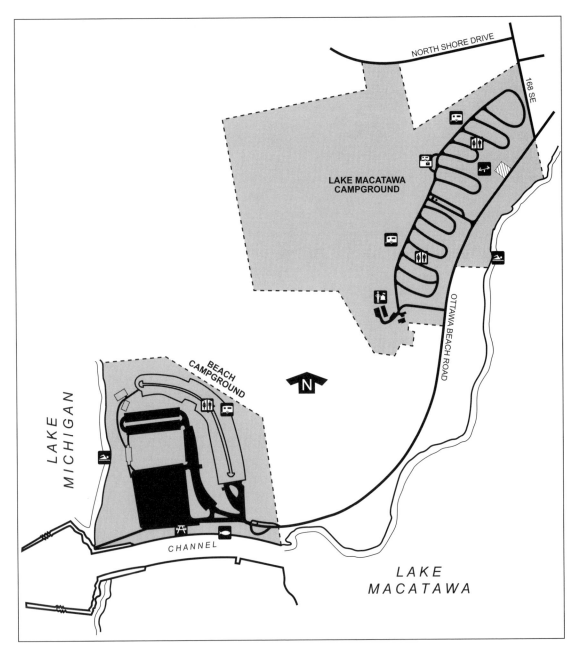

on Lake Macatawa. If you plan to stay at the Lake Macatawa unit, bring your 3- or 10-speed and take it on a pedaler's path to the Lake Michigan beach and other area bike tours.

During peak summer months, especially on weekends, the only sure way of getting a spot at either unit is by reservation. Even in mid-week, if you arrive late in the day without a reservation, you risk being turned away.

Water skiers skim across Lake Macatawa and fishermen hook walleyes and perch in its sheltered waters. On the Great Lakes, spring runs of lake trout, brown trout and salmon provide good action. Pier fishermen, too, pull out salmon and trout in the spring, plus perch throughout the summer, from a breakwater that marks the mouth of Lake Macatawa on the park's southern border. Shore fishing along the channel is popular as is ice fishing on the smaller lake after winter freeze up. Boaters can gain access to both lakes from a boat launching ramp a mile east

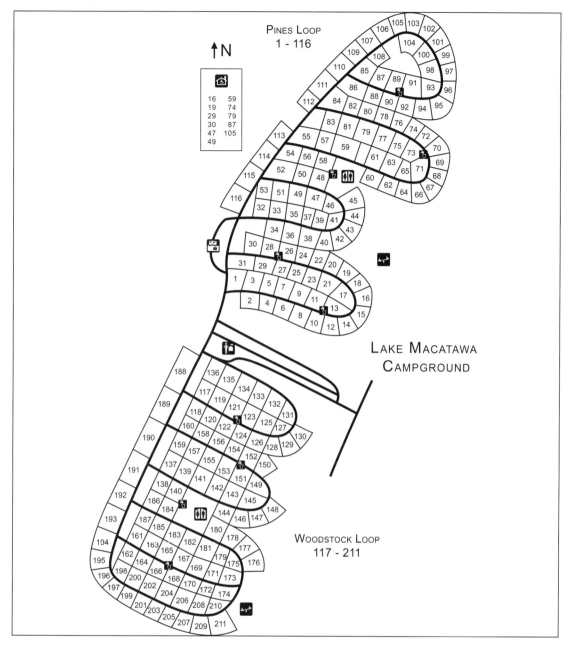

Pines Loop
1 - 116

↑N

16	59
19	74
29	79
30	87
47	105
49	

Lake Macatawa
Campground

Woodstock Loop
117 - 211

of the Lake Macatawa Campground.

Wireless internet access is available within a radius of about 150 feet from the concession stand. Metal detectors can be used in certain areas, but the possession or consumption of alcohol is prohibited throughout the park.

COUNTY: OTTAWA

CAMPING SITES: 309, ALL MODERN.

SCHEDULE: THE BEACH CAMPGROUND IS OPEN MAY 25 THROUGH THE DAY AFTER LABOR DAY. THE LAKE MACATAWA CAMPGROUND IS OPEN APRIL 1 THROUGH OCTOBER 31.

DIRECTIONS: FROM DOWNTOWN HOLLAND DRIVE NORTH ON RIVER AVENUE ACROSS THE MACATAWA RIVER, THEN TURN LEFT (WEST) AND DRIVE ON OTTAWA BEACH ROAD ABOUT 5 MILES.

FURTHER INFORMATION: HOLLAND STATE PARK, 2215 OTTAWA BEACH ROAD, HOLLAND, MI 49424; 616-399-9390.

*S*augatuck Dunes
STATE PARK

31

OVERNIGHT ACCOMMODATIONS: NONE

ACTIVITIES:

The DNR calls Saugatuck Dunes a "day-use park." That's false advertising. True, there's no campground, and the park is open only from 8 a.m. to 10 p.m. But it's impossible for anyone to absorb its 1,100 acres, over two miles of Lake Michigan beach, and 13 miles of marked hiking/cross ski trails in just one day.

It might be fun to try, but not many people even do that. Saugatuck Dunes is not only one of the Michigan's newest (established in 1977) state parks, but also, with only 30,000-plus annual visitors, one of the Lower Peninsula's least used. So if you're after exceptional scenic beauty without large crowds, look no further.

The park's glistening Lake Michigan beach is among the least-used in the state park system, and for good reason. You don't drive up, park and drag all your beach paraphernalia a few yards to the water's edge. The shortest route to the beach is a sand-sucking, one-mile slog over wooded dunes from the parking lot. It not only reduces your list of beach necessities, it's a great hedge against overcrowding.

Adjacent to the 50-car parking area, just inside the park's eastern boundary, picnic tables, grills and a covered picnic shelter lie scattered under a mix of evergreens and hardwoods. Vault toilets are found next to the picnic area, and they are the park's only concession to that other call of nature.

The rest of Saugatuck Dunes is almost totally undeveloped, wild and scenic, and the south end is a designated natural area. Twen-

ty- to 180-foot-high dunes frame the waters of Lake Michigan, and back from them a mixed hardwood/pine forest partially covers the rolling landscape.

Thirteen miles of sandy, well-marked trails, all of which begin at the parking lot, network the park and range in length from the 2.5-mile roundtrip to the beach to a 5.5-mile loop through the southern end of the park. Two paths end at scenic overlooks of the lake from the crest of barrier dunes. Metal detectors are allowed in certain areas of the park.

When the snow flies, the trails, which range in difficulty from novice to expert, welcome cross-country skiers.

COUNTY: ALLEGAN

CAMPING SITES: NONE.

DIRECTIONS: TAKE EXIT 41 (BLUE STAR HIGHWAY) FROM I-96 AND GO WEST LESS THAN A HALF MILE TO 64TH STREET. TURN RIGHT (NORTH) ONTO 64TH AND DRIVE 1.5 MILES TO 138TH AVENUE. TURN LEFT (WEST) ONTO 138TH AND GO ABOUT A MILE.

FURTHER INFORMATION: SAUGATUCK DUNES STATE PARK, C/O VAN BUREN STATE PARK, 23960 RUGGLES ROAD, SOUTH HAVEN, MI 49090; 269-637-2788.

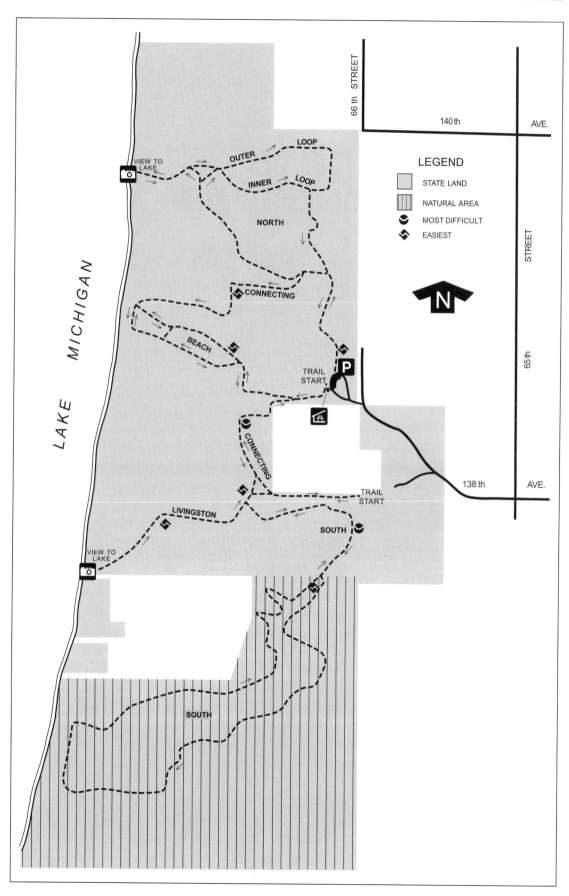

Yankee Springs
RECREATION AREA

32

OVERNIGHT ACCOMMODATIONS:

ACTIVITIES:

On hot summer weekends at Yankee Springs Recreation Area, a narrow peninsula that pokes into Gun Lake resembles Times Square on New Years Eve. Before lunch on Saturdays and Sundays, the long, continuous parking lot that centers the finger of land has filled with swimmers' and picnickers' vehicles who have claimed tables and parcels of beach lining both sides of the peninsula.

But though it may sometimes seem like it, not everybody who crosses into park territory disappears into the massive quilt of beach blankets. For those who'd rather tiptoe through something other than sunbathers, there's plenty to do and plenty of room to do it in the park's 5,000-plus acres, which take in three beautiful campgrounds, miles of hiking and mountain bike trails, and good opportunities to birdwatch, hunt and fish.

There's no doubt, though, that most of the 800,000 people a year who come to the park end up in the beautiful picnic beach areas lining the peninsula that juts so far out into the water it almost cuts Gun Lake, the park's largest, in half. Dozens of tables and grills there, plus two large picnic shelters and playground equipment are scattered in open meadows and under shade trees. On the west shore, two bathhouses back the day-use area's most popular feature, two swimming beaches that gently slope under the water to only knee depth far from shore. A third swimming beach lies on the peninsula's east side.

Power boaters and water skiers launch down a ramp on the east shore then, along with those who navigate sailboards and sail-boats, put on a continuous show for the land-bound crowd.

Near the peninsula's base, cut off from the busy day-use area by a narrow inlet, is the largest of the park's camping areas. All 200 large, level lots there have electrical hookups and access to modern restroom facilities. Though mature hardwoods shade the sites to the point that in the center of the area the only ground cover is fallen leaves, there is little or no privacy. The campground boasts 16 lakefront lots and 11 handicapped accessible sites. A large, sandy stretch of gently sloping Gun Lake shoreline that fronts the area is reserved exclusively for campers. Overnighters who tow boats can launch them at a campers-only ramp in the inlet and then moor their craft to posts that line the bank of the ready-made basin.

Reservations are a must from Memorial Day to Labor Day. If you have no choice or insist on trying your luck without booking a site, arrive late on Sunday afternoon or early in the morning during midweek.

In less demand and well removed from the Gun Lake crowds are two small, rustic campgrounds near the park's eastern bound-

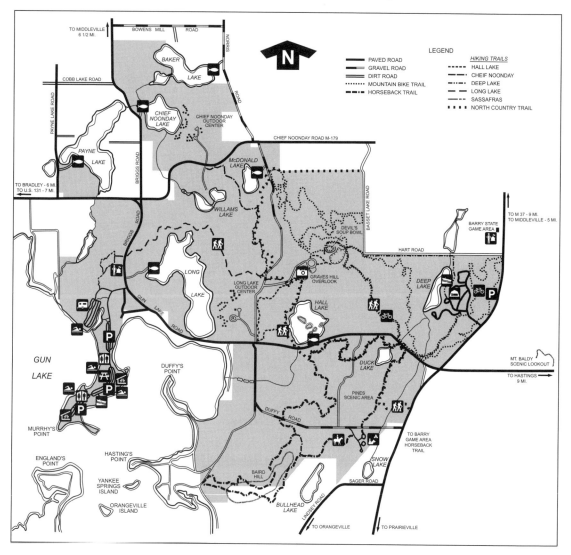

ary. The 120-site Deep Lake Campground is spread across a bluff overlooking the lake. Facilities include a fishing pier and boat ramp but no swimming beach. Tucked into the southeast corner of the sprawling park is a 25-site equestrian campground that gives immediate access to miles of bridle trails.

Hikers have six trails totaling more than 15 miles to choose from. The diverse routes, which range from 0.5 to 5 miles long, cut through an array of wildflowers, pass several interesting geological features, and rise to numerous scenic overlooks. Birdwatching is good, and the area, once the hunting grounds of the Algonquin Indians, is still rich in wildlife. Six miles of the 1,500-mile North Country Trail furrows the park on its

long tramp from New York to North Dakota. The Gun Lake Trail, the park's shortest, is handicapped accessible.

All but one (Duck) of the park's nine lakes have boat ramps, which fishermen use to go after panfish, bass, northern pike, walleye and muskies. Gun Lake is stocked annually with walleyes, but don't fish there on weekends unless you're prepared to be a pylon for speedboaters, sailboats and water skiers.

A 12 mile-long mountain bike trail starts at the Deep Lake Campground and takes pedalers from flat, easily biked terrain to some of the park's most rugged landscape. Long uphill climbs, deep sand pockets and creek crossings tests the mettle of even advanced mountain bikers.

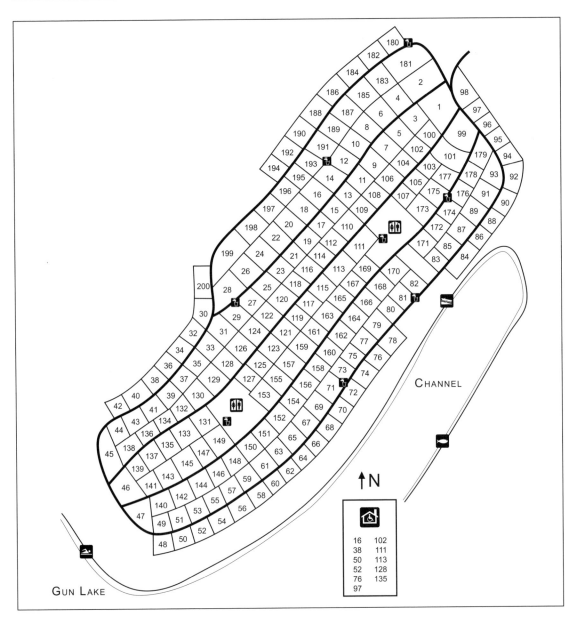

CHANNEL

↑N

GUN LAKE

🏠	
16	102
38	111
50	113
52	128
76	135
97	

In the winter cross-country skiers can track on 7 miles of groomed trails, and snowmobilers can leave tracks over their own large, open area. Ice fishing is also popular.

Hunters pursue game both in the park and in the adjoining 15,000-acre Barry State Game Area. Deer are the favored quarry, but rabbits, squirrels and ruffed grouse are also hunted. All but two of the park's nine lakes are open to waterfowl hunters.

Informal hikes and programs that explore the park's natural features, wild life, and human heritage are offered throughout the year. Metal detecting is allowed within specified areas. The park also has a large outdoor conference center that contains 12 rustic cabins including other facilities.

COUNTY: BARRY

CAMPING SITES: 345 (200 MODERN, 145 RUSTIC).

DIRECTIONS: FROM THE INTERSECTION OF US-131 AND M-179 (EXIT 61 ON US-131) DRIVE EAST 8 MILES ON M-179.

FURTHER INFORMATION: YANKEE SPRINGS RECREATION AREA, 2104 SOUTH BRIGGS ROAD, MIDDLEVILLE, MI 49333; 269-795-9081.

Kal-Haven Trail

State Park

OVERNIGHT ACCOMMODATIONS: NONE

ACTIVITIES:

At 100 feet wide and 34 miles long, Kal-Haven Trail is one of Michigan's most unusually shaped state parks. The route follows an old, unused stretch of the Penn Central Railroad from South Haven, on the shores of Lake Michigan, to Kalamazoo. The crushed limestone that has replaced the rails and ties accommodates bikers, wheelchairs, and foot traffic. In winter cross-country skiers and snowmobilers share the entire route.

Walking, pedaling, or skiing is easy, with no steep grades or hills. The trail passes through numerous small towns (Alamo, Kendall, Pine Grove, Gobles, Bloomingdale, Berlamont, Grand Junction, La-Cots and Kibbie), crosses picturesque streams on several old railroad trestles and one covered bridge, and passes a variety of scenic vistas.

Camping is not allowed on the trail itself, but state and private campgrounds are located on the South Haven end. Or you can even choose to spend the night at one of several bed-and-breakfasts in towns along the route. You can get a detailed map (see Further Information) that locates public rest areas and staging areas along the way and also lists grocery stores, restaurants, bike rentals and lodging options. Picnic areas are located at the trailheads at both ends of the park.

A vehicle permit is not required, but you will need a trail pass, available at both trailheads. Prices range from $3 for an individual day pass to $7 for a family day pass, and $15 and $35 respectively for annual passes.

COUNTIES: KALAMAZOO, VAN BUREN

CAMPING SITES: NONE

DIRECTIONS: KALAMAZOO TRAILHEAD: FROM US-131 NORTHWEST OF KALAMAZOO, EXIT ONTO M-43 AND DRIVE WEST LESS THAN A QUARTER MILE TO 10TH STREET. TURN RIGHT (NORTH) ONTO 10TH AND DRIVE APPROXIMATELY 2 MILES TO THE TRAILHEAD. SOUTH HAVEN TRAILHEAD: GO ONE MILE NORTH OF TOWN ON THE BLUE STAR HIGHWAY.

FURTHER INFORMATION: KAL-HAVEN TRAIL, C/O VAN BUREN STATE PARK, 23960 RUGGLES ROAD, SOUTH HAVEN, MI 49090; 269-637-2788.

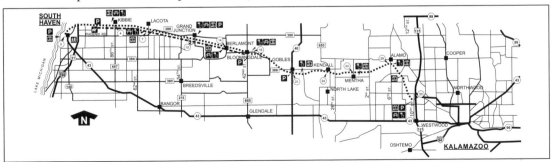

Van Buren STATE PARK

OVERNIGHT ACCOMMODATIONS:

ACTIVITIES:

Van Buren State Park hides a secret behind the partition of high, wooded sand dunes that line its west boundary. A wide sidewalk leads through a single narrow opening, and it's not until you're almost completely through the sand wall that the view opens to reveal the park's main attraction: the limitless blue waters of Lake Michigan edged by a broad sweep of fine, soft sand. The dune-backed shore disappears into the horizon on the north, and nearly a half mile to the south, park property ends at the Palisades Nuclear Power Plant.

Just back from the beach, nestled in the narrow gap that cuts through the dunes, are a large bathhouse and a few picnic tables. A little farther inland, more tables, grills, and a shelter are spread over an open, grassy meadow that separates the back of the dunes from the large day-use parking lot. (Note: Alcoholic beverages are prohibited on the beach and in the day-use area.)

Also just a few minutes' walk from the beach, tucked into the park's southeast corner away from the mainstream of traffic, is a fully modern campground. The 220 well-worn sites are arranged in five loops, with a mix of both sunny and shaded lots. And though the lots are large, they are close together, with little or no privacy. Campground use is heavy throughout the summer, filling to capacity on weekends.

Though there are no marked hiking trails in the 407-acre park, the main entrance of the 14-mile-long Van Buren Trail State Park lies next to the parking lot at the end of Ruggles Road in the park's day-use area. The state park trail is open to biking and hiking as well as cross-country skiing and snowmobiling in the winter. Within the park, well-worn foot paths probe the barrier dunes. Some of the huge, fragile sand mountains, however, are posted with no-trespassing signs to prevent human erosion from adding to the natural wear. You can stretch your legs along the lengthy shoreline and also wander through the large, rolling, wooded undeveloped parcel in the park's northeast corner.

Parts of the park are open to hunting in season, with deer and squirrel the game most often taken. Metal detector hobbyists can pursue their pastime in specific areas. Nature programs are offered throughout the summer.

There's no place to launch a boat or fish within park boundaries. If you want to go after the area's salmon, lake trout, and perch, it's only three miles north to public launches, marinas, a pier, and charter boats at South Haven. The village caters to the tourist trade and also boasts one of the finest maritime museums to be found anywhere in the Great Lakes.

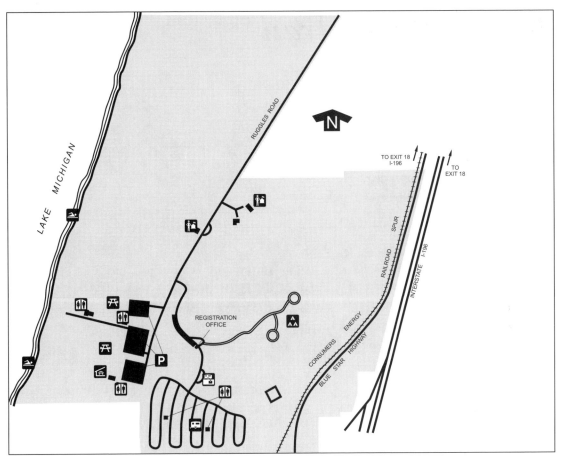

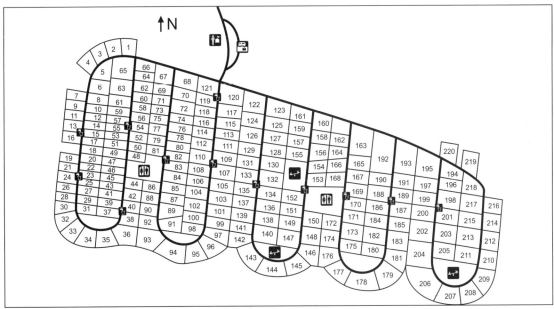

County: Van Buren

Camping Sites: 220, all modern.

Directions: Take Blue Star Highway south out of South Haven for 3 miles to Ruggles Road. Turn right (west) onto Ruggles Road and drive about a mile.

Further Information: Van Buren State Park, 23960 Ruggles Road, South Haven, MI 49090; 269-637-2788.

Van Buren Trail
State Park

OVERNIGHT ACCOMMODATIONS: NONE

ACTIVITIES:

This 14-mile-long, multi-use trail runs from Van Buren State Park to the northern edge of Hartford, Michigan. During spring, summer and fall hikers and bikers can explore the lush southwestern Michigan landscape from the dirt and gravel surfaced trail. The area through which the trail passes holds the promise of good birding. In winter the linear park is open to cross-country skiers and snowmobiles are welcome when the trail is blanketed with four-or-more inches of snow.

COUNTY: VAN BUREN
CAMPING SITES: NONE, BUT THE PARK'S MAIN ENTRANCE IS IN VAN BUREN STATE PARK WHICH BOASTS MORE THAN 200 CAMPSITES.
DIRECTIONS: TAKE THE BLUE STAR HIGHWAY SOUTH OF SOUTH HAVEN FOR 3 MILES TO RUGGLES ROAD. TURN RIGHT (WEST) ONTO RUGGLES AND GO A MILE TO VAN BUREN STATE PARK. FOLLOW ENTRANCE ROAD TO LAST PARKING LOT AND TRAILHEAD.

FURTHER INFORMATION: VAN BUREN TRAIL STATE PARK, C/O VAN BUREN STATE PARK, 23960 RUGGLES ROAD, SOUTH HAVEN, MI 49090; 269-637-2788.

Fort Custer
Recreation Area

OVERNIGHT ACCOMMODATIONS:

ACTIVITIES:

A little something for everyone and a lot of potential outdoor enjoyment for anyone is packed into the sprawling year-round playground named Fort Custer Recreation Area.

This is a mecca for mountain bikes. With 25 miles of rugged trails divided into three loops there's plenty of opportunity for off-road pedaling. The park and its trails even serve as a site for mountain bike races. Additionally, the extensive system of park roads coupled with the distance between facilities, not only add up to long aerobic rides, but also make bicycles a convenient means of getting around the far-flung park. Many bikers also pedal to the small village of Augusta, to the west.

Hikers have the same 25 miles of multi-use trails on which to wear out their boots plus a 3-mile-long, hikers-only loop that circles three small lakes – Jackson, Whitford and Lawler – in the southwest corner of the park. The trail weaves through a wildfowl management area, so you can usually see ducks and geese on the wing and in the water. Equestrians also make use of the 25 miles of trail. When the snow flies, the three loops become a thoroughfare for dog sleds, snowmobiles and cross-country skiers who court exhaustion by working any or all of the trails.

You can bring your own small boat and launch it at ramps on all the area's lakes and the Kalamazoo River, or you can rent one at the Eagle Lake day-use area and go after bluegills, bass, and pike. A no-wake speed limit is in effect on all the lakes.

The recreation area's only swimming beach edges the north shore of the largest body of water in the park, Eagle Lake. The long, wide stretch of sand and beachhouse are backed by large, open picnic grounds that overlook the water from a low bluff. Extensive tree plantings are just beginning to pay shade dividends. But the best protection from the sun comes from two picnic shelters.

A smaller, scenic, and much-more-private picnic area hugs the west shore of the two-lakes-in-one, Whitmore and Lawler. You can plop your cooler on a table right at the water's edge or under shade trees in full view of the lily pads, rushes, and marshy edges of the inlets that ring the shore. The trails that circle the lakes are only a step away, and shoreline fishing near the picnic area looks promising.

North of Jackson Lake, 219 sites divided between two loops make up the park's campground. Mature trees, which guard most sites, plus dense shrubs and wide spacing, create excellent privacy, and all lots have paved slips. Eleven of the sites are handicapped accessible and the campground's southern loop holds two mini-cabins. Campers on both loops have access to modern restrooms and electrical hookups. The campground is only moderately used throughout most of the

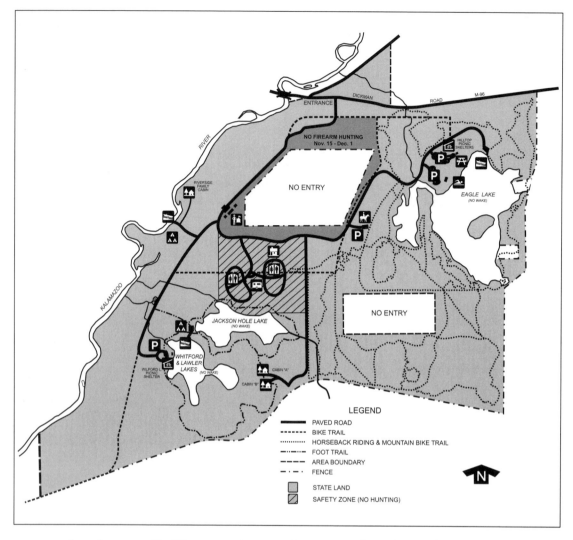

LEGEND

———	PAVED ROAD
– – –	BIKE TRAIL
·········	HORSEBACK RIDING & MOUNTAIN BIKE TRAIL
–·–·–	FOOT TRAIL
– – –	AREA BOUNDARY
–·–·–	FENCE
▨	STATE LAND
▧	SAFETY ZONE (NO HUNTING)

summer, but does usually fill to capacity every weekend in July and August. Both campers and day-users are welcome to take part in informal programs and hikes highlighting the park's natural history and heritage.

The park has three frontier cabins for rent: two on the east side of Whitford Lake that sleep 16, plus a smaller and more recently built family cabin on the banks of the Kalamazoo River that sleeps six. Many winter sportsmen spend the night in one of the cozy cabins, including snowmobilers who can run the gas tanks of their machines empty anywhere on the park's 2,962 acres except marked ski trails. Obviously, cabin reservations are a must.

The park offers excellent deer and rabbit hunting and is open to all species during regular seasons from September 15 to March 31.

And lastly, if you seek to enjoy and observe the kind of event that is far removed from the everyday experience in southern Michigan here's your chance. The park hosts dogsled races each winter; call the number below for dates and time.

County: Kalamazoo
Camping Sites: 219, all modern, plus two mini-cabins and three rustic cabins.
Directions: Approximately 10 miles west of Battle Creek on M-96.
Further Information: Fort Custer Recreation Area, 5163 Fort Custer Drive, Augusta, MI 49012; 269-731-4200.

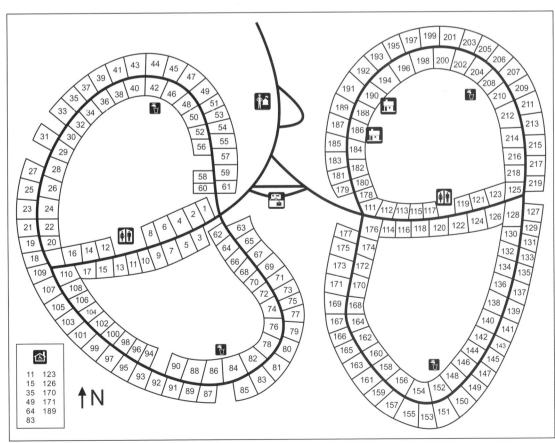

Grand Mere State Park

37

OVERNIGHT ACCOMMODATIONS: NONE

ACTIVITIES:

Many visitors come to Grand Mere State Park because it is an extremely secluded spot of uncommon beauty. The dunes, forests, Lake Michigan shoreline, and string of small interdunal lakes are part of the reason that Grand Mere is one of only a dozen Michigan areas listed among the country's National Natural Landmarks. If you're a backwoods pro, dedicated birdwatcher, or experienced naturalist, you'll revel in the isolation and nearly total undeveloped beauty.

The vegetation that grows in the park is an almost classic example of plant evolution and succession – from aquatic to terrestrial, from bare sand to climax forest – that began shortly after glaciers retreated from the state some 10,000 years ago. Because the area is unusually protected, representatives from just about every phase of the process remain, and biologists, naturalists and other scientists comb the park looking for the often rare species.

Grand Mere has also earned a reputation as one of the finest birdwatching areas in the state. Among the 250 species that have been spotted here include such rare Michigan visitors as Yellow-throated Warblers, Dickcissels, Mockingbirds, Bell's Vireo, Summer Tanager, and Worm-eating Warblers. The spring migration season is a great time to visit with binoculars and bird books. Throughout the warm-weather months, ducks, loons, cormorants and shorebirds find refuge within the interdunal lakes, and you can usually spot a wide variety of thrushes, warblers and songbirds in the bordering cover and surrounding woods. Spring and fall are both good for observing flights of migrating hawks.

From the park's picnic area a trail heads west from the picnic shelter along the marshy shoreline of South Lake. Because the first half-mile of the route is paved and bordered by dense vegetation on the South Lake side and wooded dunes on the other, it is one of the finest wheelchair-accessible birding spots in the state. At a couple of points along this section of trail, worn paths cut off to the right and lead to a mile of pristine Lake Michigan shoreline that draws beachcombers, swimmers and sunbathers. Where the main trail pavement gives way to sand the route curves to the south, climbs a high bluff on the west side of South Lake, and winds through wooded dunes lying between the smaller lake and Lake Michigan. Cross-country skiers etch the snow-covered trails in the winter months.

Fishermen with craft less than 14 feet long can put in at an unimproved sandy launch site on Middle Lake and drop a line for a variety of panfish. The lake is shallow and weedy and electric motors only are advised.

Hunting is allowed in some areas of the park, and duck blinds, by permit only, are allowed on Middle and South lakes. Contact

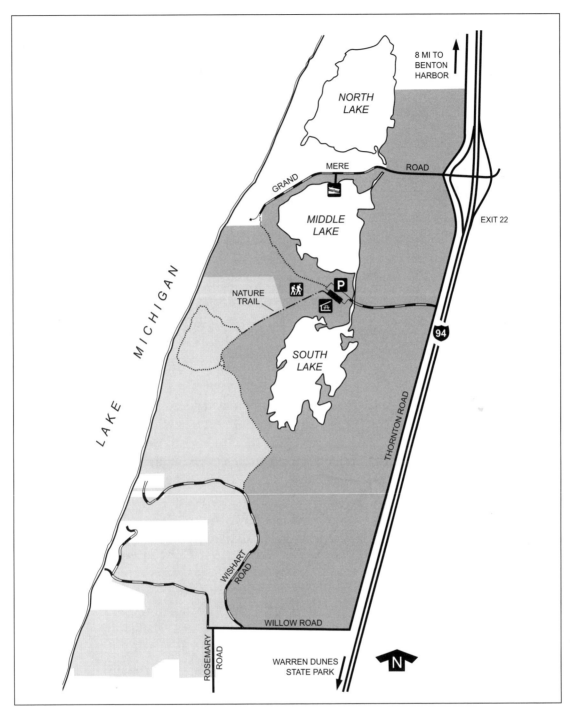

the park for other special hunting regulations.

Alcoholic beverages are prohibited from March 1 through September 30. Metal detectors are allowed in certain areas of the park.

COUNTY: BERRIEN
CAMPING SITES: NONE

DIRECTIONS: TAKE EXIT 22 (STEVENSVILLE) FROM I-94 AND DRIVE 400 FEET WEST ON GRAND MERE ROAD TO THORNTON ROAD. TURN SOUTH ONTO THORNTON AND DRIVE ABOUT A HALF MILE TO THE PARK ENTRANCE. FURTHER INFORMATION: GRAND MERE STATE PARK, 12032 RED ARROW HIGHWAY, SAWYER, MI 49125; 269-426-4013.

Warren Dunes
State Park

38

OVERNIGHT ACCOMMODATIONS:

ACTIVITIES:

We should require every out-of-state tourist who comes into Michigan from the south-west corner to stop at Warren Dunes State Park, less than 10 miles north of the state line. What a stunning introduction to our state, to a coastline that is repeated for hundreds of miles to the Straits of Mackinac, to a coastline that is only one of four. Even if you're a longtime resident who has seen what wind, water, and sand has created elsewhere along our 3,121 miles of Great Lakes frontage, you will be unprepared for your first-time visit here.

The views from the entrance road leading to the beach are so outstanding that the DNR has had to post signs advising the drivers who chauffeur in 1.3 million annual visitors that stopping is not allowed. Huge dunes tower over the asphalt on the right, while from their base to the left, the wide expanse of sand falls sharply away to deep-blue Lake Michigan waters that blend into the horizon. It's hard to keep your foot off the brake.

When you do stop, it's at one of the largest, most beautiful beaches in the state. Fine, soft sand drops none too gently to the water from two large beachhouses set on high, sandy ridges. Each of the changing facilities fronts its own immense parking lot, and directly behind the asphalt are mountains of sand that cut off the area from the rest of the park. The strenuous climb to any of the peaks ends with excellent views of the expanse of water and sand that swallows up the buildings, acres of blacktop, and thousands of visitors. To the north a virtual wilderness of sand arches past the park boundary to the horizon.

Shouldering the coast and rolling inland to blanket much of the rest of the 1,952-acre park are the Great Warren Dunes. You can get a taste of the tree-spiked dunes from eight miles of marked hiking trails (six miles of cross-country trails in the winter), or you can feast on them away

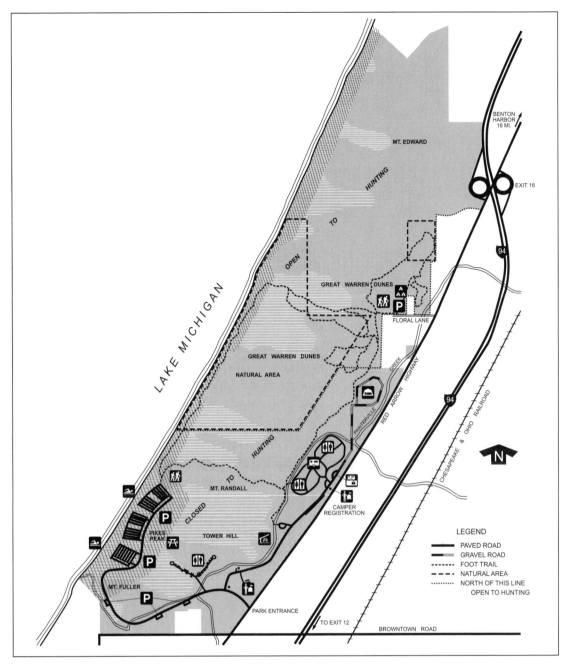

LAKE MICHIGAN

MT. EDWARD

OPEN TO HUNTING

GREAT WARREN DUNES

GREAT WARREN DUNES
NATURAL AREA

CLOSED TO HUNTING

MT. RANDALL

PIKES PEAK

TOWER HILL

MT. FULLER

PARK ENTRANCE

CAMPER
REGISTRATION

FLORAL LANE

PAINTERVILLE

RED ARROW HIGHWAY

CREEK

BENTON
HARBOR
16 MI.

EXIT 16

94

94

CHESAPEAKE & OHIO RAILROAD

TO EXIT 12

BROWNTOWN ROAD

N

LEGEND
PAVED ROAD
GRAVEL ROAD
FOOT TRAIL
NATURAL AREA
NORTH OF THIS LINE
OPEN TO HUNTING

from the crowds by heading into hundreds of open, undeveloped acres. A good way to explore the dunes plus learn a little of their natural history is to walk the one-mile Warren Dunes Nature Trail. A self-guiding brochure with numbered paragraphs that match numbered posts along the route is available at the trailhead located on the park road leading to the park's modern campground.

That overnight area is located well away from the hustle, bustle, and heavy traffic of the beach area. One hundred eighty-two large sites are arranged in two loops in such a pattern that, usually, no two lots end up back to back, which makes for good privacy. Many sites are heavily wooded, some are grass covered, and a few are well worn. The southern loop has the most heavily wooded sites, the most shade and privacy and also houses the park's three mini-cabins. A hiking trail through the dunes to the beach also begins at the southern loop. Or if you don't like playing Lawrence of Arabia across all that sand, the beach is only a five-minute drive by car. Reservations are a must for any site on either loop.

Northwest of the modern campground, 24 rustic camp-sites lie widely scattered along the looping gravel road that used to encompass an organizational campground, which has been moved farther north.

Several small, shaded picnic areas line the road to the beach. For the most beauty and se-clusion, take a short road that branches north, only a few hun-dred feet past the contact station, to its end at what is left of the park's largest picnic area, on the lee side of a giant dune. Nearly one entire wing of the picnic area has been buried under the shifting mountain of sand. At the remaining wing trees shelter tables, grills and a modern rest-room building from the sun, but not from the wall of sand that is slowly creeping closer.

All of Berrien County ranks as good birding and the park's woods and natural areas attract a wide variety of songbirds. From the beach birders regularly spot numerous waterfowl, gulls, terns and soaring birds of prey.

Some areas of the park are open to hunting, and metal de-tectors are allowed in specific areas. Contact the address or phone number below for details on both. There is a strictly en-forced ban on alcohol through-out the entire park from March 1 – September 30.

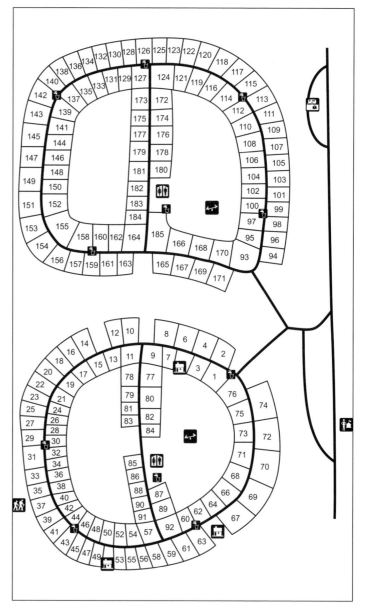

County: Berrien

Camping Sites: 182 modern, 24 rustic plus 3 mini-cabins and 2 rental tepees.

Schedule: The park and campground is open all year, but the restroom facilities are closed from October 15 to May 1.

Directions: From I-94 12 miles south of St. Joseph, take exit 16 and drive 2 miles south on Red Arrow Highway.

Further Information: Warren Dunes State Park, 12032 Red Arrow Highway, Sawyer, MI 49125; 269-426-4013.

Warren Woods

STATE PARK

39

OVERNIGHT ACCOMMODATIONS: NONE

ACTIVITIES:

Tucked away in the extreme southeast corner of Michigan are 311 acres of forest so sublimely beautiful they have not only been set aside as a state park, but are also designated as a National Natural Landmark. The forest includes the last known stand – with outstanding individual specimens – of virgin beeches and maples left in southern Michigan. Axes and saws have never touched this tract; even centuries' worth of deadfalls lie where they have fallen.

The unique area is the legacy of E.K. Warren, a local businessman who in the 1870s, when most people saw nothing but dollar signs in Michigan's forests, had the unusual foresight to purchase the virgin hardwood stand with the sole intent of saving it for posterity.

If Warren could visit the park today he would be pleased to see that it has remained as one of the least developed in the state. Pit toilets, a small parking lot, and a one-table picnic area are about the only concessions to visitors.

The lack of facilities doesn't matter, because the reason for a visit is to walk through the majestic broad-leaf hardwoods accented by the needles of the occasional huge red pines. From the parking lot, a well-worn trail heads north into the heart of the park. A quarter-mile walk brings you to a footbridge crossing the picturesque Galien River and two more miles of pathway that leads you through a cathedral of trees. Not surprisingly, fall – when the trees, trails and air are filled with bright yellow splashed with orange and red – is an especially good time to visit. The trails are open to cross-country skiers in the winter.

Warren Woods is also one of the state's premier birding sites. During spring migrations the woods attract numerous warblers, many of them uncommon to Michigan and usually only seen much farther south. Cerulean, Hooded and Kentucky warblers, along with Acadian flycatchers and Louisiana Waterthrushes, are regularly spotted all summer. The woods are also an ideal location for seeing woodpeckers, including the crow-sized Pileated Woodpecker.

COUNTY: BERRIEN
CAMPING SITES: NONE
DIRECTIONS: FROM I-94 TAKE EXIT 6 (UNION PIER) AND GO EAST ON ELM VALLEY ROAD ABOUT 2.8 MILES.
FURTHER INFORMATION: WARREN WOODS STATE PARK, C/O WARREN DUNES STATE PARK, 12032 RED ARROW HIGHWAY, SAWYER MI 49125; 269-426-4013.

Coldwater
State Park

OVERNIGHT ACCOMMODATIONS: NONE

ACTIVITIES:

Coldwater State Park is more cropland than park. Currently, more than 80 percent of the property is being farmed under a use permit, and there are no plans to develop any park facilities in the near future. But the property does contain a beautiful little lake that is fringed with swampland. Fishermen are welcome to wet hooks from the lake shore or carry in a non-motorized boat. There are no trails, but hikers can walk the fringe of the lake and wetlands looking for wildflowers and birds or just to enjoy the view.

WARREN WOODS

Hunting is allowed in season and cross-country skiers can set their own tracks in winter. Snowmobiling is permitted after 4 inches of snow has fallen, but the machines must stay off the cropland.

COUNTY: BRANCH
CAMPING SITES: NONE
DIRECTIONS: TAKE EXIT 3 FROM I-69 AND DRIVE EAST 1.8 MILES ON COPELAND ROAD.
FURTHER INFORMATION: 517-780-7866

L ake Hudson
RECREATION AREA

OVERNIGHT ACCOMMODATIONS:

ACTIVITIES:

Darkness reigns supreme at Lake Hudson Recreation Area. The park is the state's first "Dark Sky Preserve," and the 1993 law creating the preserve made Michigan the first state in the nation to so designate a tract of public land. Within the recreation area night time lighting is kept to a minimum, and where outdoor illumination is necessary, lighting fixtures are shielded and pointed downward. Although there are no legal restrictions on park users, they are requested to use nighttime lighting with moderation. The goal is to create an area where the night sky can be fully appreciated and enjoyed. This is not only a boon to astronomers and night photographers but campers will find the blackness of space, the brilliance of the stars, and glimmering celestial mist of the Milky Way in a nighttime sky unpolluted by man-made light an awe-inspiring experience.

One may well ask, "Why a dark sky preserve here?" Established in 1979 – amid rolling meadows, brush land, and forests in rural southern Michigan only seven miles from the Ohio border – the recreation area is still largely undeveloped and only lightly visited. Even if most of its 90,000 annual visitors use the park during the daylight hours, they are also there to enjoy nature.

The park's entrance road winds through wide, undulating meadows, past a large treeless picnic area overlooking Lake Hudson, a fine swimming beach on the lake's south shore, and then to the park's boat-launching ramp. The road ends at the recreation area's semi-modern campground on the shores of Lake Hudson. All 50 sites are spacious, grassy and offer views of the lake. Facilities include electric hookups, a communal hand water pump, and pit toilets. The campground does not have a dump station.

Some of the largest muskellunge found in Michigan's inland waters wait to test your tackle in the park's 700-acre, namesake lake. If that's not enough of a lure, panfish are plentiful and the bass fishing first rate. Ice fishing is the most popular winter activity in the park.

Hunters come after good numbers of waterfowl that are attracted to the open waters of the Lake Hudson. Deer and wild turkeys are common and hunted in season along with other small game.

Although there are no marked trails, cross-country skiers can cut their own if there is enough snow. Snowmobiling is permitted with 4 or more inches of snow on the ground.

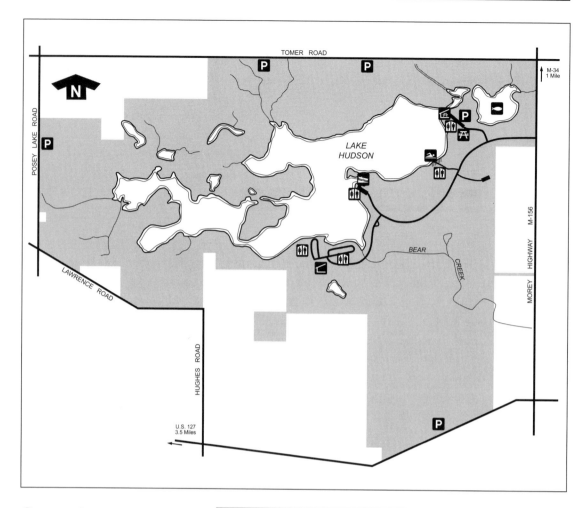

COUNTY: LENAWEE

CAMPING SITES: 50 SEMI-MODERN, ELECTRIC HOOKUPS BUT NO MODERN RESTROOMS.

DIRECTIONS: FROM M-34 11 MILES WEST OF ADRIAN, TURN SOUTH ONTO M-156 AND DRIVE ONE MILE.

FURTHER INFORMATION: LAKE HUDSON RECREATION AREA, 5505 MOREY HIGHWAY, CLAYTON, MI 49625; 517-445-2265.

STERLING STATE PARK

Sterling State Park

42

Overnight Accommodations:

Activities:

From both on the ground and on a map, Sterling State Park looks to be more water than land. Lake Erie reaches to the horizon on the east, creeks mark the park's boundary on the north and south, and turning from the Great Lake and looking inland your eyes find three large lagoons separated by dikes and causeways. One causeway extending out from the mainland is the last, thin, thread tethering most of the park's landmass to the mainland. In fact, almost half of Sterling Park's 1,000 acres is water and the principle reason why so many of its one million annual visitors are fishermen and birdwatchers.

Sterling is Michigan's only state park on Lake Erie, a water body considered a little over 40 years ago to be nothing short of a 10,000-square-mile stagnant, polluted pool. The lake was near death after years of taking in raw sewage and industrial poisons. But stringent anti-pollution laws and a ban on commercial fishing resulted in a remarkable rebirth of water quality and sport fishing.

Today, at the right time, in the right place on western Lake Erie, you can't bait a hook fast enough to please hungry walleyes, the lake's number-one game fish. Anglers also pull yellow perch, white bass, crappie, bullhead, black bass and pike from the lake. Park rangers say that the lakeside walkway, long popular with casual strollers is turning into an early spring walleye shore fishing hot spot. The lagoons are also popular with shore fishermen, and the two lagoons marking the back of the picnic area come equipped with their own parking area and fishing piers.

Boat fishermen have quick and easy access to Lake Erie from a multi-ramp launching facility (with an immense parking lot for cars and trailers) onto a large, protected basin off the Sandy Creek Outlet. Boaters will find modern restrooms and a fish cleaning station near the launch ramp.

The park's extensive shoreline, sheltered lagoons and location make for very good birdwatching. You can spot herons, gulls, waterfowl, terns and an occasional osprey, often without leaving your car. Birders also use 2.9 miles of trails that wander through the park, with the best chances for a variety of sightings coming from a path circling the park's largest lagoon and the observation tower located on its southern edge. This is a paved, ADA-accessible trail which means the wheelchair bound can fully explore the park and bicyclists have miles of pedaling. All trails are open in the winter for cross-country skiing.

Sterling State Park makes a good base for exploring a region experts count as one of Michigan's best birdwatching areas. The park sits about dead center in a string of wetlands edging the western end of Lake Erie that attracts huge numbers of waterfowl and shorebirds, including some rarely found in the rest of the state. During spring and fall

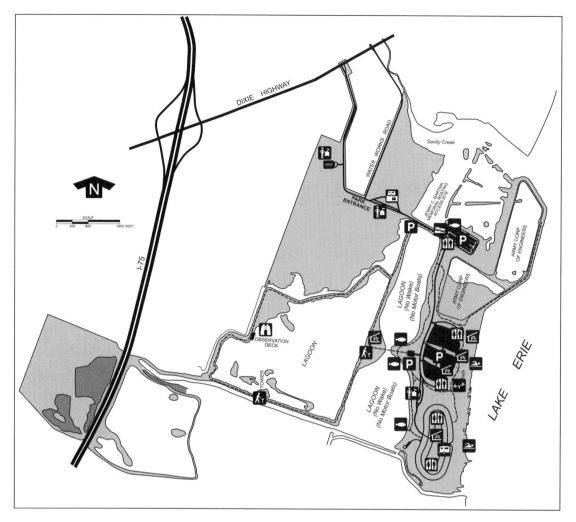

migration periods, hundreds and sometimes thousands of birds a day will fly through or over the western Lake Erie area. You can set up camp at Sterling, and then make the easy drive to several excellent spots – such as Pointe Mouillee State Game Area and Lake Erie Metropark to the north, and the Erie Marsh Preserve to the south – that will always reward you with numerous sightings.

Birders, along with fishermen and other overnighters, pitch tents or set up RVs in a modern, 256-site campground opened in 2003. The new campground spreads over a vast, grassy lawn bounded on the east by Lake Erie and on the west by a lagoon. Either the lagoon or the lake is visible from most sites, and plenty of young trees will deliver on their promise of shade sometime in the future. Each site features a paved slip

and 35-amp electrical service but nearly 100 sites come with full hookups – meaning water and sewer connections, as well as 50-amp electrical service are available at these prime sites. In addition, there are 13 handicapped accessible sites and nearly 40 pull-through sites. Two new restroom buildings with hot showers lie at either end of the campground's concentric loops. Campground use remains heavy throughout the summer, but park officials report you can usually find a vacant site in midweek and on many weekends.

The park's sprawling picnic area provides commanding views of Lake Erie from a grass-covered, tree-clad lawn that rises from a sandy swimming beach. Picnic tables, grills and five picnic shelters dot a lawn big enough to swallow up a football field. A large bathhouse with change courts stands between

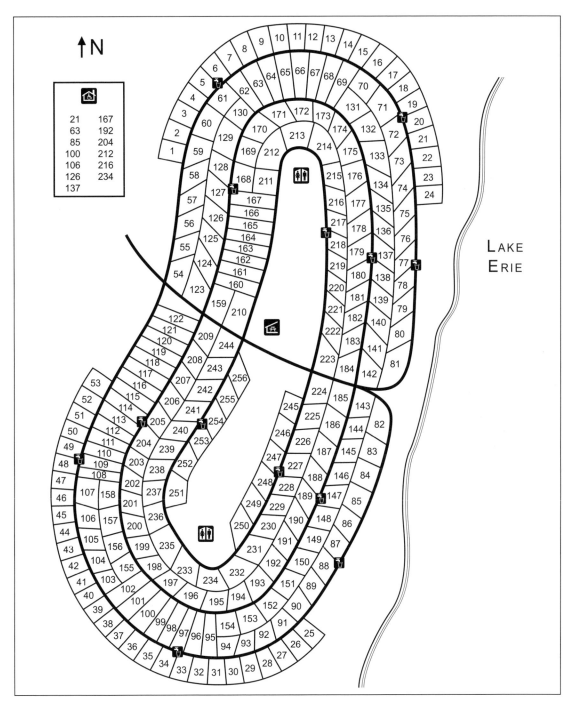

the parking lot and the day-use area. Alcohol is prohibited in the day-use areas of the park from April 1 through September 30 except with the written permission of the park manager. Metal detector enthusiasts can operate their devices within certain restricted areas of the park.

COUNTY: MONROE

CAMPING SITES: 256, ALL MODERN.

DIRECTIONS: FROM I-75, NEAR MONROE, TAKE EXIT 15 AND GO NORTHEAST ON DIXIE HIGHWAY ABOUT ONE MILE.

FURTHER INFORMATION: STERLING STATE PARK, 2800 STATE PARK ROAD, MONROE, MI 48162; 743-289-2715.

Cambridge Junction
HISTORIC STATE PARK

43

OVERNIGHT ACCOMMODATIONS: NONE

ACTIVITIES:

In the 1830s a trip by wagon or stagecoach through south central Michigan over the road that connected Detroit and Chicago was hell on wheels. The spine-crunching route, called the Chicago Military Road, was "constructed" basically by cutting trees low enough to the ground for wagons to clear the stumps. It snaked around as many obstacles – hills, bogs, streams, and swamps – as possible and gave the appearance of abhorring a straight line. Wetlands that couldn't be avoided were made passable by lashing logs crossways over the soft ground, but wagons still commonly became stuck up to their axles in mud while traveling those sections of "corduroy" roads.

After a day of such travel, the food, tap room, blazing fire, and rustic beds of the Walker Tavern, built on a low hill overlooking the road in the northeast corner of Lenawee County, must have seemed like heaven to weary travelers. The inn, one of many built along the 250-mile route, was greeting travelers before Michigan achieved statehood in 1837 and was at its busiest in the 1840s, when passengers from several stagecoaches a week stepped into the two-story, clapboard-sided structure.

Walker Tavern still stands on its original spot, at the junction of today's US-12 and M-50. Although traffic whips past the inn at 55 mph, it isn't hard to imagine how welcoming it would have been to road-weary travelers 160 years ago.

Start at the visitors center, where a tour guide, an exhibit gallery, and an audio-visual program give you a glimpse into the history of taverns and stagecoach travel when Michigan was young.

From the visitors center a short walk leads to the large, white saltbox-style tavern. Inside, two first-floor rooms have been restored to reflect a "busy/in use" 1840s' tavern. In the tap room a scattering of straight-back chairs, trunks, and a cargo bar overlook US-12.

Across the narrow hall, several Hitchcock chairs, a side table and a stove fill a sitting room. Exhibits in the restored first-floor rooms illustrate the tavern's daily operations, but the entire second story is closed.

Behind the tavern stands a reconstructed barn, complete with a New England basement and cobblestone floor. The cellar contains a carriage, buckboard, and sleigh. A scale model stagecoach (unfinished), representative of those used during the tavern's hey day, is stored on the first floor.

A small picnic area in back of the visitors center is the only other developed facility in this field museum administered by the Michigan Bureau of History.

COUNTY: LENAWEE
CAMPING SITES: NONE.
SCHEDULE: OPEN DAILY 10 A.M. – 5 P.M. FROM MAY THROUGH OCTOBER.
DIRECTIONS: THE PARK ENTRANCE IS ON M-50 A QUARTER MILE NORTH OF THE INTERSECTION OF US-12.
FURTHER INFORMATION: CAMBRIDGE JUNCTION HISTORIC STATE PARK, 13220 M-50, BROOKLYN, MI 49230; 517-467-4414.

Walter J. Hayes
STATE PARK

44

OVERNIGHT ACCOMMODATIONS:

ACTIVITIES:

With 654 acres of rolling, wooded hills and open meadows, all nearly framed by the shores of two lakes, Walter J. Hayes State Park would be a nice vacation destination in itself. But there's more. Located in the heart of an area that has drawn vacationers for decades, the park makes a fine base for exploring the attractions in the beautiful section of the state known as the Irish Hills.

Highway M-124 neatly divides the park into a day-use area on the west side and large campground on the east. Several small, quiet picnic areas strung along the entrance road to the day-use area are great places to spread a blanket and drowse away a few hours under a shade tree.

If you prefer sun, crowds, and people watching, plus the convenience of having only a short walk until you're up to your knees in water, try the sprawling, open picnic grounds that nearly surround the park's beach at Wampler's Lake. The large swimming area – with its long, wide stretch of sand and gently sloping lake bottom – is heavily used. The boat launch ramp at the north end of the beach allows boaters access to Wampler's Lake but also – via a narrow channel, navigable by most pleasure boats – to Round Lake on the park's northeastern edge.

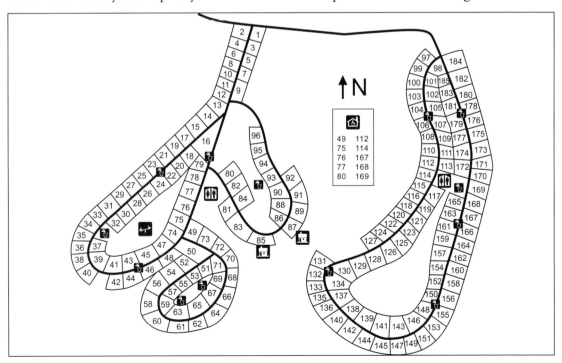

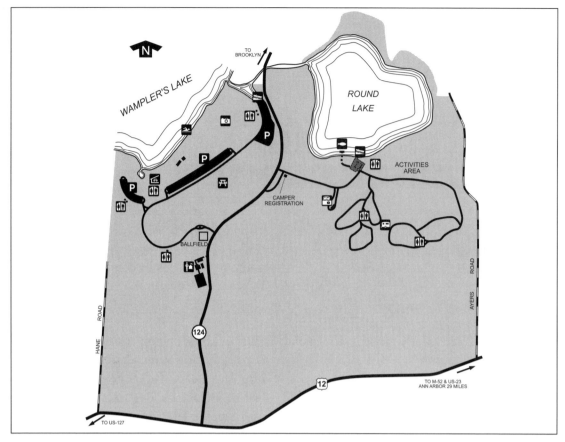

Hayes' large 185-site, modern campground receives heavy use throughout the summer months and fills up almost every weekend. The campground contains two mini-cabins and 10 handicapped accessible camping sites. Informal interpretive programs and hikes, led by park personnel, focusing on Hayes' unique natural and historic resources are scheduled throughout the summer.

Nearly half the park's acreage is underdeveloped, and the various habitats host a variety of flora and fauna. The marsh, wetlands and woods provide shelter and food to many bird species, so bring binoculars and bird books.

Fishermen pull bass, a variety of panfish, and a few pike and walleye from both Round Lake and Wampler's Lake. Fishermen who left their boats at home can wet tackle from a fishing pier on Round Lake. Nobody needs a boat when the lakes freeze over and ice fishing has consistently proven to be the most popular winter activity here.

Snowmobiling and cross-country skiing is permitted, but there are no marked trails. Metal detectors are allowed in certain areas in the park.

Within a short drive of the park there are enough attractions to keep a family busy for several days. Fun parks, a wild-west town, a "mystery spot," and antiques shops all lie close at hand. Michigan International Speedway and Cambridge Junction are a few miles west, and Hidden Lakes Gardens, one of the most unique outdoor botanical showcases in the state, is a few miles southeast, near Tipton.

County: Lenawee

Camping Sites: 185 all modern with several handicapped accessible camping spots, plus 2 mini-cabins.

Directions: From the intersection of US-12 and M-50, drive 4 miles east on US-12.

Further Information: Walter J. Hayes State Park, 1220 Wampler's Lake Road, Onsted, MI 49265; 517-467-7401.

Waterloo
Recreation Area

45

OVERNIGHT ACCOMMODATIONS:

ACTIVITIES:

> With 16 fishing lakes, a swimming beach, picturesque picnic grounds, four diverse campgrounds, miles of hiking and bridle trails, the Gerald E. Eddy Discovery Center, and most of its land open to hunting, it's sometimes hard deciding what you want to do at Waterloo Recreation Area.

And once you do choose, it's not always easy to find your way. The huge area – at 20,000 acres, the Lower Peninsula's largest state park – sprawls across two counties in a crazy quilt-patchwork of state land intermingled with private property. You have to pay attention to roadside park signs and the park map to negotiate your way along the twisting, picturesque dirt roads to the many fine facilities and activities hidden in the wooded, rolling hills. Whatever your outdoor interests, the park rewards your efforts.

Amateur naturalists, for instance, will have a literal field day here and should start with a visit to the Gerald E. Eddy Discovery Center. The center introduces visitors of all ages to the world of natural history through an array of hands-on exhibits, displays, programs, and paths that explore Michigan's diverse habitat.

From the Center, beautiful, serene nature trails wander over rolling hills and through deep woods, swamps and open fields. Rated among the most interesting (and fragile) is a route through a magnificent stand of mature beech and another that crosses a floating bog. From two of the park's campgrounds, Sugarloaf and Big Portage Lake, short nature trails loop into the surrounding scenery. If you like wildflowers, you can often wade through a near-riot of color here.

Looking for more of a challenge than a nature trail? Then test yourself on part or all of the longest hiking trail in southern Michigan. The 39-mile-long route winds through both Waterloo and Pinckney recreation areas, and by connecting to the trail networks in both you have access to a tremendous variety of week-long trips. The main trail – which runs from Big Portage Lake Campground, on the west side of the Waterloo Recreation Area, to Silver Lake, on the east side of the Pinckney Recreation Area – delves into some of the most beautiful countryside in southern Michigan, including 13 lakes, pine plantations, meadows, hardwood forests and wetlands. Maps available at both recreation areas show trail details, including campgrounds along the route.

Three of the camping areas lie in the Waterloo Recreation Area, but hikers have to share them with other overnighters. Least used is Green Lake Campground, just off M-52 on the park's east side, probably because its 25 sites, though well-shaded, have no electricity or modern restrooms.

Campers who like seclusion but prefer modern comforts gravitate to Sugarloaf Campground, located at the end of a winding, seldom-traveled dirt road near the center of the sprawling park. Surrounded by dense woods, marshes and Sugarloaf Lake, the open, level, grassy campground almost looks like a putting green set down in the wild. Its 164 sites, only about a third of which have any shade, are far from the day-use facilities, but campers do have their own beach, and there is playground equipment for children. Park personnel report this campground is heavily used on summer weekends but say you can usually find a spot in midweek.

A second modern campground covers a low bluff a hundred yards back from the brushy edge of Big Portage Lake, on the park's west side. Pluses at this 136-site area include modern restrooms, electrical hookups, and glimpses of the lake from shaded, grass-covered lots. Uneven terrain, which breaks the camping sites into different elevations, adds to the beautiful setting. The lots are quite close together, however, and privacy is limited. Also, the unevenness makes it difficult to set up large trailers and motor homes on at least half the sites. Both Portage Lake and Sugarloaf campgrounds have handicap accessible sites. Like the Sugarloaf unit, this campground also fills almost every summer weekend.

The park's fourth campground is a 25-site rustic area for equestrians. From an adjacent day-use staging area riders have ready access to more than 12 miles of bridle trails that loop through the southern edge of the park. This campground receives its heaviest use, sometimes filling, on weekends in early spring and late summer. Another overnight option is a stay in one of the park's three frontier cabins. Two of the cabins can hold up to 20 people and the third accommodates eight.

Only a few hundred feet from the Big Portage Lake Campground is Waterloo's major day-use area. A swimming beach there stretches for almost 150 yards along the lakeshore.

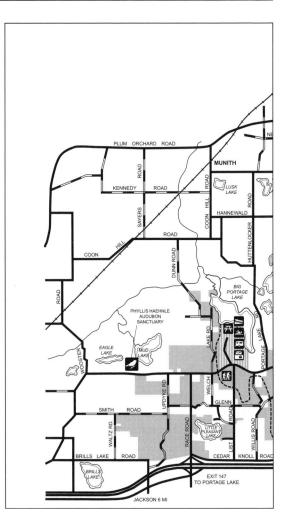

There's plenty of space on the wide ribbon of sand, plus an immense open lawn that extends back 200 yards from it, for hundreds of sun worshippers to rotisserie themselves. A large bathhouse and camp store perch on a slight rise at the back of the meadow like a southern mansion overlooking its front lawn.

Picnickers, too, have room to spread out on the rolling grounds and can set up around a table and grill overlooking the lake or in a quiet corner well back from the water in the shade of huge, old hardwoods. Playground equipment is scattered over the lawn along with two picnic shelters. Alcohol is prohibited in the Portage Lake Campground and day-use area from April 1 through Labor Day. Metal detecting is permitted in roughly a dozen specific sites throughout the park.

The Portage Lake day-use/camping area

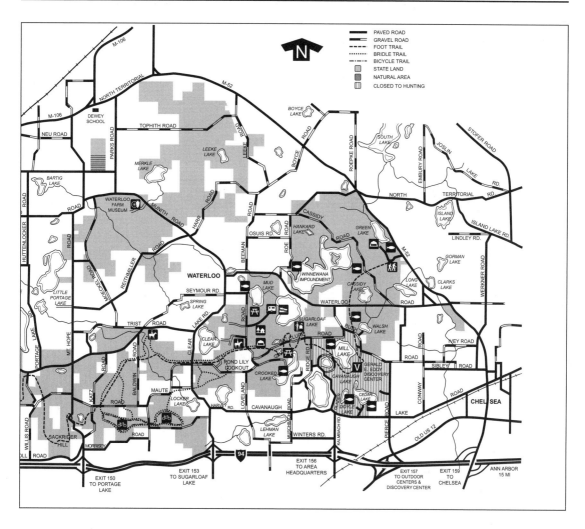

and the Discovery Center are among the few sections of the park closed to hunting. Sportsmen who carry guns or bows can pursue game over much of the rest of the park's acreage. Deer hunting here is excellent. Rabbits, ducks, and geese are plentiful, and there are enough grouse, quail, woodcock and pheasants to make hunting them worthwhile. Wild turkeys were released within the park in the mid-1980s and their numbers have increased enough to support hunting.

Birdwatching is good in the diverse habitat. And for a memorable sighting of Sandhill Cranes, visit the Haehnle Audubon Sanctuary, a roosting area for the huge birds that abuts one of the park's western parcels.

Anglers go after panfish, bass and pike in the park's many lakes. Crooked and Big Portage lakes sport fishing piers with the one at the latter rated as ADA accessible. Boat launching ramps can be found at 8 lakes and another five are accessible by foot across state land.

Mountain bikers will find 5 miles of challenging trails. In the winter, cross-country skiers have 15 miles of ungroomed trails to explore, and snowmobiles are welcomed in other areas of the park.

COUNTIES: JACKSON AND WASHTENAW
CAMPING SITES: 350 (300 MODERN, 50 RUSTIC OF WHICH 25 ARE IN AN EQUESTRIAN ONLY CAMPGROUND) PLUS 3 FRONTIER CABINS.
DIRECTIONS: FROM I-94 WEST OF CHELSEA TAKE ANY OF EXITS 147, 150, 156, OR 157.
FURTHER INFORMATION: WATERLOO RECREATION AREA, 16345 MCCLURE ROAD, CHELSEA, MI 48118; 734-475-8307.

Pinckney
RECREATION AREA

46

OVERNIGHT ACCOMMODATIONS:

ACTIVITIES:

The Pinckney Recreation Area's near-11,000 acres are jam-packed with a variety of facilities and opportunities for enjoying the out-of-doors for a day, weekend, or week.

Canoeists, for instance, can put in at Bruin Lake, then glide eastward across a chain of a half-dozen quiet, undeveloped lakes, plus make short portages to others, all in the heart of the recreation area. Some paddlers simply ferry a picnic lunch to a deserted shore, then return. Others use one of the park's two campgrounds as a base for extended day trips.

Hikers can explore the area on more than 60 miles of trails. One, the 17-mile-long Potawatomi Trail, circles the entire park. That well-marked route travels through completely wild, scenic country abundant in small lakes, creeks, streams, and wildlife. Blind Lake Campground and its 5 rustic campsites can only be reached via the Potawatomi Trail. The triple-stacked loops of the Losee Lake Trail connect wetlands east of Losee Lake to the day-use area at Silver Lake. If you're after even more of a challenge you can start at Silver Lake and walk the 35-mile Waterloo Trail, the longest trail in southern Michigan. If you'd prefer just a casual stroll, you'll like a pair of easy 3-mile-long trails that swing through the backcountry from the Silver Lake beach parking lot. Mountain bikes are welcome on all the above trails except Waterloo and Losee Lake Trails. Horseback riders will find 8 miles of bridle trails in the northeast corner of the recreation area.

Day-use visitors have their choice of two swimming beaches. On the east side of the recreation area, a grassy meadow wraps around a beach on Silver Lake. In the center of the park, on the east tip of Half Moon Lake is a larger swimming area with more facilities. Picnic grounds, with pleasing views of the water, flank that sandy beach on both ends. On the grass just back from the beach are tables, grills, a picnic shelter, a beachhouse, and a concession stand that rents kayaks, canoes, paddle boats, and boats. A boat-launching ramp marks the west end of the area.

Located well away from roads and day-use areas on top of a low, wooded plateau and extending well back from the west side of Bruin Lake are 216 sites that make up the park's modern campground. A small camper's beach, playground equipment, and a boat ramp line the shore in front of the lots. This campground is heavily used, and you will need reservations on weekends. Or, if you don't mind going without flush toilets, showers and electricity, you can set up housekeeping on one of 25 camping sites in the park's rustic campground that edges Crooked Lake. The latter campground sports a boat-launch ramp and a fishing pier. Either campground makes a good base for exploring nearby Ann Arbor's many museums, shops, and the Uni-

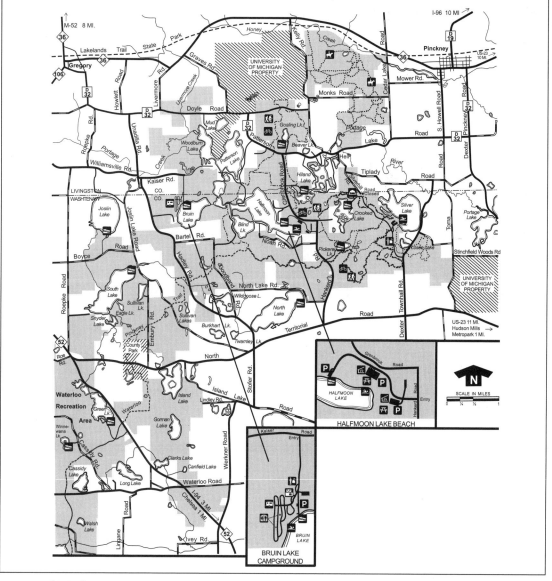

versity of Michigan campus.

Boat-launching ramps provide access to seven other lakes scattered within park property. Fishing, especially for bluegills and pike, is reportedly good on all of them, and canoeists and boaters will find great bass action on the chain of lakes.

Hundreds of the park's acres are open to hunting, with deer and rabbits the most-sought-after game. Metal detecting is also allowed within certain areas of the park.

Much of the winter activity is centered around Silver Lake. From the parking lot in back of the swimming beach two skiers-only trails – one two miles in length, the other

four – strike out into the park's low, rolling, wooded hills and valleys. Snowmobilers will find 5,700 acres set aside for their use when the snow depth reaches four inches.

COUNTIES: WASHTENAW AND LIVINGSTON.
CAMPING SITES: 216 (185 MODERN, 30 RUSTIC) AND 1 YURT.
DIRECTIONS: FROM US-23 6 MILES NORTH OF ANN ARBOR, TAKE EXIT 49 AND DRIVE WEST ON NORTH TERRITORIAL ROAD APPROXIMATELY 7 MILES.
FURTHER INFORMATION: PINCKNEY RECREATION AREA, 8555 SILVER HILL ROAD, PINCKNEY, MI 48169; 734-426-4913.

Lakelands Trail
State Park

OVERNIGHT ACCOMMODATIONS: NONE

ACTIVITIES:

Lakelands Trail State Park joins three other state rails-to-trails parks that have converted old railroad grades into non-motorized trails. Hikers, bikers, and equestrians all share this level, gravel-covered, 13-mile-long route that runs generally east/west through rolling, rural farmland and forested areas between the small villages of Pinckney and Stockbridge. Cross-country skiers frequent the trail in winter.

A spring walk is especially rewarding because of the spectacular displays of wildflowers through which the trail passes.

Plans call for the trail to be blacktopped on the north half so hikers, bikers and those in wheelchairs can be separated from horseback riders, who will use the south side.

COUNTY: LIVINGSTON
CAMPING SITES: NONE
DIRECTIONS: FROM M-36 IN DOWNTOWN PINCKNEY DRIVE NORTH ON D-19 A QUARTER MILE TO THE TRAILHEAD. THE WEST TRAILHEAD IS LOCATED ON M-52 CARPOOL LOT ON THE SOUTH SIDE OF STOCKBRIDGE.
FURTHER INFORMATION: LAKELANDS TRAIL STATE PARK, C/O PINCKNEY RECREATION AREA, 8555 SILVER HILL ROAD, PINCKNEY, MI 48169: 734-426-4913.

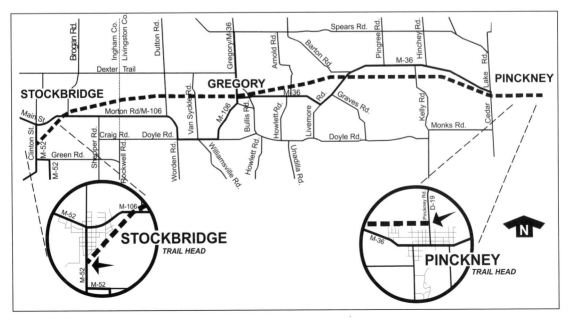

Brighton
Recreation Area

OVERNIGHT ACCOMMODATIONS:

ACTIVITIES:

More than a quarter of a million people visit the Brighton Recreation Area each year and for good reasons: fine facilities, lots of room, and plenty of choices year round for outdoor fun.

Picnickers and swimmers have two attractive options. At the park's original day-use area, on the northeast shore of Bishop Lake, tables and grills dot the spacious, hardwood-canopied picnic grounds that gently slope to the water. Good views of the lake and the newly expanded, ADA accessible swimming beach come from every corner of the picnic grounds. At Chilson Pond an open, grassy picnic area outflanks both ends of the swimming beach and extends well back from the water. Modern restroom facilities can be found in both day-use areas. The Chilson Pond area additionally features four picnic shelters with water and electricity. Each shelter will hold up to 120, and volleyball and

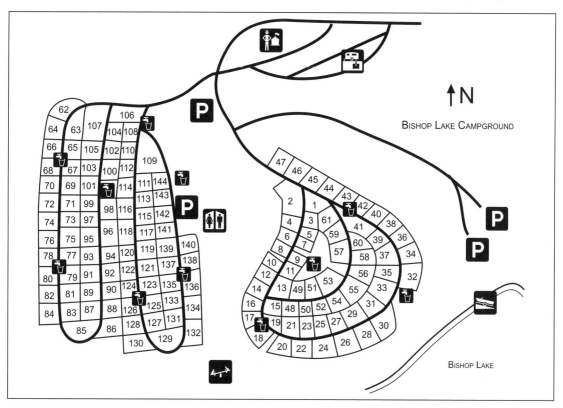

BISHOP LAKE CAMPGROUND

BISHOP LAKE

horseshoe courts are immediately adjacent. The shelters are available for rent by contacting the park office.

Hikers also have choices. A pair of well established trails – 2-mile-long Kahchin and 5-mile-long Penosha – step off from Bishop Lake Beach parking lot and then circle through the heart of the 4,913-acre park over old, rolling farmland and through deep woods. Chances are good for seeing the plentiful deer, fox, raccoon, pheasant and other wildlife on a hike.

Mountain bikers have their own trail system, off Bishop Lake Road east of Bishop Lake. The 5-plus miles of the Torn Shirt Trail will challenge even the most advanced mountain biker, while the 9-mile-long Murray Lake Trail presents bikers with easier pedaling.

If you want to rough it, you can choose from two primitive campgrounds. A total of 50 large, relatively private, shaded, rustic lots are divided among campgrounds on Murray and Little Appleton lakes. Park officials say that you can easily get a site, even on summer weekends, at these moderately used areas.

Five rustic cabins, which can accommodate 8 – 20 people, are located in isolated areas of the park and can be reserved by contacting the park office.

If you prefer modern camping facilities, including electrical hookups and restrooms with flush toilets and showers, head for the 144 sites spread along the north shore, near the narrow "waist," of hour-glass-shaped Bishop Lake. It is the park's most heavily used campground and usually fills on weekends. Lots 1-61 border the edge of a low bluff over-looking the east section of the lake. All those sites are roomy, grass-covered and level, and about half provide some shade. Lots 61-144 are spread over a sunny, open meadow near the shore of the lake's west half. The sites there are dead-level and spacious enough to pull even the largest RVs into and out of with ease. Throughout the summer infor-

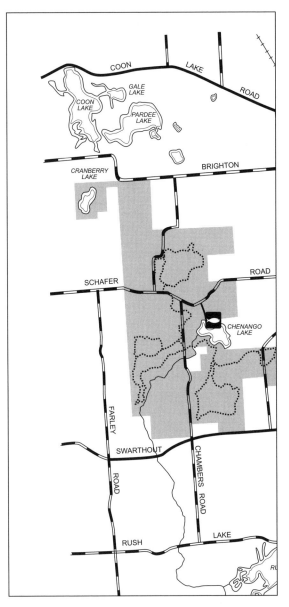

mal, ranger-led programs and hikes – open to campers and day-users – explore the park's cultural and natural resources.

Equestrians have 18 miles of bridle trails to ride, as well as their own 17-site horsemen-only campground, adjacent to a riding stable off Chilson Road on the west side of the park. If you'd like to ride but don't have your own mount, they can be rented at the stable.

Fishermen can drop hooks into any of the park's 10 quiet lakes and go after bluegills, sunfish, bass, pike and perch. Appleton Lake is stocked with rainbow trout. Three lakes have fishing access sites, three others have

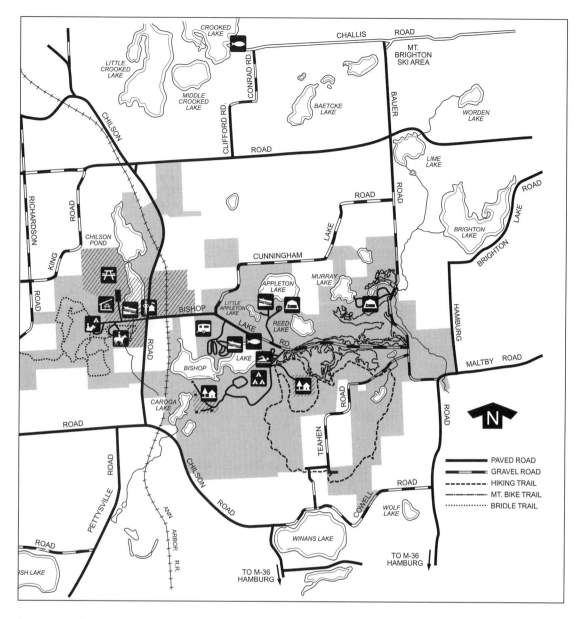

boat launches, and if you don't have a fishing boat you can shore fish most lakes or from the ADA accessible fishing pier at Bishop Lake.

Much of the park is open to hunters, who take squirrels, rabbits, deer, fox, geese, ducks, pheasants, partridge, woodcock, and raccoon. Those who like to hunt with metal detectors can do so in specific areas of the park.

During the cold months, cross-country skiers and snowmobilers make heavy use of the park.

COUNTY: LIVINGSTON

CAMPING SITES: 211 (67 RUSTIC, 144 MOD-ERN), PLUS 5 RUSTIC CABINS.

DIRECTIONS: FROM I-96 APPROXIMATELY 0.5 MILES WEST OF US-23, TAKE EXIT 147 (SPENCER ROAD) AND GO WEST THROUGH BRIGHTON. CONTINUE WEST ABOUT 6 MILES OUT OF TOWN TO CHILSON ROAD. TURN LEFT (SOUTH) ONTO CHILSON AND GO 1.5 MILES TO BISHOP LAKE ROAD. TURN LEFT (EAST) ONTO BISHOP LAKE ROAD AND GO ONE MILE TO THE PARK.

FURTHER INFORMATION: BRIGHTON RECRE-ATION AREA, 6360 CHILSON ROAD, HOW-ELL, MI 48843; 810-229-6566.

Island Lake

Recreation Area

49

OVERNIGHT ACCOMMODATIONS:

ACTIVITIES:

The name of this 4,000-acre park gives no hint as to what the high point is for most visitors. True, two lakes (including one named Island Lake) guard the park's eastern and western boundaries, but most first-time visitors are surprised to find that the beautiful, gently flowing Huron River is the area's prime attraction. The 7.5-mile section of the steam that makes lazy loops through deep woods, small marshes and open meadows in the heart of the park was designated "Country Scenic" in 1977 under the Natural Rivers Act. After pulling up a picnic table or spreading a blanket along its banks, it's hard not to be hypnotized by the gentle sweep of current as it quietly, effortlessly makes its way to Lake Erie.

The 40- to 60-foot-wide river and the park are ready-made for canoeists, even novice paddlers. Near the center of the area and accessible only by canoe is one of the state park system's few canoe campgrounds, Facilities at the two sites include vault toilets, picnic tables and fire circles. Contact park headquarters before planning an outing. Also nestled along the river's edge are two small picnic areas – reachable by car or canoe – which include one of the park's seven picnic shelters. Rental canoes are available at a livery on Kent Lake. If you bring your own, you can put in at either Kent Lake or an access point not quite halfway along the river's course through the park.

If the Huron River is the recreation area's most spectacular feature, an arm of Kent Lake that pokes into the east end of the park is the most heavily used. Visitors gravitate to a sandy beach and bathhouse near the bay's west end and a picnic area, the park's largest, which stretches along its southern shore. Picnickers there have plenty of space to spread out over the attractive, sprawling, partly shaded grounds, which cover a hill overlooking the lake. Two picnic shelters rest on the east side Kent Lake.

At the opposite (west) end of the park a spacious picnic area, with three picnic shelters, nearly rings the southern end of Island Lake. The park's southern section features a sandy swimming hole, with a modern toilet building, located on 8-acre Spring Mill Pond. The waters of the spring-fed pond stay cool and clear all summer.

In the middle of the park, the sunny, open Meadow Picnic Area is the site of the first and only balloon port in a Michigan state park, and you can down your hotdogs, hamburgers and potato salad while watching colorful hot-air balloons rise into the sky and drift away on a gentle breeze.

The park is enjoying a growing popularity with bicyclists who have discovered its 14-miles of paved, one-way biking and hiking trail. Divided into two connecting loops, the 9-mile West Loop features fewer hills

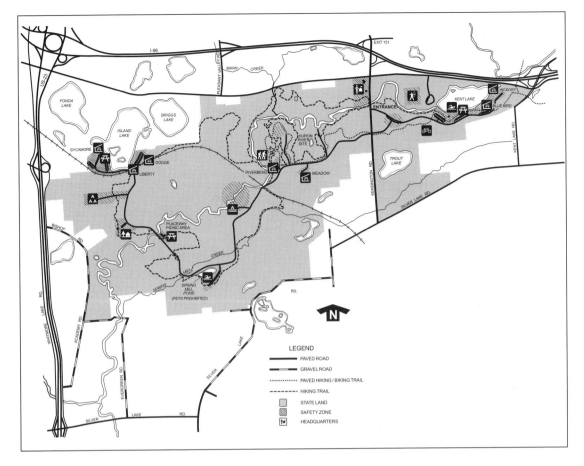

as it crosses fields, woodlands and borders wetlands. The shorter, East Loop edges the Huron River in several places on its 5 mile circuit. The latter loop also connects to the Kensington Metro Park paved trail and many more miles of bicycling. The wide diversity of habitat along the trail and in the park promises good birdwatching and abundant wildflowers. In winter cross-country skiers usurp the trail.

If you want to overnight here, your only option if you're not a canoe camper are two secluded frontier cabins nestled in the woods not far from the river on the park's western edge.

Fishermen will find action good for crappies, perch, bluegills and bass on Kent Lake; Spring Pond is stocked with trout in the spring; and panfish, bass and an occasional pike are pulled from both Island Lake and the Huron River. There's no boat ramp in the park.

Most of Island Lake Recreation Area's acreage is open to hunters during the fall and winter. Pheasants are released in the park, and other small game, as well as deer, are also taken. Hunters can sharpen their skill at the park's modern handicap-accessible shooting, skeet and trap ranges.

Snowmobiling is permitted in the winter. Hobbyists are allowed to use metal detectors in specified areas of the park.

County: Livingston
Camping Sites: Two canoe-camping only sites, and two frontier cabins.
Directions: From I-96 2.5 miles east of US-23, take exit 151 onto Kensington Lake Road and drive 0.75 miles south.
Further Information: Island Lake Recreation Area, 12950 East Grand River Avenue, Brighton, MI 48116; 810-229-7067.

Maybury
State Park

50

OVERNIGHT ACCOMMODATIONS:

ACTIVITIES:

Looking at a map and trying to make sense of the multitude of trails within Maybury State Park is harder than visually untangling a plate full of spaghetti. It's only when you're in the park and following a trail on foot, bike, ski, or horse that you come to appreciate how the park's variety of pathways whisk you away from the sight and sound of the Detroit metropolitan area and replace the urban experience with a healthy dose of Michigan's natural environment.

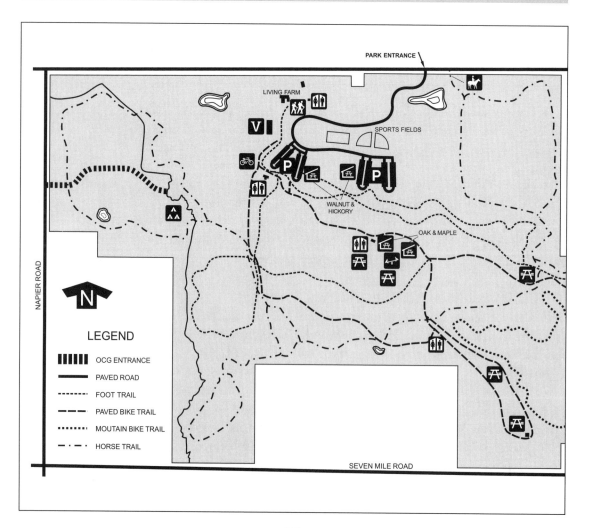

The park's 945 acres of rolling hills, alternately covered with dense stands of mixed hardwoods and open meadows, shelter a variety of wildflowers and wildlife. In summer, a good way to get a sense of it all is along four miles of paved bicycle paths and an estimated six miles of hiking trails, which begin at two large parking areas at the end of the entrance road and wind through the rolling terrain. The park also boasts a 4-mile-long, challenging mountain-bike trail.

Small, secluded picnic sites, isolated tables, and rain shelters are scattered along all bike and hiking paths ,and most require a healthy walk or pedal from the nearest parking area. There is no large, central picnic ground, but one small area and pavilion is conveniently located about 100 yards south of the easternmost parking lot. Four picnic shelters are available; reservations are recommended.

Ten miles of bridle trails also roam into the far corners of the park from the horsemen's area, on the west side of Beck Road. Rental horses are available at a stable located near the staging area. The stable also offers hayrides in the fall. Near the stables is a small fishing pond where children can get hooked on the sport.

In winter both beginning and experienced cross-country skiers can pick from over 10 miles of groomed trails, more than half of which are rated as difficult. The park no longer rents cross-country ski equipment but continues to maintain a warming building where skiers can rest and gather around a blazing fire.

The park's very popular working farm burned to the ground a few years ago. The farm reopened in September of 2005, but it is no longer a part of the park. The farmland is leased from the state and the farm is now an independent entity supported by the Northville Community Foundation, all of which means the farm has a separate entrance from the park, has its own entrance fee, and a state park sticker is not required.

COUNTY: WAYNE
CAMPING SITES: NONE
DIRECTIONS: DRIVE 6 MILES WEST OF I-275 ON EIGHT MILE ROAD. OR DRIVE 3.8 MILES SOUTH OF I-96 ON BECK ROAD TO EIGHT MILE ROAD, THEN ONE MILE WEST ON EIGHT MILE.
FURTHER INFORMATION: MAYBURY STATE PARK, 20145 BECK ROAD, NORTHVILLE, MI 48167; 248-349-8390. THE RIDING STABLE NUMBER IS 248-347-1088.

Proud Lake
Recreation Area

51

OVERNIGHT ACCOMMODATIONS:

ACTIVITIES:

In a setting of natural beauty only minutes from metropolitan Detroit, the Proud Lake Recreation Area has catered to the widely varying interests of millions of outdoor lovers since its establishment in 1944. Within a valley framed by gently rising hills, the park's 4,000 acres straddle both the scenic Huron River and a chain of lakes created by the damming of it. Marshes, meadows, bogs, pine plantations and large expanses of natural forest add variety to a landscape dominated by the river.

That wide variety of habitat makes the area ideal for wildflower hunters, birdwatchers, and walkers, who can take anything from a casual stroll to a challenging hike on the park's 21-mile-long trail system. East of Wixom Road and the park's headquarters, two hiking/ski trails crease the land on either side of the Huron River. Across Wixom Road from the headquarters, eight miles of bridle trails, also open to mountain biking, quilt the park's western-most terrain. Horsemen can saddle up in a staging area off Garden Road.

The park's canoe-rental concession is also off Garden Road. The Huron River in this west section of the recreation area is an ideal setting for paddlers. Old channels, bayous, and islands mark the flow as the river continuously loops back on itself. Arrangements can be made for drop off and pick up services. If you bring your own canoe it can be launched at the Huron River Fishing Site on Wixom Road just north of the park's headquarters.

Day-use picnic grounds overlook the river at the end of a long entrance road a few doz-

en yards north of the above fishing site on Wixom. Sheltered by a stand of impressive oaks, picnickers are favored with panoramic views of the river and valley from a grass-covered hill. Two picnic pavilions are available for rent.

At the opposite end of the recreation area, a modern campground stretches along the crest of a hill on the south side of Proud Lake. The 130 lots and two mini-cabins line the hill in

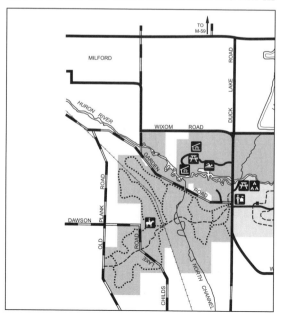

four long rows well up from the lake, making the entire shoreline – including a campers-only beach and boat-launching ramp – accessible to all overnighters. Most sites are small and lack shade and privacy, but because of the area's long, narrow layout, there is little feeling of being cramped. Best shade and views of the lake come from sites at the extreme western edge. Depending on traffic conditions, campers are rarely more than 30 or 40 minutes from most metro Detroit attractions. The heavily used campground is almost always full on summer weekends, but during the week you can usually find an open site. Throughout the year a wide variety of nature programs and guided interpretive walks are offered to the public.

The Huron River and its chain of lakes yield panfish and some bass and pike, and fly-rod aficionados come after the 16-inch rainbow and brown trout released into the river each spring. From April 1 through the last Saturday in April a 2-mile stretch of the Huron River, within the park, features catch and release fishing for trout. The easiest access site for trout fishing is from a parking lot next to the river on Wixom Road. Regular fishing rules apply during the rest of the year. A public boat-launching ramp lies on the north shore of Proud Lake off Bass Lake Road.

More than half the recreation area is open to hunters, who take rabbits, squirrels, deer and the occasional pheasant. Metal detectors are allowed in certain areas. During the winter, snowmobiles run 10 miles of trails.

COUNTY: OAKLAND

CAMPING SITES: 130, ALL MODERN, PLUS TWO MINI-CABINS.

DIRECTIONS: FROM I-96 APPROXIMATELY 12 MILES EAST OF US-23, TAKE EXIT 159 (WIXOM ROAD) AND GO NORTH ABOUT 6 MILES TO THE PARK HEADQUARTERS. THE CAMPGROUND IS ON GLENGARY ROAD, ABOUT A MILE EAST OF WIXOM ROAD.

FURTHER INFORMATION: PROUD LAKE RECREATION AREA, 3500 WIXOM ROAD, MILFORD, MI 48382; 248-685-2433.

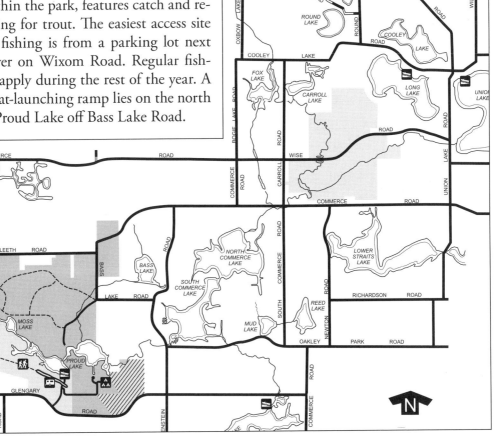

Highland
Recreation Area

52

Overnight Accommodations:

Activities:

For its size, nearly 6,000 acres, Highland Recreation Area is the least developed of the many state parks that arc around the northwest Detroit area. There are no large facilities and thus no large crowds to be found in this big chunk of land spread across western Oakland County. The campground, picnic areas, and swimming beach are not only small but are located on the fringes of the park, leaving a large, undeveloped, wide-open central portion to roam on foot, horseback, mountain bike, snowmobile or cross-country skis.

A couple of other features set Highland apart from most other state parks. The first is Haven Hill Natural Area, a 550-acre parcel in the northwest corner of the park, in which grows every forest type found in southern Michigan. This National Natural Landmark abounds with wildflowers and birds. The park's bird list tops a hundred. Nature Trails from Goose Meadows Picnic Area follow the shoreline of Haven Hill Lake and penetrate to the heart of the nature area north of the lake.

Second is a 25-site, hitching-post equipped equestrian campground on the east side of the park. The camping area is primitive – no showers, flush toilets, or electricity – but is conveniently close to miles of bridle trails that range through the heart of the park, climbing to several panoramic vistas from some of the highest elevations in the region. You don't have bring along Mister Ed to stay in the campground, and the trails can be walked rather than ridden. You can rent a mount at a riding stable on the main park road and "Hi-yo, Silver!" to your heart's content.

The park's lone modern cabin sits in splendid isolation near Bass Lake just off Pettibone Lake Road and offers modern comforts seldom found in state park cabins. The year-round cabin has an L.P. furnace, 5 twin-sized beds, 2 small bedrooms, a loft, kitchen with stove and refrigerator, living/dining room, and a bath with shower. The cabin also comes with coffee pot, toaster, pots, pans, flatware, dishes, and cutting knives. A row boat with life jackets sits next to the cabin in the summer.

Also just off Pettibone Lake Road north of the cabin is the quiet, peaceful and wooded Dodge #10 picnic area. Two newer picnic areas on the west side are accessible from Livingston Road. One overlooks a large field trial area, and the other snuggles up to a small lake. Three more picnic areas are strung along the twisting main road. Facilities at Goose Meadow, in a large open field beside Haven Hill Lake, include a pavilion, a ball field, and immediate access to the natural area. At another picnic area farther south, tables and grills perch on a high hill with scenic views over the north shore of Teeple Lake.

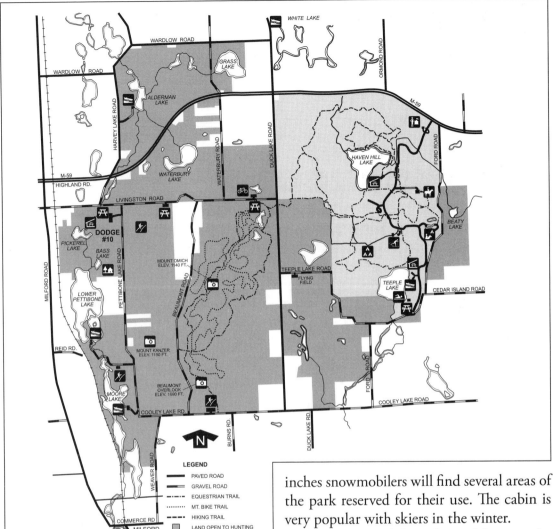

WHITE LAKE

WARDLOW ROAD
WARDLOW ROAD

GRASS LAKE

ORMOND ROAD

ALDERMAN LAKE

HARVEY LAKE ROAD

M-59

WATERBURY LAKE

WATERBURY ROAD

DUCK LAKE ROAD

HAVEN HILL LAKE

FORD ROAD

M-59

BEATY LAKE

M-59
HIGHLAND RD.

LIVINGSTON ROAD

DODGE #10

PICKERELL LAKE

BASS LAKE

PETTIBONE LAKE ROAD

MILFORD ROAD

LOWER PETTIBONE LAKE

MOUNT OMICH ELEV. 1140 FT.

BEAUMONT ROAD

TEEPLE LAKE ROAD

FLYING FIELD

TEEPLE LAKE

CEDAR ISLAND ROAD

REID RD.

MOUNT KANZER ELEV. 1150 FT.

MOORE LAKE

BEAUMONT OVERLOOK ELEV. 1090 FT.

FORD ROAD

COOLEY LAKE ROAD

COOLEY LAKE RD.

BURNS RD.

DUCK LAKE RD.

N

WEAVER ROAD

COMMERCE RD.
MILFORD

LEGEND
PAVED ROAD
GRAVEL ROAD
EQUESTRIAN TRAIL
MT. BIKE TRAIL
HIKING TRAIL
LAND OPEN TO HUNTING
LAND CLOSED TO HUNTING

From the end of the park's main road, a short walk leads to the last picnic ground, which consists of a few tables hugging the shore near the park's only swimming beach on the southeastern shore of Teeple Lake. Nestled behind the small beach are restrooms, a pavilion and grills.

Mountain bikers who like a challenge can depart from a trailhead on Livingston Road and set out on 15 miles of very technical trails featuring steep climbs, big rocks, off-camber runs, sharp dips, and very tight turns. Novices have 2 miles of easier trails to enjoy.

When the snow flies, cross-country skiers have three marked trails totaling 12 miles to glide over, and when snow fall reaches 4, inches snowmobilers will find several areas of the park reserved for their use. The cabin is very popular with skiers in the winter.

Fishing is good for pike and bass in the park's 10 lakes, four of which have boat-launching ramps. More than half the property is open to hunting with deer, rabbit and pheasant all successfully taken. Hunters can sharpen the skills of their bird dogs at three field trial areas.

Hobbyists are allowed to operate metal detectors in specified areas of the park.

COUNTY: OAKLAND
CAMPING SITES: 25, ALL RUSTIC PLUS A MODERN CABIN.
DIRECTIONS: DRIVE 15 MILES WEST OF PONTIAC ON M-59.
FURTHER INFORMATION: HIGHLAND RECREATION AREA, 5200 EAST HIGHLAND ROAD, WHITE LAKE, MI 48383; 248-889-3750.

Dodge Brothers #4
State Park

53

OVERNIGHT ACCOMMODATIONS: None

ACTIVITIES:

The main attraction at Dodge Brothers #4 State Park is Cass Lake. Nearly encompassed by water, the park spreads across the tip of a peninsula that nudges out into the lake. The mile-long, scalloped shoreline is beautifully distinctive, with narrow beach-hugging islands, odd-shaped little promontories, three foot bridges, backwater bayous, and an old channel.

The narrow channel, in fact, creates a small peninsula within the larger one. At the tip of that thin finger of land and nearly cut off from the rest of the park is a narrow, sandy 150-yard-long swimming beach. After crossing a foot bridge to get to the picturesque area, you have the option of spreading a blanket on sand in full sun or, back from the beach, on a thick carpet of grass in the heavy shade of stately trees. Nearby is a concession stand and bathhouse. On the shore just west of the swimming beach you can rent a sailboat.

You can also bring your own craft and join the steady stream of fishing boats, speedboats, sailboats, and runabouts put in and pulled out of Gerundegut Bay at the park's ramp. Anglers who dare to brave the busy waters of Cass Lake, Oakland County's largest, will discover some of the best fishing in southeastern Michigan, particularly for smallmouth bass. Fishing for largemouth bass and northern pike is also good, especially in the less-heavily used waters of Gerundegut Bay. Panfish, channel catfish, and lake trout are also taken from the 1,200-acre lake.

Any of Dodge #4's 139 acres that aren't paved, sand-covered, or reserved for boat launching are set aside for picnickers, who have their choice of three attractive, distinctly different areas. One, on top of a hill near the center of the park, radiates out from a circular parking lot into the deep shade and seclusion of a stand of mature pines. The other two are near water. Across the channel from the swimming beach, picnic tables and young trees dot a grassy meadow that spreads from the parking lot to the shore of both channel and lake. Many of the tables are right at the water's edge, with a full view of all the activity on Cass Lake. On the opposite (west) side of the park, tables are widely spaced in full sun along Gerundegut Bay. And, in spite of the availability of a large pavilion, this area appears to be the most quiet and least used of any in the park. Although there are no hiking trails, there is plenty of room for an after dinner stroll. The possession or consumption of alcohol is not allowed within the park.

When the snow flies, the park offers an eyeful of scenic beauty to cross-country skiers who don't mind cutting their own trails. Ice fishing is also very popular here when Cass Lake freezes over.

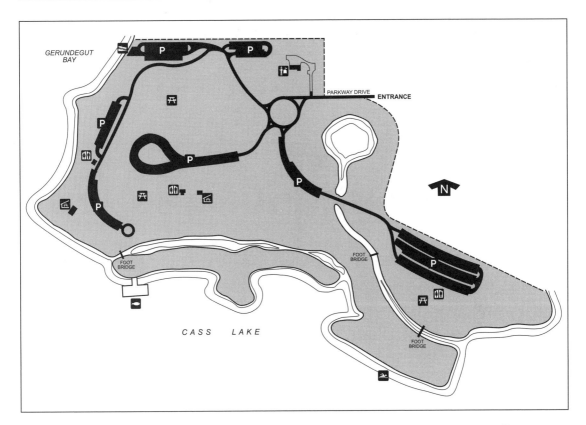

County: Oakland

Camping Sites: None

Directions: From the intersection of M-59 (West Huron) and M-24 (Telegraph Road) in Pontiac, go west on M-59 approximately 1.5 miles to Cass Road. Turn left (south) onto Cass and drive about one mile to Cass-Elizabeth Road. Turn right (west) onto Cass-Elizabeth and go one mile to Parkway Drive. Turn left (south) onto Parkway and go 0.75 miles.

Further Information: Dodge Brothers #4 State Park, 4250 Parkway Drive, Waterford, MI 48327; 248-682-7323.

Pontiac Lake
Recreation Area

54

Overnight Accommodations:

Activities:

For visitors to the Detroit metro area, the Pontiac Lake Recreation Area is an inexpensive base from which to take advantage of the Detroit Zoo, Pontiac Silverdome, Meadowbrook, Ford Field, Joe Louis Arena, Greenfield Village, The Palace, and a host of other Detroit-area attractions and facilities. Big city dwellers, on the other hand, can enjoy open spaces and a true sense of the out-of-doors only minutes from the end of their driveways.

The park's wide diversity of habitat and ecosystems makes for such good wildlife observation that local colleges use the area for biology field trips and bird study. An excellent cross section of Michigan wildflowers grace the area's woods, fields, and wetlands. Morel mushroomers forage through the park each spring, and modern-day hunter-gathers pick a wide variety of fruits and berries throughout the summer. The park offers a variety of nature programs for the public.

The best way to explore is on foot or horseback along the 17 miles of bridle trails that cut through the heart of the park, border the Huron River, and rise to several scenic overlooks. The main trail access is at the horsemen's staging area and riding stable where, in addition to horses, hay rides and pony rides are available. Call the stable at 248-625-3410 for current rates and hours. A small, rustic equestrians-only campground abuts the staging area. A 1.9-mile hiking trail runs from the campground to the swimming beach on Pontiac Lake, and the area's 11-mile mountain bike trail has been ranked among the top 100 in the country.

A mile west of the horsemen's staging area

and campground rests an inviting, lightly used modern campground far removed from busy roads and crowded day-use facilities. One hundred seventy-six sites are divided between two widely separated wings that spread over rolling, partially wooded hills in the heart of the park. The sites, with few exceptions, are large, well shaded, and fairly private. Generally, those in the west loop are the most-shaded and private. Every site features a paved slip and is served by modern restrooms with flush toilets and showers. Park officials recommend reservations for peak summer weekends.

Campers can reach the large day-use area by walking 1.9 miles on the park's sole hikers-only trail or by driving 5 miles on gravel and paved roads. A swimming beach there stretches nearly 400 yards along Pontiac Lake's northeast shore, and just back from the water are a large bathhouse and snack bar. Immense grass-covered, tree-shaded picnic grounds dotted with grills, tables, a ball field, swings, slides, two picnic shelters, volleyball courts, and horseshoe pits wrap around the beach and extend several hundred yards inland.

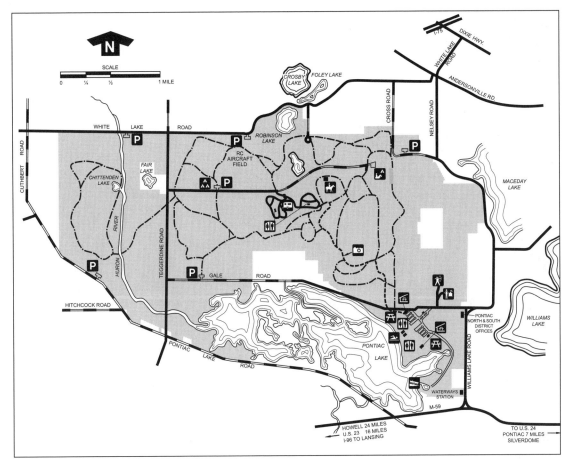

At the extreme southeast end of the day-use area, pleasure boaters, water skiers and fishermen all use a boat-launching ramp to get onto the popular lake. Panfish, catfish, walleye, and pike are regularly pulled from the water, and in the recent past the lake has been the site of bass-fishing tournaments. A wheelchair-accessible fishing dock serves handicapped fishermen.

Much of the area is open to hunting with squirrels, pheasant, grouse, woodcock, rabbit, and deer all taken in season. Experienced hunters can sharpen their aim at a modern shotgun, rifle, pistol, and archery range across Gale Road from the day-use area.

No groomed cross-country ski trails crease the park's snow during the winter, but skiers are welcome to break their own paths through the property. Snowmobilers may do the same in a large portion of the park after four or more inches of snow has fallen.

COUNTY: OAKLAND

CAMPING SITES: 176 MODERN AND A FEW RUSTIC SITES IN THE EQUESTRIAN CAMPGROUND.

SCHEDULE: THE PARK IS OPEN ALL YEAR, BUT THE CAMPGROUND IS CLOSED FROM OCTOBER 26 TO APRIL 30. THE SHOOTING RANGE IS OPEN 10 A.M. TO 6 P.M. WEDNESDAY-SUNDAY IN THE FALL AND THURSDAY-SUNDAY THE REST OF THE YEAR.

DIRECTIONS: FROM US-23 AND M-59 DRIVE APPROXIMATELY 15 MILES EAST ON M-59. FROM I-75 AND M-59 DRIVE APPROXIMATELY 11 MILES WEST ON M-59.

FURTHER INFORMATION: PONTIAC LAKE RECREATION AREA, 7800 GALE ROAD, WATERFORD, MI 48327; 248-666-1020.

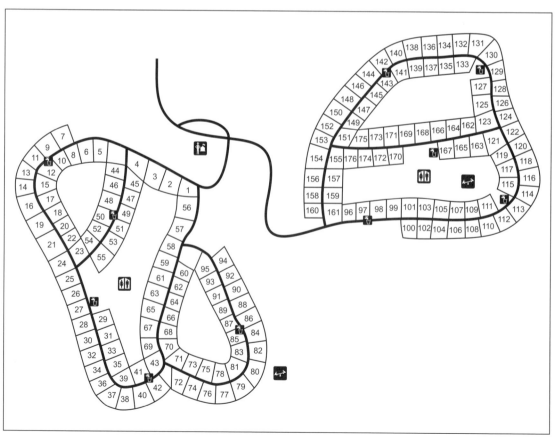

Seven Lakes
State Park

55

Overnight Accommodations:

Activities:

Seven Lakes State Park is a pleasing 1,378-acre blend of water, woods, and large, open meadows that embraces a wide variety of uses. The area does not, however, include seven lakes. At one time it did, but the seven small lakes were flooded to create one large one – Big Seven Lake.

The park's completely modern campground – opened in the spring of 1992 – is hidden away in the southeast corner of the property. The 71 grassy, sunny sites with asphalt pads line the north side of tiny Sand Lake. The lake and campground are nestled at the bottom of a bowl shaped depression surrounded by wooded hills on three sides. Four of the campsites are handicapped accessible. A wide, sandy camper's-only beach is only steps away from any site.

On the west shore of Big Seven Lake, the park's 800-foot-long day-use swimming beach fronts a large picnic area. Warm water, a gently sloping lake bottom, and a wide expanse of sand draws large summer crowds to the sun-drenched area. A large concession stand with restrooms and changing courts stands just back from the beach. Picnic shelters anchor each end of the beach. Around the shore on the north side of the large lake, less-crowded, slightly shadier picnic grounds overlook the water from a hill. Facilities there include two large pavilions.

A third, shade-dappled picnic area, which overlooks Dickinson Lake from a wooded bluff, is considerably less crowded than the two on Big Seven Lake. Still, the small, quiet area seems to be the third choice of most visitors, probably because it's the farthest from the swimming beach. A no-alcohol ban is in effect for the entire park from April 1 through Labor Day.

Fishermen walk the shores of all the park's lakes and cast lures for walleye, trout, panfish, and bass, including some good-sized largemouths in Big Seven Lake. Others rent boats or canoes from a concession, open Memorial Day to Labor Day. You can bring your own craft and launch it from ramps at Big Seven and Dickinson Lake. A no-wake speed is in effect. Dickinson Lake also boasts a fishing pier.

The park's diverse habitat and small lakes undisturbed by boat motors make for very good birdwatching. A wide variety of species find cover in the large meadows bordered by wooded groves, shrubs, and thickets. The open waters in spring attract numerous migrating waterfowl, and special efforts to attract bluebirds have been very successful. The same conditions that create good birdwatching opportunities are equally good for wildflower hunters.

You can roam just about anywhere in the park, but if you're more comfortable with es-

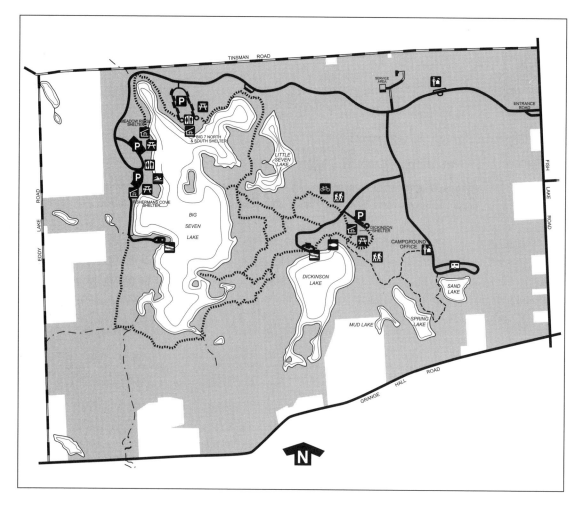

tablished routes, you can confine your wandering to the more than six miles of well-marked trails that run between Big Seven Lake, Dickinson Lake, and Sand Lake. Except for the 0.7 mile Nature Trail, which circles south of Sand Lake, and the even shorter Dickinson Trail, all trails are open to mountain bikes.

In the winter, through-the-ice anglers go after pike, and snowmobilers and cross-country skiers set tracks over the large, open park.

Much of the acreage is also open to hunters in season. Rabbits, deer, and pheasants are the game most often taken. Metal detectors are allowed in several areas within the park.

COUNTY: OAKLAND
CAMPING SITES: 71, ALL MODERN.
DIRECTIONS: FROM I-75 TAKE EXIT 101 (GRANGE HALL ROAD) WEST ABOUT 5 MILES TO FISH LAKE ROAD. TURN RIGHT (NORTH) AND DRIVE ONE MILE TO PARK. FROM US-23 TAKE EXIT 79 AND DRIVE EAST ON SILVER LAKE ROAD INTO FENTON. AT THE STOPLIGHT, SILVER LAKE ROAD BECOMES GRANGE HALL ROAD. CONTINUE EAST ON GRANGE HALL ROAD 3 MILES TO FISH LAKE ROAD AND TURN NORTH.
FURTHER INFORMATION: SEVEN LAKES STATE PARK, 14390 FISH LAKE ROAD, HOLLY, MI 48442; 248-634-7271.

Holly
Recreation Area

OVERNIGHT ACCOMMODATIONS:	🚐 🏠 ♿ ⛺ 🏕️ 🏕️
ACTIVITIES:	🚴 🦅 🛶 🛶 🎿 🐟 🏃 🔫 🏃 🎣 🎪 🛷 🛷 🚤 🏊

A crowded swimming beach and picnic areas are likely to be your first impression of the Holly Recreation Area, especially if you come on a weekend. You'll turn onto the entrance road, roll over the crest of the hill that hides Heron Beach from view, and see the area covered beach blanket to beach blanket with young people who come to troll for dates, show off tan lines, and soak up the sun and anything they can carry past the sharp-eyed park attendants.

Don't turn around and go home. As so often happens, first impressions can be misleading. There's plenty of both space and quiet corners in this sprawling 7,800-acre recreation area. And, except for the flood of visitors at Heron Beach, Holly Recreation Area's hilly, wooded landscape, wet with more than 20 lakes, seems to soak up visitors like a dry sponge.

The park's centerpiece is a large day-use area that surrounds three connected lakes – Heron, Valley, and Wildwood. The first turnoff from the day-use entrance road leads to Heron Lake and its largely treeless, sun-baked picnic area and large, usually jam-packed beach. Just back from the sand is a large bathhouse, a concession stand, and canoe and boat rentals.

Past the Heron Beach turnoff, the road winds between Heron and Valley lakes, then sweeps to its end at picnic grounds on the south side of Wildwood Lake. Both sides of the road along the route are marked by secluded, grass-covered, tree-shaded picnic areas. Each either overlooks one of the three lakes from atop a hill or is nestled into one of the wooded, serpentine shorelines. You can also take easy walks around both Valley Lake and Wildwood Lake. Alcohol is not allowed in the day-use area from April 1 through Labor Day.

Also common along the drive is the sight of anglers slouched in folding chairs – tackle boxes, coolers, and portable radios within arm's reach. The shore-fishermen eye floating bobbers on all three lakes, and a parking lot near the isthmus that separates Heron and Wildwood lakes is reserved specially for them. Both Heron and Valley lakes have boat-launching ramps (as do other area lakes – more in a moment). Only electric motors

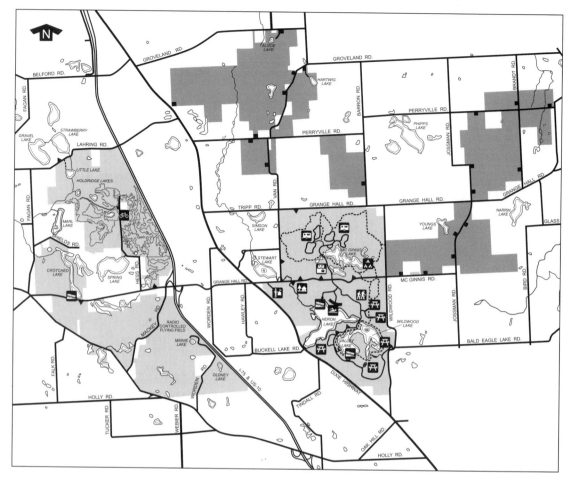

are allowed on Heron Lake. Gas motors are permissible on Wildwood and Valley but at no-wake speeds.

Across McGinnis Road from the day-use area is the undiscovered gem of the entire recreation area, a 161-site campground perched on hills north of McGinnis Lake. The large lots are arranged around four loops off the access road, and most are heavily shaded and screened from other campers by thick stands of trees. Paved slips, which alternate off each side of each loop, make for easy setup of trailers and motor homes. Facilities include two mini-cabins, modern restrooms, a dump station, and electrical hookups (except for lots 147-161). On weekends during the summer and fall months, the campground usually fills.

The semi-rustic Rolston Cabin offers overnighters a third option. Located in the woods with a small pond out the front door, the cabin has electricity, lights, and a kitch-

en with stove, refrigerator, table and chairs. The living room comes with chairs, a bunk bed, and a fireplace/wood burning stove for heat. The four mattresses in the loft make the sleeping capacity six. Outside, a hand pump for water, picnic table, fire ring, and a pit toilet round out the amenities. The cabin can be rented year round. No pets are allowed.

Many visitors use the campground as a base for making use of the park's other half dozen parcels, which horseshoe around the day-use/campground areas. Holly Recreation Area's lakes, many with fishing-access and boat-launching sites, yield good catches of sunfish, walleyes, muskie, bass, bluegill, perch, bullheads and crappies.

Much of the park is open to hunters who bag everything from game to photographs, mushrooms, and memories. Deer, rabbits, grouse, squirrels, and turkey are all taken by hunters in season. Mushroom hunters, wild-

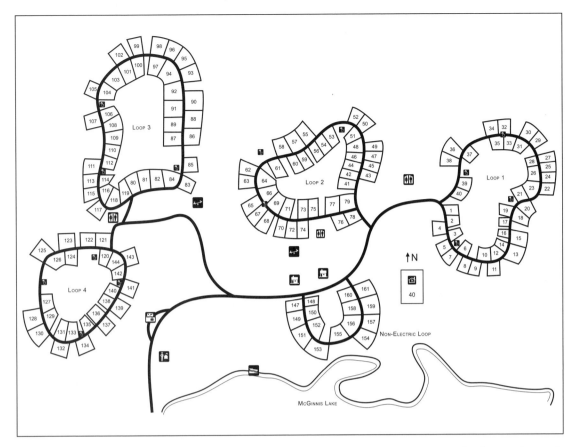

flower enthusiasts, and nature photographers will not be disappointed by a search through the park's wide range of habitat. Birdwatchers have spotted 190 different species, including such rare visitors as American avocets, osprey, and Caspian terns. All the above hunters and those just looking to burn some calories in pleasant surroundings make use of the ten miles of hiking trails that probe some of the park's remotest corners. Metal detectors are permitted in specific areas of the park.

In the winter, snowmobiles are permitted on 1,000-plus acres of the park lying on the west side of I-75, and cross-country skiers take over the hiking trails. In recent years, ice fishing has become very popular on Heron Lake.

Mountain bikers will find an extensive and challenging labyrinth of trails off Hess Road on the recreation area's west side. The trails cross some of the region's highest and most scenic hills and range in length from an easy 0.75-mile pedal great for kids, to a slightly more challenging 2.25-mile loop through fields and woods, to a gut-busting 18-mile, 3-hour-plus slog that includes log jumps, off-camber climbs and more hairpin turns than you can find in a box of paperclips.

For detailed descriptions and routes of all trails in the park, inquire at the headquarters building, just west of Dixie Highway on Grange Hall Road. Park staff hold informal nature programs and hikes throughout the summer.

County: Oakland
Camping Sites: 160 (all but 16 completely modern), including two mini-cabins and a semi-rustic frontier cabin.
Directions: From I-75 north of Pontiac take exit 101 (Grange Hall Road) and go east about 2.5 miles.
Further Information: Holly Recreation Area, 8100 Grange Hall Road, Holly, MI 48442; 248-634-8811.

Ortonville Recreation Area

57

OVERNIGHT ACCOMMODATIONS:

ACTIVITIES:

The 5,400-acre Ortonville Recreation Area spills across the extreme southwest corner of Lapeer County like a giant Rorshach ink-blot test. If while studying the abstract-looking map of the area, you envision fishing, hunting, swimming, trap shooting, horseback riding, hiking, mountain biking, and a myriad of other outdoor activities, you're not only sane but also in the perfect frame of mind to enjoy this great outdoor playground.

Nineteen lakes are nestled in the park's rolling wooded terrain. Three – Big Fish, Davison, and Algoe – have boat-launching ramps. Big Fish Lake, the area's largest, is popular with water skiers and power boaters, most of whom come from the cottages and homes on the lake's east shore. High speed boating is only allowed on the lake between 11:00 a.m. and 7:30 p.m.

The park's other lakes, though smaller, are generally quieter and less congested and make the angling for bass, bluegills, and trout the solitary, contemplative sport it was intended to be. Round, Mud and Tody lakes all have fishing access sites.

If, on weekends, Big Fish Lake resembles a watery drag strip rather than a quiet fishing hole, so be it. Many find drag strips fun to watch, and a large picnic/swimming area that rims the lake's west side makes an excellent grandstand for all the water borne activity. The huge expanse of lawn with grills and picnic tables extends down to a 20 to 25 feet wide beach that welcomes those who enjoy playing in the sand. Facilities include two rental pavilions, a playground, and horseshoe and volleyball courts, with occasional shade provided by several scattered groups of stately, old trees.

Hikers and mountain bikers share a 2.75-mile loop at the Bloomer #3 area off State Park Road, and cross-country skiers can access a 1.5-mile loop from the same trailhead in the winter. The park's seven miles of bridle trails are also open to hikers.

A 25-site equestrian campground, off Fox Lake Road, features vault toilets and a hand pump for water. The sites are restricted to campers with horses. It operates on a first-come, first-served basis – no reservations are

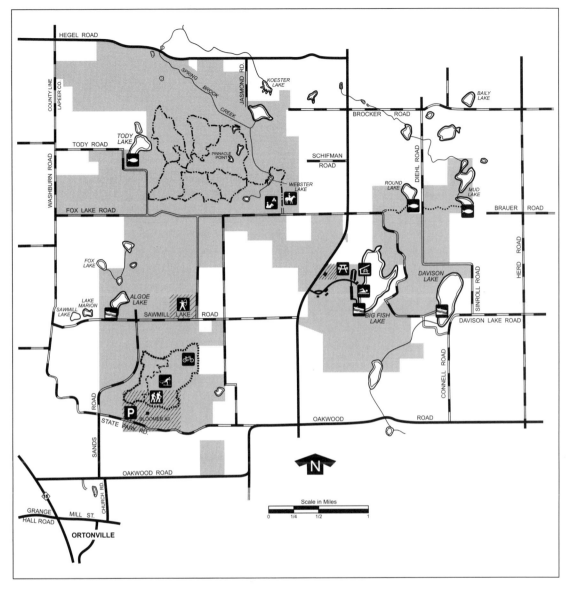

taken. From the staging area near the campground, the bridle trails lead into some of the park's most remote sections. The paths border several small lakes and pass over many of the area's highest hills, with striking views of the surrounding countryside.

Even after subtracting areas set aside for picnicking, hiking, and camping, sportsmen will find nearly 4,500 acres open to hunting. Park officials report deer and rabbit are the most often taken.

During limited dates and times, shooters can sharpen their skills at the park's rifle/trap range on Sawmill Lake Road. Call 248-627-5569 for a current schedule.

COUNTIES: LAPEER AND OAKLAND.

CAMPING SITES: 25 RUSTIC SITES FOR EQUESTRIAN CAMPERS ONLY.

DIRECTIONS: FROM ORTONVILLE, GO WEST ON OAKWOOD ROAD ABOUT ONE MILE TO HADLEY ROAD. TURN RIGHT (NORTH) ONTO HADLEY, WHICH CUTS THROUGH THE PARK AND PROVIDES ACCESS TO MOST POINTS OF INTEREST.

FURTHER INFORMATION: ORTONVILLE RECREATION AREA, 5779 HADLEY ROAD, ORTONVILLE, MI 48462; 248-627-3828 OR 810-797-4439.

M etamora-Hadley

RECREATION AREA

58

OVERNIGHT ACCOMMODATIONS:

ACTIVITIES:

Only minutes from urban sprawl, yet tucked into an out-of-the-way corner of Lapeer County far from major expressways or even busy secondary roads, the Metamora-Hadley Recreation Area offers welcome respite from everyday metropolitan life. This quiet, heavily wooded park, with rolling hills that overlook Lake Minnewanna, might even make you feel like you're several hundred miles farther north.

The park's facilities circle Lake Minnewanna, a twisting, narrow body of water created by the damming of a small creek that flows through the center of the property. Stretching along nearly the entire west shore is a 212-site campground, divided into roughly equal north and south sections. The south loop overlooks the water from a low bluff and is roofed by a mature stand of hardwoods. Panoramic views of the lake can be had from about a quarter of the sites that are perched right at the edge of the bluff. All lots are roomy, deeply shaded, and fairly private. The park's mini-cabin is nestled in among the loop's camping sites.

The lots making up the northern half of the campground are smaller, less private, and sparsely covered with small hardwoods and evergreens. On the plus side, you can fish, sunbathe, or relax on the lawn-like shore just a few yards from your tent or trailer on a quarter of the lots that are immediately adjacent to the lake. The campground usually has vacancies Sunday through Thursday nights, but unless you have made a reservation, you'll have trouble getting a spot on weekends during the peak summer months.

A camp store is located at the entrance to the campground.

Swimming is not allowed in the campground area, but it's just a short walk to the day-use area on the east shore. There, a long sandy swimming beach with a bathhouse and concession stand fronts a grass-covered almost treeless picnic area. Plenty of tables and grills are scattered throughout the large, open grounds, with many close enough to the beach to keep a wary eye on children in the water. If you want a little more privacy and a lot more shade, take your basket and cooler to an area nestled in heavy woods on a bluff that overlooks the water about halfway down the lake's east side.

You can get into the lake, too, with a canoe, rowboat, or pedal boat, all available for rent at the day-use area's concession stand. There is a boat-launching ramp next to the dam on the lake's north end. A no-wake speed limit is in effect.

Two fishing piers jut into the water, one at each of the camping areas. Shore fishing is an equally popular way to go after the lake's bluegill, crappie, bass, and northern pike. In the fall, hunters take grouse, rabbit, squirrel,

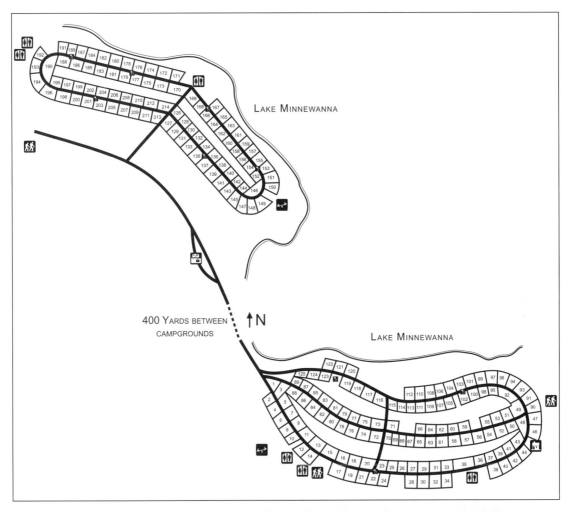

LAKE MINNEWANNA

400 YARDS BETWEEN
CAMPGROUNDS

↑N

LAKE MINNEWANNA

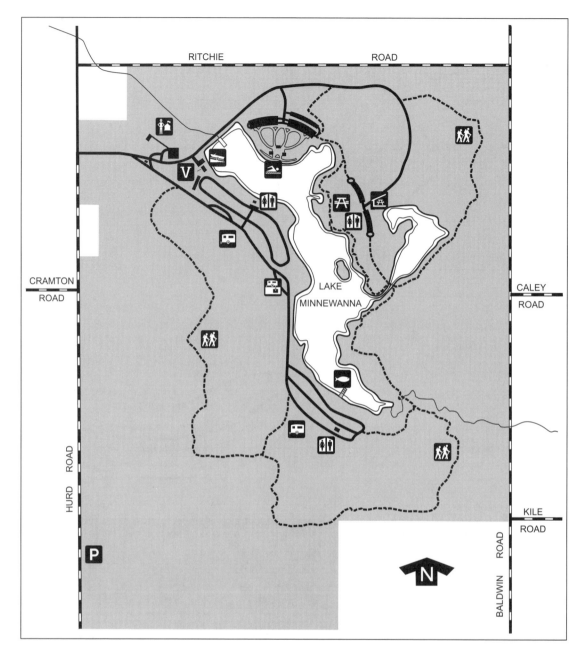

deer, raccoon, pheasant, and geese.

Wildflower enthusiasts (picking not allowed), mushroom hunters, and birdwatchers will also usually be rewarded, although the area is not a prime location for those pursuits. The six miles of hiking trails that circle the lake, climb gentle hills, and pass through deep woods on the outer edges of the 723-acre park are quiet, secluded leg stretchers.

Ice fishing, cross-country skiing, and snowmobiling are enjoyed in the winter. Metal detectors are also allowed in the park.

COUNTY: LAPEER

CAMPING SITES: 212, ALL MODERN, PLUS ONE MINI-CABIN.

DIRECTIONS: FROM M-24 APPROXIMATELY 7 MILES SOUTH OF LAPEER OR 10 MILES NORTH OF OXFORD TURN WEST ONTO PRATT ROAD AND DRIVE 2 MILES TO HURD ROAD. TURN LEFT (SOUTH) ONTO HURD AND GO ABOUT A HALF MILE.

FURTHER INFORMATION: METAMORA-HADLEY RECREATION AREA, 3871 HURD ROAD, METAMORA, MI 48455; 810-797-4439.

Bald Mountain

RECREATION AREA

59

OVERNIGHT ACCOMMODATIONS:

ACTIVITIES:

A prominent Detroit-area magazine rates the swimming beach in Bald Mountain Recreation Area the best in southeast Michigan for small children. The wide, sandy shore, gently sloping lake bottom, and shallow waters that reach far out into Lower Trout Lake add up to peace of mind for parents and near-perfect water play place for small fry.

Back from the shore, a bathhouse fronts a large grass-covered picnic area. There's a bonus for parents: the long entrance road to the swimming/picnic area crests some of the highest elevations with sweeping views in northeast Oakland County.

If you want or need to escape the noise and activity of the swimming beach, the park provides you with options. Away from that south-shore area, several quiet, picnic areas with shelters ring Lower Trout Lake. You can drift through the lake's colonies of lily pads and past its forested edges in a canoe or paddle boat, available for rent at the beach concession.

If you really want to roam, then step or pedal onto the 15.1 miles of hiking/mountain biking trails that crisscross two of the three large tracts that make up the 4,637-acre recreation area. Trail maps, available at park headquarters, detail both a 7.1-mile circuit that explores an area north of Lower Trout Lake and an 8-mile network connecting a dozen small lakes in the park's northernmost parcel. The trails traverse some of the most rugged and steep terrain in southeastern Michigan.

Although Bald Mountain lacks a camp-ground, it boasts two rustic cabins on Tamarack Lake. Each can sleep up to twenty. And at the door of either cabin lies eight miles of hiking, biking, and cross-country ski trails leading to a double-handful of lakes.

Several of the small lakes in the northern unit have either fishing access sites or boat-launching ramps. A no-wake speed limit is in effect on Upper and Lower Trout lakes, and just about all lakes in the recreation area yield bass, bluegills, crappies, and northern pike. Fly fishermen can test their skill against the brown trout found in Trout and Paint creeks, which flow through the southern section of the park.

Bald Mountain's diverse habit and cover make for such excellent birdwatching that the Oakland County Chapter of the Audubon Society holds its annual Christmas bird count here. Wildflowers also abound, and if weather conditions cooperate, mushrooms pop up throughout the area.

At Bald Mountain, hunters and firearm enthusiasts can practice at one of the country's most up-to-date shooting ranges, complete with skeet, trap, pistol, and archery areas. The complex, located on the west side of Kern Road, includes a classroom, lounge,

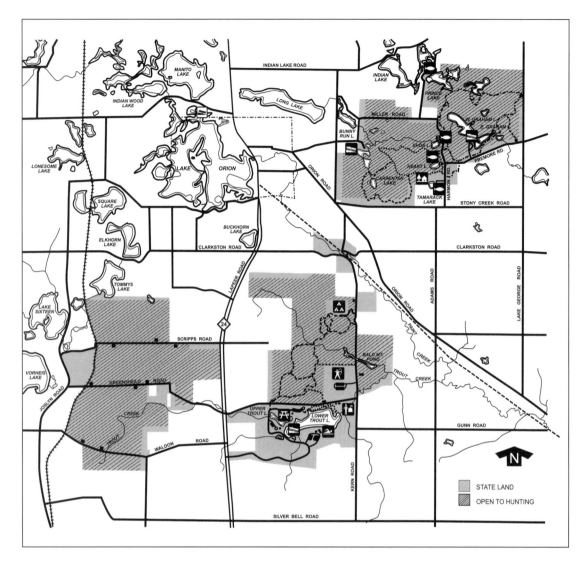

STATE LAND

OPEN TO HUNTING

and sales area where guns can be rented. A ranger is always on duty.

Hunting is allowed in approximately 3,500 acres of the recreation area. Deer and rabbits are the most plentiful game, but pheasants and ruffed grouse are also taken. Metal detectors are allowed in certain areas.

In the winter, ice-fishing and sledding bring the bundled-up to the park, as does the eight miles of groomed, cross-country ski trails. Snowmobilers have their own seven miles of marked trails and another 2,500 acres set aside for their use when snow depth reaches four inches.

COUNTY: OAKLAND
CAMPING SITES: TWO FRONTIER CABINS.
SCHEDULE: THE SHOOTING RANGE SCHEDULE VARIES ACCORDING TO THE SEASON.
CALL 248-814-9193 FOR HOURS.
DIRECTIONS: APPROXIMATELY 3 MILES SOUTH OF LAKE ORION ON M-24.
FURTHER INFORMATION: BALD MOUNTAIN RECREATION AREA, 1330 EAST GREENSHIELD ROAD, LAKE ORION, MI 48360; 248-693-6767.

Tri-Centennial
STATE PARK AND HARBOR

OVERNIGHT ACCOMMODATIONS:

ACTIVITIES:

Dedicated on May 20, 2005, Tri-Centennial State Park and Harbor ranks not only as Michigan's newest state park but also its first urban park. Located on the Detroit River in the heart of downtown Detroit, the 31-acre park serves as both a harbor of refuge for Great Lakes boaters and a refuge for city dwellers looking for a respite from urban sprawl in the state's largest city.

A 63-foot-tall replica of the Tawas Point Lighthouse marks the river entrance to the harbor of refuge. Amenities at the park's 52 boat slips include water, electricity, showers, pump out, grills and picnic tables, 24-hour security, and a laundry. Boaters will find they have tied up within a few blocks of Hart Plaza and the Ren-Cen Towers. The slips are for transient boats only and reservations can be made online. The harbor is open May to September and the Harbor Master is on duty from 8 a.m. to 8 p.m. and can be reached on Radio Channel 16. There are no seasonal slips available.

No boat, no problem. Landlubbers can fish from shore in a waterway famed for producing walleyes or simply stroll the river bank and take in the continuous flow of Great Lakes ore carriers, pleasure boats, and ocean going freighters from around the world that ply the narrow waters of the Detroit River. Better yet, spend the day anchored at a picnic table and grill enjoying the sights and sounds of this unique park or invite the extended family and settle in at a picnic shelter.

The park remains under development and it is foreseen that additional services and at-tractions will be phased in over the coming years.

COUNTY: WAYNE
CAMPING SITES: 52 BOAT SLIPS.
DIRECTIONS: FROM I-375 AND EAST JEFFERSON IN DOWNTOWN DETROIT DRIVE EAST ON JEFFERSON ABOUT THREE BLOCKS TO ST. AUBIN STREET. TURN RIGHT (SOUTH) ON ST. AUBIN AND DRIVE TO PARK ENTRANCE.
FURTHER INFORMATION: TRI-CENTENNIAL STATE PARK AND HARBOR, 1900 ATWATER STREET, DETROIT, MI 48226; 313-396-0217. HARBOR MASTER PHONE NUMBER: 734-289-2715.

WC *Wetzel*
STATE RECREATION AREA

OVERNIGHT ACCOMMODATIONS: NONE

ACTIVITIES:

For more than 30 years Wetzel State Park was a park in name only. It lay undeveloped, and except for a few hunters and the Radio Control Club of Detroit – which established a flying field for model airplanes with bleachers and parking lot off 27 Mile Road – the 844-acre tract of land was all but forgotten and ignored. That is, until a simple change of name and a not so simple law-breaker had as revolutionary an impact on this park as a glass slipper had on Cinderella's life.

In November of 2004, Wetzel was designated a State Recreation Area instead of a State Park which allowed a wider variety of hunting to take place on the land including an early goose season and a spring turkey hunt. Ducks, geese, upland game birds, rabbit, squirrel, and deer are also hunted with success here.

Then, somewhere in the state, a contractor was caught destroying wetlands. To atone for his transgressions, legal and environmental, the contractor turned a good deal of the acreage at Wetzel into wetlands at his own expense. The recreation area is now dotted with ponds of various sizes ringed with marshes and wetlands, transforming farm fields into prime habitat for a wide variety of game and non-game birds and wetland mammals.

The finishing touch at the new recreation area includes two new parking areas and two walking trails that loop through the new terrain. The 1.16-mile long South Trail departs from the old parking lot next to the model airplane field on 27 Mile Road and heads south skirting several ponds. The Pondo Trail begins in a new parking lot on the east side of the park on Werderman Road just south of New Haven Road and makes a 1.06 mile circuit around a large pond before returning to the parking lot. The third parking lot is off Omo Road on the west side of the park and is primarily for hunters. Vault toilets are located at the Werderman Road and 27 Mile Road parking lots.

Trails are open to skiers in the winter, and snowmobiles are welcome when four or more inches of snow cover the ground.

COUNTY: MACOMB
CAMPING SITES: NONE
DIRECTIONS: FROM NEW HAVEN DRIVE NORTHWEST ON NEW HAVEN ROAD APPROXIMATELY 1.5 MILES TO WERDERMAN ROAD. TURN LEFT (SOUTH) ON WERDERMAN AND DRIVE ABOUT 0.25 MILES TO THE PARKING LOT. TO REACH THE 27 MILE ROAD PARKING LOT, CONTINUE SOUTH ON WERDERMAN FOR ABOUT 0.75 MILES TO 27 MILE ROAD AND TURN RIGHT OR WEST AND PROCEED TO THE PARKING LOT AT THE END OF THE ROAD.
FURTHER INFORMATION: WETZEL STATE RECREATION AREA, C/O ALGONAC STATE PARK, 8732 RIVER ROAD, MARINE CITY, MI 48039; 810-765-5605.

Algonac
State Park

Overnight Accommodations:

Activities:

Since its establishment in 1937, Algonac State Park has been providing one of the best seats in the state for watching the world go by. The park stretches for a half mile along the banks of the St. Clair River, one of the world's busiest shipping lanes. Huge Great Lakes and ocean-going vessels, many with international markings, continuously ply the narrow waters, and freighter-watching is one of the park's chief attractions. Nearly as much attention is directed at the constant of parade of large pleasure boats making their way up and down the waterway connecting lakes Huron and St. Clair.

Each year a quarter of a million visitors spread blankets or set up lawn chairs on the picnic and campground areas across M-29 from the river, then spend the day mesmerized by the passing show. Campers on the two rows of sites closest to the highway experience the astonishing sensation of watching 1,000-foot-long ore carriers and other ships pass what appears to be less than a boat length from their tents and RVs. From the narrow strip of bank on the river side of the highway, the huge slow-moving vessels seem to block out almost everything else.

Don't tell fishermen that freighter-watching is the main attraction unless you're prepared to hear a long lecture on just how good fishing is on the river and, a few miles downstream, Lake St. Clair. Following spring breakup of river ice comes smelt dipping and good catches of king and coho salmon. In spring, summer and fall walleyes and yellow perch are abundant throughout both the river and lake. Anglers also hook white bass, channel catfish, sturgeon, and muskies, and the village of Algonac, a couple of miles to

the south, is known as the "pickerel capital of the world."

There is a small boat ramp near the park's scenic turnout, but better-equipped public-launch facilities are available in Algonac or north of the park at Marine City. Judging from the number of anglers who toss lures from the riverbank, fishing from shore is as popular as from boats.

Much of the 1,459-acre park, which stretches well back from the river and is covered by a sometimes-dense mixed-hardwood forest, is also open to hunting. Rabbits and squirrels are plentiful, some deer are taken, and a few lucky hunters get at shot at a pheasant. In the off season, sportsman can sharpen their shooting skills at the park's trap and archery ranges.

Other interesting but less obvious attractions are also available if you can tear your attention away from the show on the river. Hidden amid the park's lush landscape, for instance, is a special treasure: four patches of original Michigan lakeplain prairie, the last remnants of the great grasslands that once

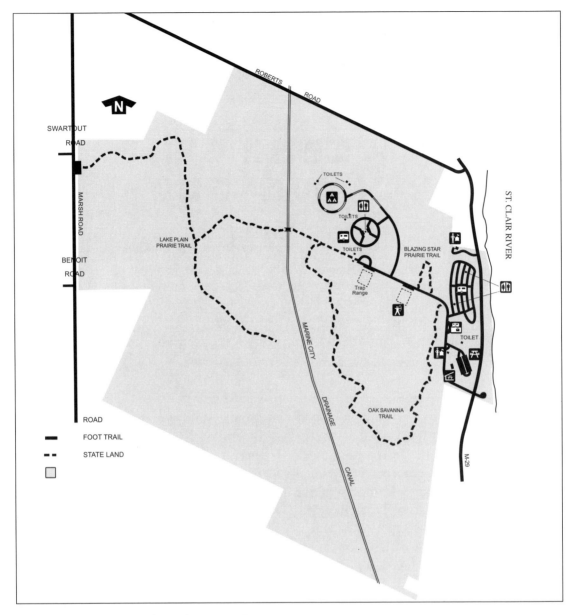

spread across much of southern Michigan. The four plots total roughly 62 acres and, according to the Michigan Natural Areas Council, support nearly 300 types of grasses and plants, including many rare and threatened species.

The park is also home to a wide variety of birds, mushrooms, and wild flowers. Three hiking trails, totaling about six miles, penetrate the park's interior and lead to three of the four prairie areas. Informal lectures and nature hikes are conducted by park rangers that explore the park's natural history and heritage. Cross-country skiers ply the trails in winter.

Campers have a choice of 296 sites divided between two separate campgrounds. Generally, the most desired lots are the 220 in the Riverfront Campground, which borders M-29 and the St. Clair River. The very best for freighter watching are the lots closest to the river. There is a trade-off for the great view, however. Campers at those sites have to put up with being within a few feet of a fairly busy state highway. The rest of the lots in the Riverfront Campground spread back in several rows from the highway. All sites offer little privacy, but most are shaded and

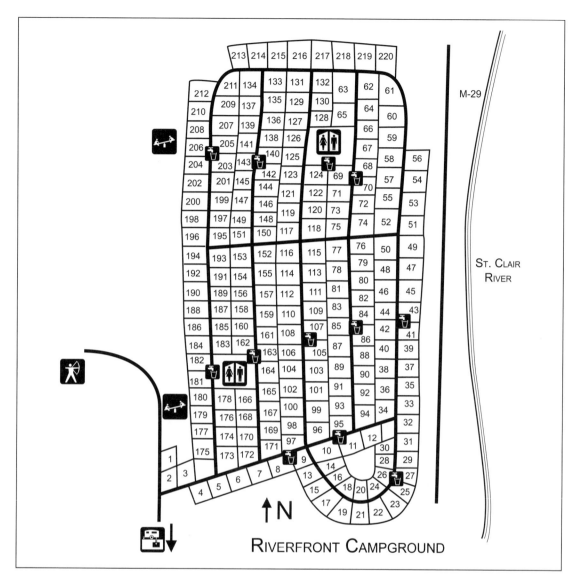

RIVERFRONT CAMPGROUND

over half have gravel pads for easier parking. There are several pull-through sites for those who don't like to back-in their rig, and many sites offer 50 amp electrical service.

The newest and prettiest campsites are located in the Wagon Wheel Campground, three-quarters-of-a-mile inland from the river. This heavily shaded area features electrical hookups, blacktop roads and pads, and three handicapped accessible sites. All campers have access to modern restrooms and showers. Although the Riverfront Campground has a number of non-reservable sites, the campgrounds are heavily used throughout the summer, so make a reservation to ensure a site for a weekend visit.

Day visitors have plenty of room to enjoy a cookout and the scenery from a sprawling grass-covered, partially shaded picnic area that borders the west side of the highway, just south of the Riverfront Campground. The use of metal detectors is permitted in specific areas of the park.

COUNTY: ST. CLAIR
CAMPING SITES: 296, ALL MODERN.
DIRECTIONS: ON I-94 NORTHEAST OF DETROIT TAKE EXIT 243 AND TRAVEL 20 MILES EAST ON M-29 TO THE PARK ENTRANCE.
FURTHER INFORMATION: ALGONAC STATE PARK, 8732 RIVER ROAD, MARINE CITY, MI 48039; 810-765-5605.

Lakeport State Park

63

OVERNIGHT ACCOMMODATIONS:

ACTIVITIES:

For day-users and campers alike, the focal point at Lakeport State Park is a mile and a half of beautiful Lake Huron shoreline. The park lies just three miles north of where the lake empties into Lake St. Clair, and from the park's low bluffs come distant views of freighter traffic heading in and out of that gateway to the upper Great Lakes. Most visitors, however, don't come here to look at freighters but rather to build sand castles, sunbathe, swim, picnic, and laze away the day on a golden ribbon of sand that is easily reached from nearly anywhere in the park.

The small village of Lakeport splits the park into two unequal sections. Abutting the village's southern border is a day-use area (Franklin Delano Roosevelt Unit), and to get to its half mile of Lake Huron frontage you have to cross over busy M-25 on a pedestrian bridge. It's a long way to lug a heavy cooler but worth the effort. Panoramic views of the lake come from a picnic area that lines the low bluff. There's plenty of room for sunbathers and swimmers to spread out blankets and towels on the beach and even more room on the grassy bluff overlooking the lake. The lake bottom shelves steeply here and the water gets deep fast, so keep a close eye on youngsters. Centrally located on the beach side of the highway is a large bathhouse and restrooms. Children's playground equipment is found throughout the grounds.

If you don't want to mount a caravan to get your baskets, bags, and coolers across the highway, you can use a spacious picnic area, including pavilion, adjacent to the large parking lot.

North of the village, 250 sites that make up the park's modern campground are divided into two areas. Farthest from the highway and closest to a mile of beach reserved for campers only are lots 1-194. The sites in this area, the park's original campground, are shaded and much less crowded after the wing was reconfigured and reduced by 30-plus campsites. The redesign allows for several new pull-through sites. The best views come from even-numbered lots 18-34, which are closest to the water. The park store is located at the shore edge of this wing.

About a quarter mile south of the original campground, the park's newest camping sites, 301-356, are arranged in four loops near the contact station. Though somewhat less shaded than those in the older unit, these lots are generally roomier and have paved slips for easy parking and setup of RVs. The park's two mini-cabins are located here. The beach is less than a 100-yard walk past a play area and through a dense stand of trees.

Both units fill to near capacity June through Labor Day, so make reservations if you're coming in the summer. Many overnighters

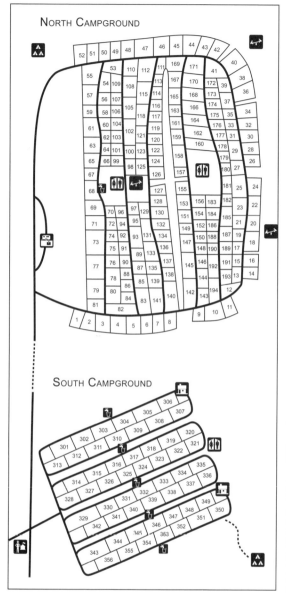

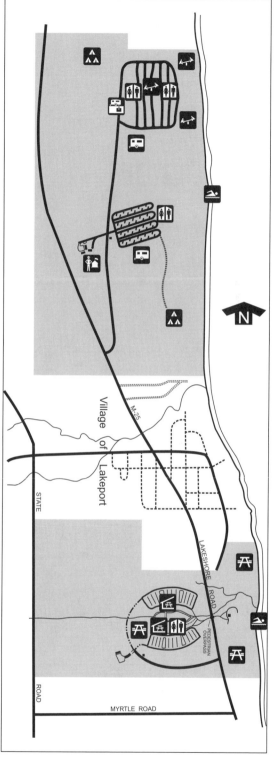

use the campground as a base for excursions into Canada over the Blue Water Bridge, just 10 miles south. Ten miles to the north is the quaint village of Lexington and a state-operated boat launch that will get fishermen and pleasure boaters afloat on Lake Huron. Park personnel present natural history programs and guided hikes throughout the summer, and hobbyists can operate metal detectors in certain areas of the park.

COUNTY: ST. CLAIR
CAMPING SITES: 250, ALL MODERN AND TWO MINI-CABINS.

DIRECTIONS: DRIVE 10 MILES NORTH OF PORT HURON ON M-25.
FURTHER INFORMATION: LAKEPORT STATE PARK, 7605 LAKESHORE DRIVE, LAKEPORT, MI 48059; 810-327-6224.

Sanilac Petroglyphs

Historic Site

64

OVERNIGHT ACCOMMODATIONS: NONE

ACTIVITIES:

In an area known for its quiet towns, large farms, and billiard-table flat landscape lies one of Michigan's most haunting and intriguing mysteries. Poking only a couple of feet out of the ground on the banks of the Cass River in Sanilac County is a 20- by 40-foot sandstone outcropping etched with strange markings.

Scientists have known what the figures are ever since a forest fire cleared the land and exposed the rock in 1881. They're the best known petroglyphs – that is, prehistoric carvings or line drawings on rock – in the state. Ancient artists – using stones, bones and antlers – laboriously gouged, scraped and chiseled animals, hunting scenes, animal tracks, human figures and abstract designs into the soft rock.

The mystery here is when and why? Man has roamed the Cass River basin off and on for more than 10,000 years, according to archaeological evidence. But traditional methods, such as carbon dating or links to other artifacts found in the area, have so far failed to conclusively determine the carving's age. Most researchers theorize that they were done during what is called the Late Woodland Period, making them anywhere from 300 to 1,000 years old.

Why were the 100 or so figures carved? Speculation ranges from the recording of dreams, visions, or significant events to their being done during hunting rituals or religious ceremonies.

You don't have to know the answers to get caught up in the spell cast by this very special place. Little known and far from any major tourist center in the Thumb, the Sanilac Petroglyphs receive few visitors. So you can sit in quiet solitude and contemplate the art work and wonder just what the unknown artists were preserving for posterity.

Sadly, walking on the rock and even brushing the carvings with your hand wears the soft sandstone, albeit imperceptibly. Rain, snow, and other forms of precipitation also take their toll, but nothing is as harmful as the thoughtless fools who have defaced the outcropping with graffiti. As a result, the state first covered the rock with a large roof to protect it from the weather and then fenced it to protect the artwork from vandalism. See below for hours when the public can view the carvings.

Hikers and walkers will find the park's 240 acres etched with two miles of trails that wander through some of the most beautiful country in the Thumb. The south fork of the north branch of the Cass River winds along the southern edge of the park. Large, majestic hardwoods form cathedral-like arches across the narrow stream, which is bordered in several places by sandstone outcroppings. Away from the river, the trails traverse open

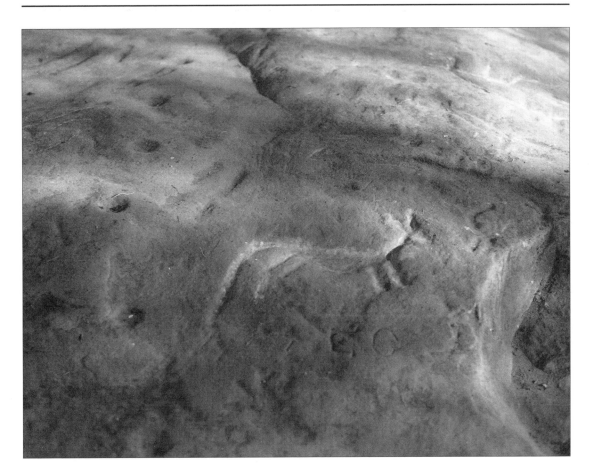

meadows, dense thickets, and stands of second growth forest. Cross-country skiers can take to the trails in the winter months.

COUNTY: SANILAC
CAMPING SITES: NONE
SCHEDULE: THE HIKING TRAIL IS OPEN ALL YEAR. THE FENCED AND GATED PETROGLYPHS AREA IS OPEN TO THE PUBLIC FROM 10:30 A.M. TO 5 P.M. WEDNESDAY THROUGH SUNDAY FROM MEMORIAL DAY TO LABOR DAY. THESE HOURS ARE SUBJECT TO CHANGE AND BEFORE A VISIT IT'S BEST TO CALL THE NUMBER BELOW.
DIRECTIONS: FROM THE JUNCTION OF M-53 AND M-81 DRIVE 4 MILES NORTH ON M-53 TO BAY CITY-FORESTVILLE ROAD. TURN RIGHT (EAST) ONTO BAY CITY-FORESTVILLE ROAD AND DRIVE 4 MILES TO GERMANIA ROAD. TURN RIGHT (SOUTH) ON GERMANIA AND GO ABOUT A HALF MILE TO THE PARK ENTRANCE.

FURTHER INFORMATION: FOR HOURS OF OPERATION, CONTACT SLEEPER STATE PARK, 6573 STATE PARK ROAD, CASEVILLE, MI 48725; 989-856-4411. FOR HISTORICAL AND INTERPRETATIVE INFORMATION, CONTACT THE MICHIGAN HISTORICAL CENTER, P.O. BOX 30740, 702 WEST KALAMAZOO STREET, LANSING, MI 48909; 517-373-3559.

Port Crescent
State Park

65

OVERNIGHT ACCOMMODATIONS:

ACTIVITIES:

When you first see Port Crescent State Park's three miles of unsurpassed Saginaw Bay shoreline, blanketed with low dunes and white sand so fine it was used for smelting, you'll immediately realize that you are at one of the premier parks in southeastern Michigan. By the time you leave, after experiencing its exceptionally fine, beautiful facilities, you'll probably have decided that this 605-acre park rates as one of the best in the Lower Peninsula.

No matter where you stay in Port Crescent's modern campground, you will be drawn to a beach covered in a sand so soft that even with shoes on you often sink to your ankles. Only a few of the 137 sites are immediately on the water. Many of those sites and some across the narrow campground street are so inundated with sand they have been partially paved so cars and RVs can park without getting stuck. A dozen sites line an old channel of the Pinnebog River and offer campers the most level spots in the campground.

The remaining lots are back from shore, most on a grassy shelf. Almost all of these sites are just a walk away from the camper's beach, and from many you can catch glimpses of the lake through trees that provide both shade and privacy. The campground has one mini-cabin and a new (handicapped accessible) rustic cabin with a covered front porch overlooking its own stretch of shoreline. Every evening, campers from all lots make their way to the beach to watch the sun go down over a distant point of land.

The campground (the site of the former village of Port Crescent, which gave up the ghost in the 1930s and left only the stump of a smoke stack to mark its passing) is heavily used from June 15 to Labor Day, and the only sure way to get a spot then is to reserve one.

Almost two miles west of the campground on M-25, an entrance road leads to a day-use area with panoramic views of Saginaw Bay, miles of beach, and acres of low dunes that wet their toes along the shoreline before reaching back into the interior. Scattered between the twisting Pinnebog River and lakeshore throughout the large area are secluded, private picnic tables and grills. From a change house and large, covered picnic shelter at the swimming beach, boardwalks lead to two of the best picnic spots on the east side of the Lower Peninsula with large decks perched on the lip of dunes overlooking Saginaw Bay. Stretching east, the expanse of low dunes nearly disappears over the horizon. Four miles of marked cross-country/hiking trails wander over the singular landscape.

An additional 2.5 miles of beautiful hiking and cross-country ski trails explore a large, undeveloped parcel that lies between the picnic area and campground. The Pinnebog River and Saginaw Bay all but surround the area, and the foot paths pass through quiet, secluded woods, over low sand ridges and dunes, along the beach, and to several scenic spots overlooking the lake and river. Park rangers conduct nature walks and interpretive programs throughout the summer.

The entire park offers excellent birding with the trail bordering the old river channel a prime area for warbler watching in late April and early May. Campers can reach the trails from a spot on their beach where shifting sands have blocked the river's original mouth. Day visitors have to cross over the Old Pinnebog River Channel on a footbridge directly across M-25 from the end of Port Crescent Road.

Canoeists can spend an entire day nosing around the Pinnebog, a river that seems to tie itself in knots as it searches for an outlet to Saginaw Bay. The nearly four miles of river that slowly moves through the park also attracts fishermen, who take trout, walleye, salmon, and perch from both the river and the channel. The day-use area has a small fishing

pier on the river, and there's plenty of shore space for anglers to spread out. A launch site limited to car-top boats and canoes is located on the river just inside the day-use area. The village of Port Austin, about five miles east of the park, has a modern harbor and state boat-launching facility, and pier fishing is allowed there.

Sections of the park are open to hunters, who take deer with bows or firearms, plus small game in season.

County: Huron
Camping Sites: 137, all modern, plus one mini-cabin and one frontier cabin.
Directions: Five miles west of Port Austin on M-25.
Further Information: Port Crescent State Park, 1775 Port Austin Road, Port Austin, MI 48467; 989-738-8663.

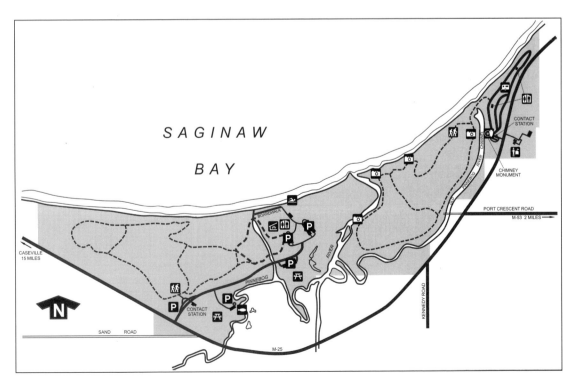

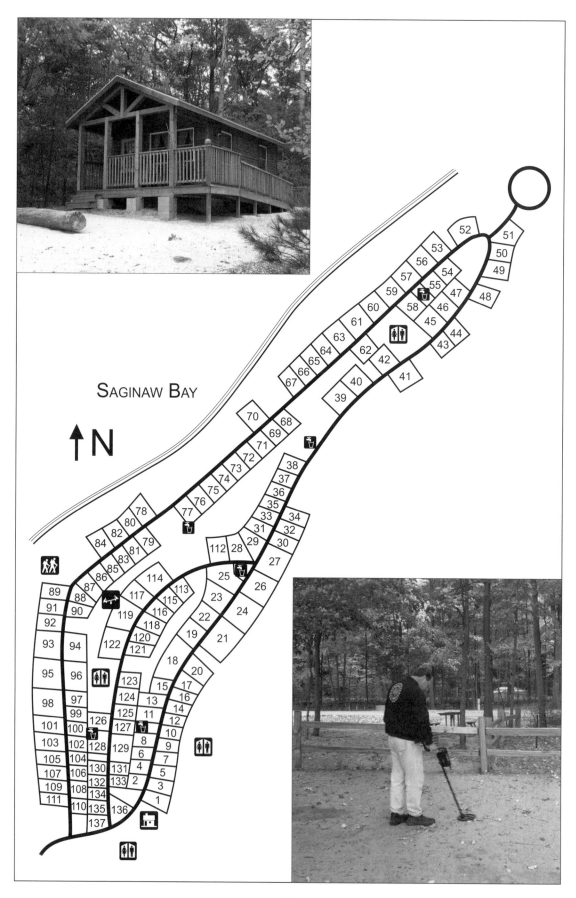

SAGINAW BAY

↑N

Albert E. Sleeper
State Park

66

OVERNIGHT ACCOMMODATIONS:

ACTIVITIES:

Practically from the day it first opened as a county park in 1925, Albert E. Sleeper State Park has attracted vacationers from southeast Michigan who want the feel of being in the northern parts of the state without the long drive. Vast and largely undeveloped, the park's heavily forested 723 acres extend well back from a half-mile strip of beautiful, sandy Saginaw Bay beach in a series of sand ridges and ancient shorelines. The pine-scented realm is ideal for hiking, cross-country skiing, nature study and enjoyment, hunting, and other outdoor pastimes. Park personnel lead informal hikes and programs that explore the park's rich environment, wild life, and resources.

Highway M-25 separates the day-use area from the rest of the park. The half-mile of white-sand beach plus the gently sloping bottom and warm waters of Saginaw Bay lure swimmers, waders, beachcombers, and sunbathers. Back from the shore, widely scattered picnic tables and grills are tucked into a stand of mature trees between low, wooded dunes and the highway. Although the dunes cut off views of the lake, picnickers have extraordinary privacy and only have to share their space with troops of busy chipmunks. Other facilities at the day-use area include a bathhouse and a picnic shelter.

Directly across the highway from the beach is Sleeper's grass-covered, heavily shaded campground. All 226 sites have electrical outlets – either 30/20 amp or 50/30/20 amp service – and access to modern restrooms with flush toilets and showers. The campground, including its one mini-cabin, fills nearly every summer weekend, and park personnel strongly encourage reservations. The resort town of Caseville, with its many attractions, lies five miles to the west.

Schools, church groups, and other organizations can rent the wilderness cabins, kitchen/dining hall, and the adjacent toilet/shower building that comprise the park's large outdoor center. Set well away from other facilities, the center can accommodate groups up to 120.

Except for the center, park property in back of the campground is wild and undeveloped. Most of the acreage is unscarred by any path, to the joy of "bushwhackers" who like to plunge into the area.

Conventional hikers will find 4.5 miles of formal trails probing the area immediately south of the campground. Along one, the Ridges Nature Trail, you can use a self-guiding brochure to not only identify the fascinating array of native trees, shrubs, and flowers along the route, but learn how Indians used the plants in everyday life. Other trails follow ancient Saginaw Bay shorelines and skirt wetlands. The wide variety of ecosystems here – lakeshore, dunes, and woodlands

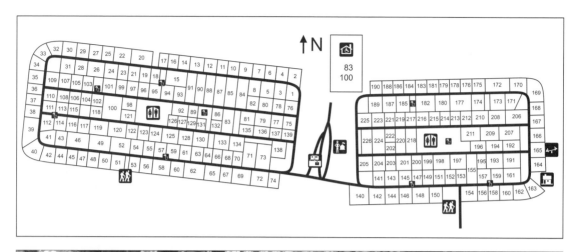

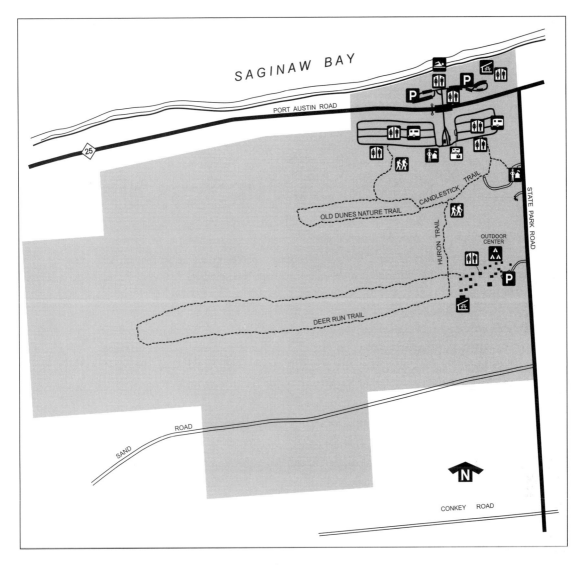

– attracts many birds. The park grooms the trails for cross-country skiers in winter.

A remote, well-posted corner of the park is open to hunting, as is the 2,200 acre Rush Lake State Game Area that lies adjacent to the park across State Park Road. Metal detectors are allowed in specific areas of the park.

County: Huron
Camping Sites: 226 modern sites including 1 mini-cabin.
Directions: Five miles east of Caseville on M-25.
Further information: Albert E. Sleeper State Park, 6573 State Park Road, Caseville, MI 48725; 989-856-4411.

Bay City
STATE RECREATION AREA

67

OVERNIGHT ACCOMMODATIONS: 🚐 🏠 ⛺

ACTIVITIES: 🚴 🐦 🎿 🎣 🥾 🔫 🚶 🎣 🏕 🛷 🏊 V 🔭

One adjective fits just about all of the facilities – beach, picnic grounds, and one of the state's finest nature-study areas – at Bay City State Recreation Area: Expansive.

The park's soft sandy beach, for instance, stretches for nearly a mile along Saginaw Bay, and hundreds of people can stake out portions of the long, broad strip without creating a crowd. The swimming area also extends farther out than most. The lake bottom slopes so gradually that the water is barely knee deep 100-150 feet from shore, and waders there move around sand bars that nudge into or poke out of the bay. This obviously is a great beach for small children and their watchful parents. Facilities, located well back from the water's edge, include a large bathhouse, nature center, and restrooms.

Behind the beach and paralleling the bay for almost the entire length of the day-use area is an immense picnic area, with a choice of either views of the water from open, sunny meadows or shade and seclusion amidst towering hardwoods. Playground equipment is scatted along the picnic grounds/beach line, and five picnic pavilions are available.

Across State Park Drive from the picnic area and beach is the park's modern campground. Dense woods screen the area from the road and the rest of the park, and the high leafy canopy shades the 184 large, well-worn lots and two mini-cabins. Nearly a quarter of the sites, those which back up to woods, also have a fair degree of privacy.

Registered campers are the only park visitors allowed to possess or consume alcohol. The beach is only a few-hundred-yard walk from the campground. Reservations are recommended at this busy park.

Bay City State Recreation Area is one of the finest areas in the Lower Peninsula for both recreational and dedicated birdwatchers and naturalists. At the Saginaw Bay Visitor Center, north of the picnic area, you can immerse yourself in a variety of displays and exhibits that tell the natural history, geology, ecology, and wildlife of the Saginaw Bay area. The center also offers a variety of year-round interpretive programs.

Then you can experience the natural splendors of Saginaw Bay first-hand on two trails that begin at the center. The shorter of the two, which circles a small lagoon lying between the visitor center and Saginaw Bay, crosses over two boardwalks and leads to splendid views of the bay.

The longer trail heads north into 2,000-acre Tobico Marsh which, because of its, "exceptional value in illustrating the nation's natural heritage," has been registered as a National Natural Landmark. The first mile of trail is paved and cuts through deep woods and marshes before edging the eastern side of vast wetlands. There are two ob-

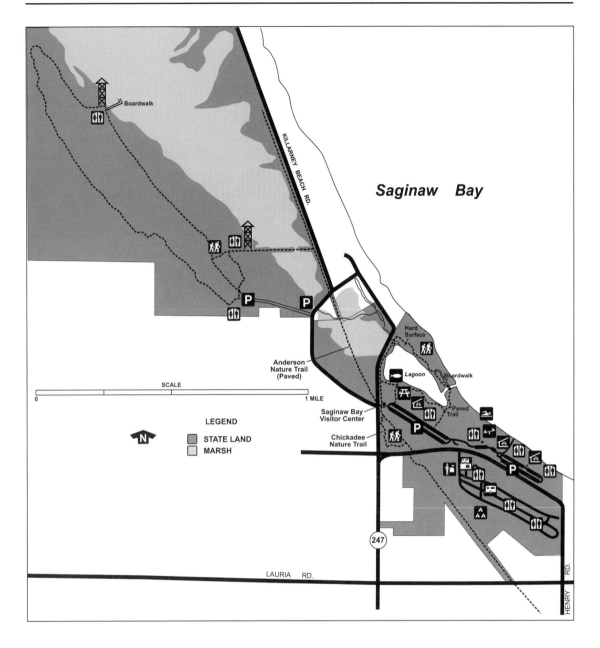

servation decks along the trail, and a paved branch trail leads to a tall observation tower on the west side of the marsh. The pavement ends at the tower, but a well-worn extension circles farther north along the west side of the marsh, slips through an impressive stand of hardwoods, and passes a boardwalk that reaches out into the marsh and another tall observation tower. Bikes are allowed on most trails, and a large part of the system is handicapped accessible. Cross-country skiers can take to the trails in winter.

One of the largest remaining coastal wet-lands on the Great Lakes, Tobico Marsh is not only one of the finest birdwatching areas in the state, but also is nationally famous for its wetland bird life. More than 200 species of birds have been spotted in the marsh, and rare Michigan species such as the Ruddy Duck and Yellow-headed Blackbird nest here. Birds aren't the only wildlife that calls the area home. Deer, beaver, mink, fox, rabbit, otter, coyote, and muskrat have all been spotted by hikers. A bird identification book isn't the only guide to bring along because the marsh shelters a wide range of wildflow-

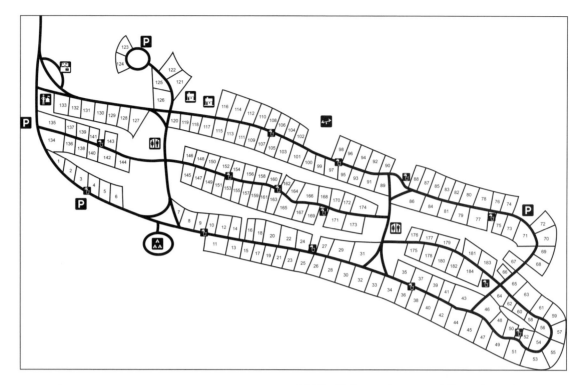

ers including some rare species.

Hunting is allowed in some areas, with waterfowl, game birds and deer being the prime targets.

Anglers catch perch and bass from a dock built on the shore of the park lagoon; perch and walleye are pulled from the open waters of Saginaw Bay. Metal detectors are allowed in specific areas of the park.

COUNTY: BAY

CAMPING SITES: 184, ALL MODERN, PLUS TWO MINI-CABINS

SCHEDULE: THE PARK IS OPEN YEAR ROUND FROM 8 A.M. TO 10 P.M. DAILY. THE SAGINAW BAY VISITOR CENTER IS OPEN TUESDAY THROUGH SUNDAY, NOON TO 5 P.M.

DIRECTIONS: FROM I-75 NORTH OF BAY CITY, EXIT ONTO BEAVER ROAD (168), AND DRIVE EAST ABOUT 5 MILES.

FURTHER INFORMATION: BAY CITY STATE RECREATION AREA, 3582 STATE PARK DRIVE, BAY CITY, MI 48706; 989-684-3020.

WILSON STATE PARK

Wilson
STATE PARK

68

OVERNIGHT ACCOMMODATIONS:

ACTIVITIES:

Granted, Wilson State Park, with only 36 acres, is small. And, yes, Old US-27 crowds the campground. And, no, there aren't any hiking trails or even any undeveloped areas to speak of in the park. So why do more than 90,000 visitors come here each year, year in and year out?

A look at a state map supplies part of the answer. Wilson is the first "up-north" state park that campers from southeast Michigan can reach in an easy drive. Geographically you could argue the point, but at least psychologically, the ambiance of the place says "up north" to a lot of tired city dwellers – so many, in fact, that the campground is filled to capacity on most weekends and holidays from mid-June to mid-August.

Another reason for the park's popularity with campers is that they have the whole place to themselves – the beach and picnic area are only lightly used by day-visitors. Shaded tables, grills and a large playground are scattered over a gentle rise that overlooks Budd Lake, and the sandy swimming beach edges a small point that juts out into the water. An historic bathhouse built by the Civilian Conservation Corp sits at the base of the little peninsula.

The 160-site modern campground wraps around either flank of the day-use area and backs up to busy US-127 Business Route. The narrow strip of

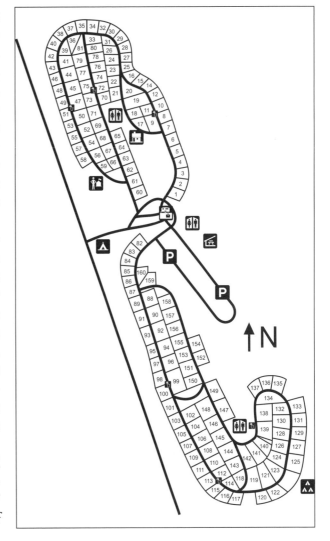

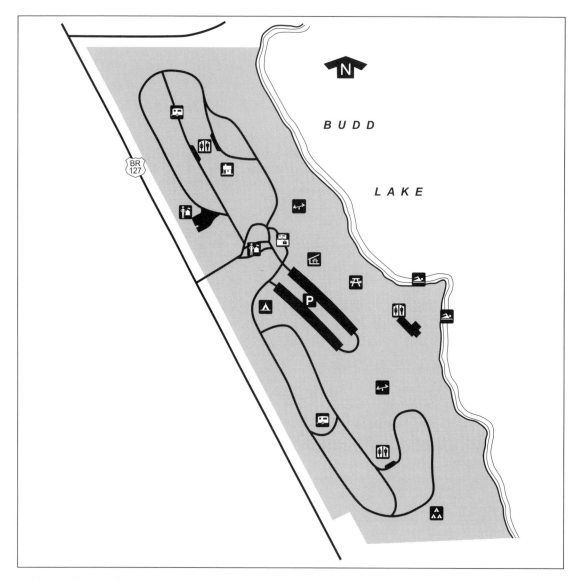

park land is sheltered by a mature stand of hardwoods and provides campers with plenty of shade but little privacy. Most campsites are worn bare of grass. If you don't own a tent or RV (or even if you do) and want a nearly unique camping experience, stay in Wilson State Park's tepee, which is permanently and visibly set up just off the highway near the entrance. The large, blinding-white, canvas-and-pole accommodation rents for $30 a night and comes equipped with cots. The campground also has a mini-cabin.

Budd Lake was one of the first in the state to be stocked with northern muskies, and in more recent years tiger muskies have also been released. Fishermen, who launch at pri-

vate marinas, also pull in good catches of bass and some panfish. Metal detecting is allowed in certain areas within the park.

The Clare County Fairgrounds lie across the road from the park and hosts a wide variety of events throughout the summer.

County: Clare
Camping Sites: 160, all modern, plus one rental tepee and one mini-cabin.
Schedule: Open April 1 – Nov. 30.
Directions: A half mile north of Harrison on Old US-27.
Further Information: Wilson State Park, P.O. Box 333, Harrison, MI 48625; 989-539-3021.

Rifle River
Recreation Area

69

Overnight Accommodations:

Activities:

One of the best ways to enjoy this scenic recreation area is on a bicycle. Several miles of paved and good dirt cycling roads cross one-lane bridges, pass forest-fringed lakes, and climb high hills to broad vistas of tangled stands of cedar cut by narrow, fast-moving streams, including the Rifle River. Some of the best views come from Ridge Road, a one-way dirt route that passes over the park's highest elevations. Campers who bring bikes even pedal to nearby villages on the lightly traveled surrounding highways.

If pedal power to you means pressing the accelerator, you can frame many beautiful scenes through the window of a slow-moving car. Or to get an even more intimate perspective than that from a bike seat, you can foot it over 14 miles of trails that skirt several lakeshores, follow countless picturesque streams, and probe the 4,449-acre park's most remote corners. The park is a riot of wildflowers every spring and quiet and careful observers may catch a glimpse of nesting loons on Grebe Lake. Beaver, deer, otter, fox, mink, trumpeter swans, and a wealth of songbirds can be seen by the lucky and the sharp-eyed visitor. Except for the 1-mile-long Pintail Pond Trail, all trails are also open to mountain bikes, and in the winter cross-country skiers have the entire trail system to choose from. Numbered posts on the trails are keyed to the park map in order for trail users to orient themselves. Yet another great way to see the park is via a canoe on the Rifle River. There are several canoe launching sites in the park.

Many of the area's 100,000-plus annual visitors arrive with fly rods and creels and for good reason: the Rifle River and its upper tributaries, particularly Gamble and Houghton creeks, have earned reputations for yielding good catches of brown, rainbow, and brook trout. Here at the beginnings of its journey to Saginaw Bay, the shallow Rifle widens to 50 feet in many stretches to accommodate several fishing methods, but waders should watch out for occasional 5-foot-plus holes. Some steelhead and chinook salmon are caught on the upper reaches of the river, and pike, bass and panfish are pulled from the park's 10 lakes and ponds, many of which have public access sites. Fisheries research is conducted on Jewett Lake and is closed to fishing without a permit, which can be obtained at park headquarters. Motors are not allowed on any of the park's lakes.

Some trout fishermen like to stay at Birch Cabin, one of five frontier cabins for rent in the park. Birch is close to the river while the other four feature lakeside locations. All are located in beautiful, secluded surroundings far from campgrounds and day-use areas, and all are rustic, with vault toilets, hand water pumps, and only the barest necessities for furnishings. Contact park officials for reservation information and a list of what to bring to set up housekeeping.

Other trout fishermen favor two rustic campgrounds that border the Rifle River. Spruce Campground, farthest of the park's overnight areas from the entrance, envelops campers in deep shade and seclusion on widely spaced lots. Upriver, equally close to the water is the larger Ranch Campground. Overnighters who stay at the third rustic area, at Devoe Lake, have easy access to a lightly used beach and a boat ramp. The shaded, private, widely-spaced lots are nestled in a dense stand of trees on the south shore of the lake.

Grousehaven Lake Campground's 75 sites offer the only camping with electricity and access to modern restrooms. A small campers' beach edges the lake, and good views of the water come from most lots. All are large and grassy but offer little shade or privacy. If you have a large RV, try to avoid the eastern loop (sites 40-plus), because many of the sites there are uneven. The campground receives heavy use throughout the summer and fills to capacity on most weekends. Interpretive programs that highlight the park's natural history and heritage are offered throughout the summer.

Up the Grousehaven Lake shoreline is a boat ramp and, even farther east, the park's day-use area, where a small picnic area, including a shelter, has been cut out of the woods bordering the lake. There's plenty of room to spread out blankets on the grass, which runs almost down to the water's edge, but swimming conditions are only fair. Metal detectors are allowed within specific areas of the park.

The land in the recreation area originally belonged to H.M. Jewett, an early auto-industry tycoon, who used it as a private hunting preserve. The park lives up to its heritage. Deer are the most plentiful game, but hunters also go after ruffed grouse, woodcock, waterfowl, rabbits, raccoon, and wild turkeys on the 90 percent of the park's acreage open to hunting.

Ice fishermen, snowmobilers and trappers use the park in the winter.

COUNTY: OGEMAW
CAMPING SITES: 174 (75 MODERN, 99 RUSTIC) PLUS FIVE FRONTIER CABINS.
DIRECTIONS: DRIVE 4.7 MILES EAST OF ROSE CITY ON COUNTY ROAD F-28.
FURTHER INFORMATION: RIFLE RIVER RECREATION AREA, P.O. BOX 98, LUPTON, MI 48635; 989-473-2258.

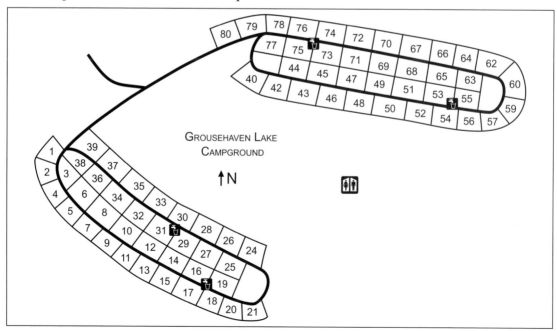

GROUSEHAVEN LAKE CAMPGROUND

↑N

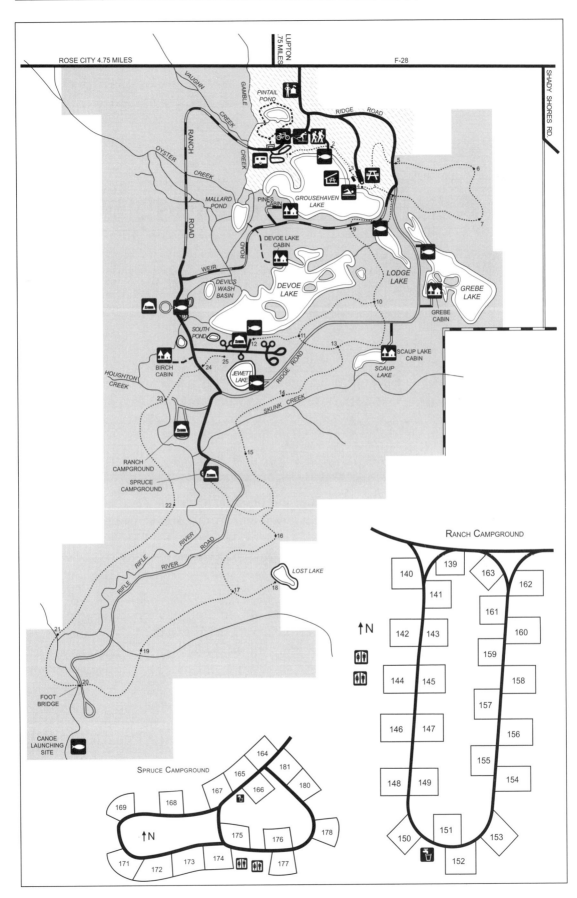

ROSE CITY 4.75 MILES

LUPTON .75 MILES

F-28

SHADY SHORES RD.

VAUGHN CREEK

GAMBLE CREEK

PINTAIL POND

RIDGE ROAD

OYSTER CREEK

RANCH ROAD

MALLARD POND

PINES CABIN

GROUSEHAVEN LAKE

DEVOE LAKE CABIN

WEIR ROAD

DEVILS WASH BASIN

DEVOE LAKE

LODGE LAKE

GREBE LAKE

GREBE CABIN

SOUTH POND

BIRCH CABIN

JEWETT LAKE

RIDGE ROAD

SCAUP LAKE CABIN

SCAUP LAKE

HOUGHTON CREEK

SKUNK CREEK

RANCH CAMPGROUND

SPRUCE CAMPGROUND

RIFLE RIVER ROAD

RIFLE RIVER

LOST LAKE

FOOT BRIDGE

CANOE LAUNCHING SITE

RANCH CAMPGROUND

↑N

140 139 163 162
141 161
142 143 160
159
144 145 158
157
146 147 156
155
148 149 154
150 151 153
152

SPRUCE CAMPGROUND

164
165 181
167 166 180
169 168
↑N 175 176 178
171 172 173 174 177

Tawas Point
STATE PARK

70

OVERNIGHT ACCOMMODATIONS:

ACTIVITIES:

You can come to Tawas Point State Park every year and never see the same place twice. Its 183 acres covers the sharp tip (barb sometimes included) of the fishhook-shaped peninsula that pokes out into Lake Huron to form Tawas Bay. Annual winter storms pummel the exposed point to create small islands where there were none, carve out chunks of shoreline, file off the barb then add it back, and otherwise rearrange the landscape. In addition to those stunning effects of wind and wave power, serious and recreational naturalists can also study a near-perfect model of interdunal wetlands, examine nature's attempts to colonize bare sand with plants, and binocular their way through one of the finest birding areas in the Midwest.

If you could care less about the finer points of nature and are after nothing more than a day's, weekend's, or week's worth of sunning, swimming, picnicking, and playing in the sand, this "Cape Cod of the Midwest," as the peninsula has been called, will also fit the bill perfectly.

Acres of glistening, white sand, sprinkled with patches of dune grass and backed by low dunes, make up the park's expansive day-use beach on the Lake Huron side of the peninsula. Ringing the parking area well back from the beach are picnic tables and grills scattered among small groupings of pines and hardwoods. Other facilities include a large picnic shelter and bathhouse with modern restrooms.

Opposite the day-use area on the shore of Tawas Bay is the park's most photographed feature – a classic, 1876-built lighthouse.

South of the lighthouse and day-use area, the peninsula quickly tapers around marshes, interdunal ponds, and shrubs to its point.

Footpaths loop through the dwindling finger of sand, skirt the shoreline, climb to decks overlooking low dunes, and edge interdunal wetlands. A dirt access road to a foghorn at the tip also cuts a broad, level swath through the heart of the area.

On foggy evenings the deep, resonant voice of the horn adds a special touch to an already-pleasant modern campground, on the sheltered bay side of the peninsula just inside the park's northern boundary. From June through Labor Day, unless you plan to arrive early in the week, it's best to reserve a spot. On weekends reservations are a must. All 193 sites – including 8 handicapped accessible – are large, level, and grass covered but lack privacy. The few trees provide scattered shade but make it easy for even the biggest trailers and RVs to pull in and out. Two mini-cabins edge a large pond near the southern edge of the campground. A campers' beach on the bay – with warmer water and fewer people than the day-use beach on

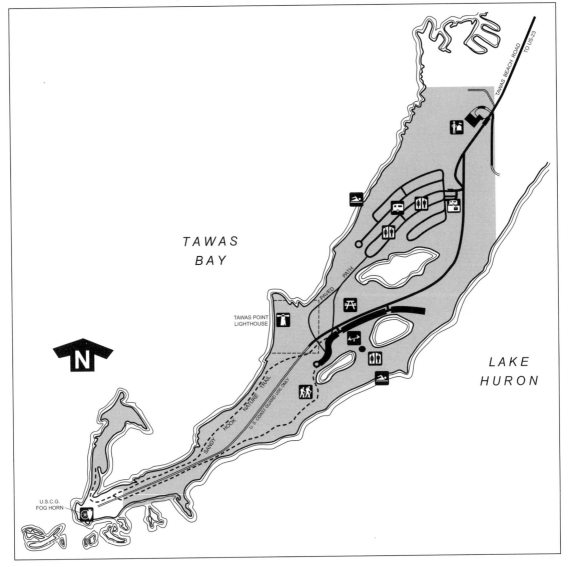

Lake Huron – is just a short walk from most sites.

Campers who tow boats can moor them in the bay, or, if small enough, beach them next to the campground. Since the park doesn't have a launch ramp, boaters must put in at a commercial marina near the park or at a DNR ramp across the bay. Tawas Bay has gained a reputation for good catches of smelt, perch, coho and chinook salmon, walleye, lake and brown trout, thanks, in large part, to an 800-foot-long limestone reef laid down in the northern waters of the bay in 1987.

Birding can be exceptional throughout the park in spring and fall, but it is especially good in May, when the tip of the peninsula is alive with migrating birds and birdwatchers. A checklist of different birds spotted within the park or surrounding waters numbers 205, including 31 species of warblers and 17 species of waterfowl.

Campers often bike the park's paved roads, and a paved bike path alongside Tawas Beach Road and the sidewalks edging US-23 make pedaling to downtown East Tawas a popular diversion. Care must be taken with children when crossing US-23 or passing the many business parking lots on the south side of the highway. Tours and nature programs are offered throughout the summer. Metal detectors are allowed in specific areas of the park.

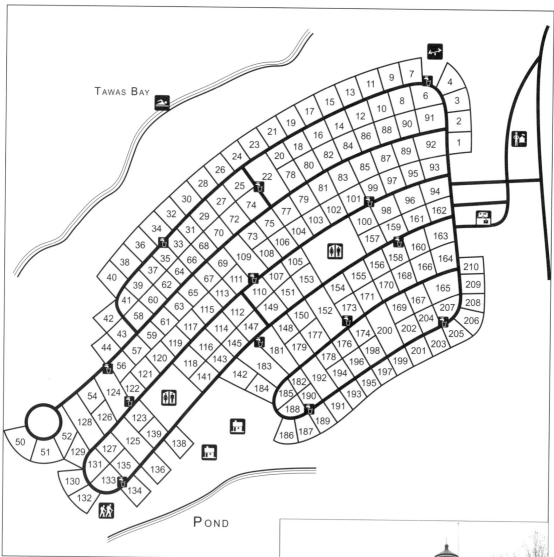

TAWAS BAY

POND

COUNTY: IOSCO

CAMPING SITES: 193, ALL MODERN INCLUDING 8 ADA CAMPSITES, PLUS TWO MINI-CABINS.

SCHEDULE: THE PARK IS OPEN MID-APRIL THROUGH NOVEMBER BUT MODERN RESTROOMS FACILITIES AND ELECTRICAL HOOKUPS ARE ONLY AVAILABLE FROM MID-APRIL TO THE FIRST WEEKEND IN NOVEMBER.

DIRECTIONS: FROM US-23 JUST NORTH OF EAST TAWAS DRIVE EAST ON TAWAS BEACH ROAD ABOUT 2.5 MILES.

FURTHER INFORMATION: TAWAS POINT STATE PARK, 686 TAWAS BEACH ROAD, EAST TAWAS, MI 48730; 989-362-5041.

Harrisville State Park

71

OVERNIGHT ACCOMMODATIONS:

ACTIVITIES:

Except for a wide swatch of sand that meets Lake Huron, trees blanket nearly all of Harrisville State Park's 107 acres. Fragrance of cedar permeates the air, and a scattering of maple, birch, ash, and balsam add visual accents. Add to that an exceptionally fine campground, picnic area, and swimming beach, and it's easy to see why this park draws 150,000-plus visitors year after year.

At Harrisville you have to look hard for a sunny camping site and even harder for an undesirable one. All 195 large, flat, grass-covered lots, with electrical hookups and access to modern restrooms, are snuggled among the trees. Most are well shaded, and the trees and shrubs create natural privacy screens around many. Even with all the vegetation, good-sized RVs will fit comfortably into most lots. About 26 of the most desirable campsites, with blacktop pads, border the shore, but all lots are only a short walk from Lake Huron's glorious shoreline. To insure a camping spot, park officials suggest making reservations for the summer months. Sites are in special demand on the last Saturday in July when the park hosts an annual sand sculpture contest.

Tucked into the park's southeast corner is the day-use swimming and picnic area. Tables and grills there are spread under towering trees, in open meadows, and along the sandy beach. A large pavilion is centered a few yards in front of the parking area, and playground equipment lies scattered throughout the grounds. Kayakers and anglers with car-top-size boats can launch both

at a small site on the south end of the day-use parking area. You can float larger craft in the village of Harrisville, less than a mile north. Brown trout, salmon, and some prodigious lake trout are pulled from the waters off the village and park.

If you want to work the chair-webbing marks out of your backside, you can hike the Cedar Run Nature Trail, which loops through deep woods in back of both the campground and day-use area. The quiet path can be walked in 45 minutes without breaking a sweat, and the observant will find wildflowers, which range with the season from ladyslippers and black-eyed Susans to marsh marigolds and trillium. Cross-country skiers set their own tracks on the trail in winter. If you seek a slice of civilization instead of wildflowers, another trail heads north from the campground to the resort village of Harrisville. Metal detectors are permitted within the park and can be used in specific areas. Informal hikes and nature programs that explore the park's natural features, wildlife, and resources are conducted throughout the summer by park personnel.

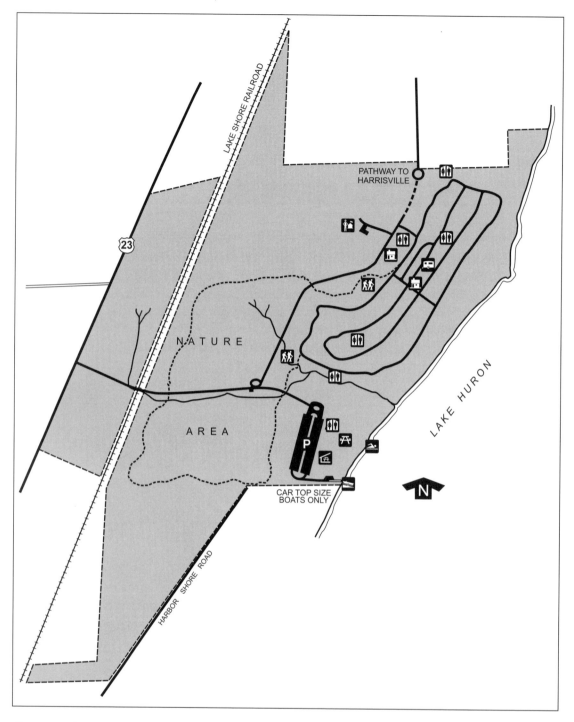

County: Alcona

Camping Sites: 195, all modern, plus two mini-cabins.

Schedule: The campground is open mid April to late October; the rest of the park is open year round.

Directions: One mile south of Harrisville on US-23.

Further Information: Harrisville State Park, 248 State Park Road, P.O. Box 326, Harrisville, MI 48740; 989-724-5126.

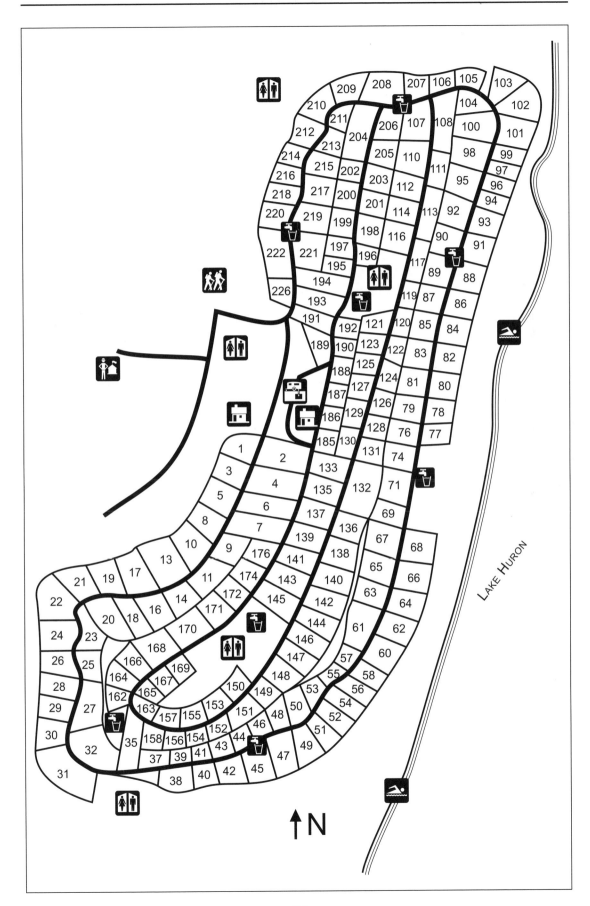

LAKE HURON

N

Sturgeon Point

Scenic Site

OVERNIGHT ACCOMMODATIONS: NONE

ACTIVITIES:

On a map Sturgeon Point hardly looks like it warrants the name. There's no digit pointing out into Lake Huron, and it would seem to be of little danger to navigation on the great lake. From the shore side of the lighthouse that has kept a light burning on the point since 1870, you can see the beginning of a long, barely submerged gravel reef that extends out into Lake Huron from nearly a mile. The reef has the potential to wreak havoc on any ore carrier or freighter that passes too close to the Lake Huron shoreline.

The still-active light is operated by the US Coast Guard, and the 70-foot tower is closed to the public, but the light keeper's house has been restored and maintained as a maritime museum by the Alcona Historical Society. The sparkling-white house and tower with the bright red trim would make any lighthouse keeper proud to call it his own. On a sunny summer day the shipshape little building stands in beautiful contrast to the blue sky, shifting aquamarine hues of the lake, and the green blanketing the land.

Although there are no formal trails, the park's 76 acres invite a lot of wandering around, and there's the ever present, incessant tug from a great lake's beach to come and explore. From Memorial Day to mid-September the restored light keeper's house is open to the public seven days a week. When snow covers the ground, cross-country skiers are welcome to break their own trails.

COUNTY: ALCONA

CAMPING SITES: NONE

DIRECTIONS: FROM HARRISVILLE DRIVE NORTH ON US-23 ABOUT 3 MILES TO LAKE-SHORE DRIVE. TURN RIGHT (NORTH) ON LAKESHORE AND DRIVE ABOUT 1 MILE TO POINT ROAD. TURN RIGHT (EAST) ONTO POINT AND DRIVE A LITTLE LESS THAN A MILE TO THE PARKING AREA ON THE LEFT. FURTHER INFORMATION: STURGEON POINT LIGHTHOUSE AND MUSEUM, STURGEON POINT ROAD, HARRISVILLE, MI 48740; 989-724-5107.

egwegon
STATE PARK

OVERNIGHT ACCOMMODATIONS: NONE

ACTIVITIES:

At Negwegon State Park, a negative is turned into a positive. The same lack of facilities that keep most vacationers away from this beautiful 2,475-acre chunk of northern Michigan real estate make it all the more appealing to those who gladly forego creature comforts in order to enjoy an unspoiled natural attraction free of crowds.

"Facilities" here amount to a gravel access road, a parking lot, pit toilets, a water spigot, and a bulletin board with a map of the park's trails. Park personnel caution that Sand Hill Trail, the route to the park, is only a two-track whose sand during dry summer months, "becomes so sugary that most two-wheel-drive vehicles are apt to get stuck."

But for adventurous outdoor lovers who can get their hands on a four-wheel drive conveyance, nature has provided a serene and beautiful retreat. The park shelters some of the most beautiful stretches of beach on the sunrise side of the state. The waters of Lake Huron have sculpted the park's 6.5 miles of shoreline into a chain of softly curving bays and coves. A wide, sandy beach reaches back from the water's edge with lake and sand framed by a palisade of green. Behind the tree-lined beach, a pine forest – accented with some hardwoods and aspen – blankets the park.

You're welcome to swim and picnic anywhere along the shore. Three trails ranging in length from 3.3 to 4.8 miles cut through the lush forest and border the beach. Or, you can beach comb where only a relatively few others have turned over a rock or weighed the possibilities inherent in a piece of driftwood. If you go out of your way in search of places that are as far removed as possible from the humdrum of the modern world, Negwegon ranks with the best in the Lower Peninsula.

The park has a great reputation among hunters for white-tailed deer, turkey, and rabbit. There are also some woodcock, squirrel, and waterfowl taken here. A limited section of the beach area is open to hobbyists with metal detectors.

COUNTIES: ALCONA AND ALPENA
CAMPING SITES: NONE
DIRECTIONS: FROM HARRISVILLE DRIVE 12 MILES NORTH ON US-23 TO BLACK RIVER ROAD. TURN RIGHT (EAST) AND GO ABOUT 1.5 MILES TO SAND HILL TRAIL (UNMARKED). TURN LEFT (NORTH) AND DRIVE APPROXIMATELY 2.5 MILES TO A GRAVEL ROAD. TURN RIGHT (EAST) AND GO 1.25 MILES TO THE PARKING LOT.
FURTHER INFORMATION: NEGWEGON STATE PARK, C/O HARRISVILLE STATE PARK, 248 STATE PARK ROAD, HARRISVILLE, MI 48740; 989-739-9730 OR 989-724-5126.

Clear Lake

State Park

OVERNIGHT ACCOMMODATIONS:

ACTIVITIES:

The focal point of this out-of-the-way park is the beautiful spring-fed lake from which the park takes its name, but the most memorable moment for a few lucky visitors may be the sighting of elk in the surrounding area. The quiet, secluded 289-acre park sits smack dab in the middle of elk country, and there are plenty of county roads to wander in hopes of spotting one of the majestic creatures. A nearby 48.5-mile scenic drive takes motorists to prime elk sighting areas as well as providing numerous opportunities for a grand sampling of Michigan wildlife including deer, bear, grouse, turkeys, bald eagles, and loons (maps are available at the park).

Inside the park a forest of dense hardwoods and evergreens frame the clear, blue waters of the small, nearly tear-drop-shaped lake. The park's day-use area and campground encompass two-thirds of Clear Lake's sandy and gently sloping shoreline.

Campers can almost always find an empty spot among the 200 campsites, which are divided into two large double-looped wings separated by a playground. The flat, partially grass-covered lots range from open and sunny to deeply shaded, and all are roomy enough to accommodate the largest RV. All sites have electrical hookups and access to modern restrooms with flush toilets and hot showers.

It's a short walk from any campsite to the large sandy campers-only beach, where parents with young children will appreciate the shallow waters that reach far out into the lake. At the east end of the campground and in the day-use area, paved boat launching ramps give fishermen a chance at the lake's trout, smallmouth bass, and pan fish.

The day-use area on the west side of the lake boasts an expanse of grassy, tree-shaded shoreline edged with picnic tables and grills. A picnic shelter at the center of the grounds overlooks a fine swimming beach.

A trail on the west side of the lake joins the park's two sections and is part of a much larger trail system whose loops go around the north and south shores of Clear Lake, rejoin southeast of the park, then continue over rolling terrain to the Jackson Lake State Forest Campground. Points of interest along the six-mile round trip include a gravel pit rich in fossils plus the lumbering-era ghost town of Valentine. A shortened four-mile round trip to where the loops rejoin makes for a pleasant outing featuring many scenic views. (A detailed map of the trial system is available at park headquarters.)

If that's not enough hiking, the Clear Lake system serves as a link in one of the longest hiking trails in northern Michigan. The High Country Pathway, which cuts through the park (blue trail markers) on its tour of the Pigeon River State Forest, crosses some of the state's most wild and beautiful country in a

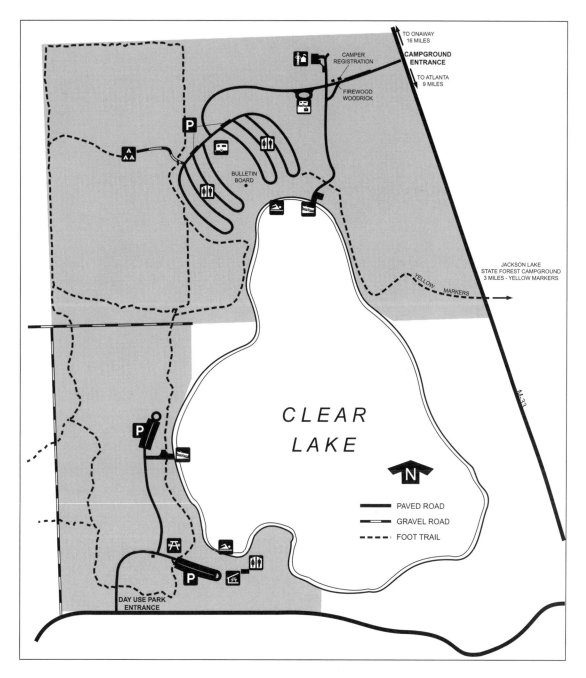

nearly circular, 70-mile loop. Clear Lake's campground is one of eight on the trail, but because it's the only one with modern facilities, it makes the best base camp for the long and difficult trek. You can get a detailed map of the High Country Pathway from almost any DNR field office.

Mountain bikers are welcome on most of the foot trails including, for the hard-core pedaler, the High Country Pathway. Metal detectors are allowed in designated areas as is hunting. Children and adults will enjoy the park's nature programs.

COUNTY: MONTMORENCY

CAMPING SITES: 200, ALL MODERN, AND ONE MINI-CABIN.

DIRECTIONS: TEN MILES NORTH OF ATLANTA ON M-33.

FURTHER INFORMATION: CLEAR LAKE STATE PARK, 20500 M-33 NORTH, ATLANTA, MI 49709; 989-785-4388.

Thompson's Harbor
State Park

OVERNIGHT ACCOMMODATIONS: NONE

ACTIVITIES:

The 5,247-acre Thompson's Harbor State Park is destined to be one of the jewels of Michigan's park system if it isn't already. As early as 1958, a survey by the National Park Service and Michigan Department of Conversation rated the place as one of the 221 sites along the state's Great Lakes shoreline most worthy of preservation. In fact, the park's continued undeveloped status may well help the area maintain its pristine condition.

The focal point of the park is 7.5 miles of absolutely gorgeous, untouched Lake Huron shoreline accented by low limestone points that break up the waterfront into a series of picturesque bays and inlets. A narrow, sandy beach lines a designated natural area and a small cove to the west. Elsewhere, a cobble shoreline gives way to a series of low dunes covered by grasses and shrubs. Farther inland a mixed coniferous/hardwood second-growth forest blankets the park. On any visit your only company may turn out to be coyotes, deer, bald eagles, osprey, and the occasional black bear.

In the summer of 1992, an access road and parking lot were constructed, a trail system totaling better than six miles was blazed, and a vault toilet installed at the trailhead. The trail's three loops (1.4, 2.4, and 2.6 miles in length) all eventually reach the shoreline, but the shortest route to Lake Huron is via Loop 1, which brushes the shore after about a third-of-a-mile walk. Several unmarked trails and faint two-tracks crisscross the area, and if you plan on wandering off the marked trails, bring along a compass and map. Cross-country skiers take over from hikers when

the snow flies. The park is open to hunting where posted.

To reach the trailhead, turn onto the park's entrance road off US-23, then take the first right. If you stay on the entrance road and

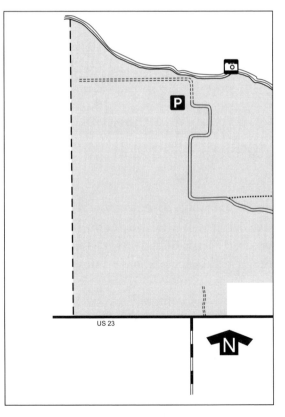

US 23

don't take the turnoff to the trail, you will eventually come to a parking area only a short walk from the beach. All park roads are undeveloped, so it's a good idea to call ahead for driving conditions.

COUNTY: PRESQUE ISLE
CAMPING SITES: NONE
DIRECTIONS: TWELVE MILES SOUTH OF ROGERS CITY OR 24 MILES NORTH OF ALPENA ON US-23.
FURTHER INFORMATION: DNR CHEBOYGAN FIELD OFFICE, P.O. BOX 117, 120 A STREET, CHEBOYGAN, MI 49721; 231-627-9011.

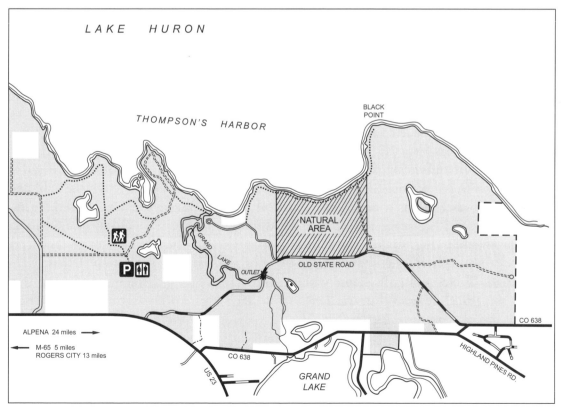

PH *Hoeft* STATE PARK

76

OVERNIGHT ACCOMMODATIONS:

ACTIVITIES:

Many rate P.H. Hoeft State Park as the most beautiful state park along Michigan's Lake Huron shore, and it's easy to see why. A near-mile-long-strip of pristine, soft, white sand gently rises from the water's edge and gradually builds into low, rolling dunes. Like ramparts guarding the park from the Great Lake, they march inland for at least 50 yards, where the land then rises more sharply in a series of shelves stacked with a mixed hardwood/conifer forest. Add to this a top-notch picnic area, as beautiful a campground as you can find anywhere in Michigan, and the clincher – an attendance record that ranks the park as one of the least visited in the Lower Peninsula – and you come very close to an outdoor-lover's Shangri-La.

The 144-site completely modern campground – set amidst mature pines and hardwoods, with plenty of shade and privacy – is only moderately used, except on summer weekends. Most sites are level, well worn, and unusually large, and more than half are arranged in single rows not backed up to other lots, which creates even greater privacy. The crème de la crème are lots 1-33, which are only steps from the beach and water. The campground includes a mini-cabin. Since every site is reservable, it's not a bad idea to make reservations when planning a vacation.

At the day-use picnic area you can dine in a degree of privacy you usually won't find at other parks. Tables and grills, some within view of the water, are nestled in small clearings cut out of the forest. Facilities include an array of playground equipment, a large picnic shelter built by the Civilian Conservation Corp in the 1930s, and one of the finest beaches in any Michigan state park, with

great swimming, hours of beachcombing, and enough sand and room to build Windsor Castle.

From the picnic area south to the park boundary, almost half the shoreline and park property behind it is totally undeveloped dunes and woods that abound in wildlife and vegetation. Some 40 species of wildflowers, including orchids and irises rare to Michigan and North America, bloom here. More than four miles of trails, most of which begin at the day-use area, loop through the wild parcel along the beach, over and around the low dunes, and across the highway into the backcountry. The trails, though not groomed, are open in winter to cross-country skiers.

Bikers can't use the above trails, but they do have their own designated path, which crosses US-23 and heads south towards Rogers City through dense, quiet woods. Bicyclists have a new and scenic alternative if they would like to pedal the four miles to Rogers City. A recently completed 10-foot

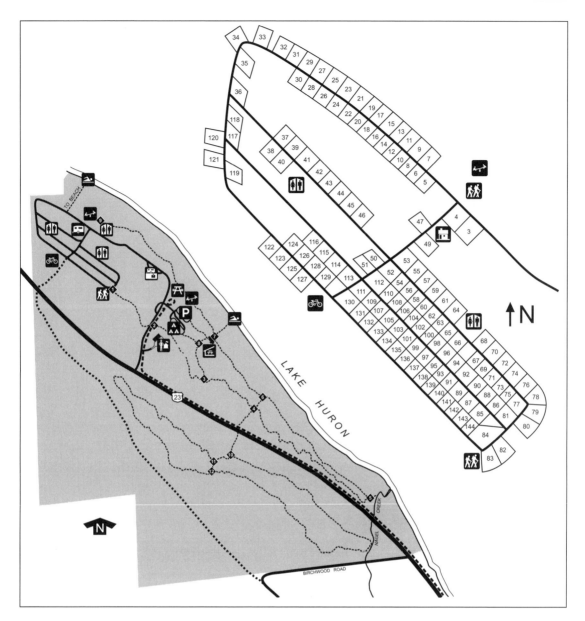

wide paved, non-motorized trail borders US-23 and the Lake Huron shoreline into and through Rogers City and ends at an overlook of the Calcite Limestone Quarry, the world's largest open pit limestone mine.

Sportsmen are permitted to hunt on park property west of US-23 with deer, bear, and squirrels the most sought after game. Although the park has no launch ramp, fishermen float their boats on the big lake from a marina in Rogers City and commit hook, line, and sinker for lake trout, steelhead, and chinook and coho salmon.

Park personnel lead informal programs

and hikes in which the park's natural and cultural heritage are explored. The park also allows hobbyists to use metal detectors in proscribed areas of the park.

County: Presque Isle

Camping Sites: 144, all modern including one mini-cabin.

Directions: Five miles north of Rogers City on US-23.

Further Information: P.H. Hoeft State Park, 5001 US-23 North, Rogers City, MI 49779; 989-734-2543.

O*naway*
State Park

77

Overnight Accommodations:

Activities:

Established in 1921, Onaway State Park has aged and mellowed like a fine wine. Yet few people come to taste. With only 44,000 visitors annually, Onaway is one of the most ignored parks in the Lower Peninsula. Probably the lack of a glorious swimming beach and the absence of nearby tourist attractions dissuade a lot of people from a first time visit. The faithful who do come here find those very features to be assets, not detractors.

Overnighters, for instance, can relax in beautiful surroundings without distractions in one of the few state-park campgrounds that rarely fills up. The 85 sites, all with electrical hookups and access to modern restrooms, are divided into two unequal sections. Most are spread over the top of a bluff under a dense canopy of virgin white pines and scattered hardwoods that both dwarf and perpetually shade tents, trailers, and motor homes. The trees, rolling terrain, and the fact that better than half the campsites do not back up to other campers translates into a fair degree of privacy. Underfoot, needles and leaves carpet the roomy sites. At the bottom of the bluff, edging the rocky shore of Black Lake is the smaller camping unit. Cedars, pines and hardwoods crowd the lots, which are slightly smaller than those above and either back up to the lake or nestle against the steep-sided bluff.

A playground area and pavilion separate the campground from the swimming beach, such as it is. The lakeshore bordering the entire park is very rocky, and the "beach" was created simply by pushing aside rocks in a postage-stamp-size area then covering it with hauled-in sand. There's enough sand for

small kids to enjoy themselves with a shovel and bucket, and if it isn't so good for swimming, the lake bottom and nearly one mile of park shoreline is a fossil hunter's treasure trove. Tables and grills near the old, rustic pavilion are wedged into small clearings in a stand of cedar that's so thick your nose will swear you're eating lunch in a cedar closet. At the extreme eastern end of the park another picnic area sits amid cedar, red pines, and hardwoods close to the shoreline.

Black Lake, 6 miles long and 3 miles wide, is not only the state's eighth-largest, but ranks among the 10 best in Michigan for walleye fishing, according to the DNR. Good catches of smallmouth bass and muskie are also pulled from its waters, and from all reports it's worth dropping a line for pike and perch. The lake is also home to lake sturgeon. Fishermen and boaters can launch at a ramp with a skid pier and parking lot for cars and boat trailers on the west side of the day-use area.

Wildflowers and morel mushrooms, in season, fill the wooded park. A 3-mile-long nature trail loops through the park's deep woods, and even better hiking opportunities come at Ocqueoc Falls Bicentennial Path-

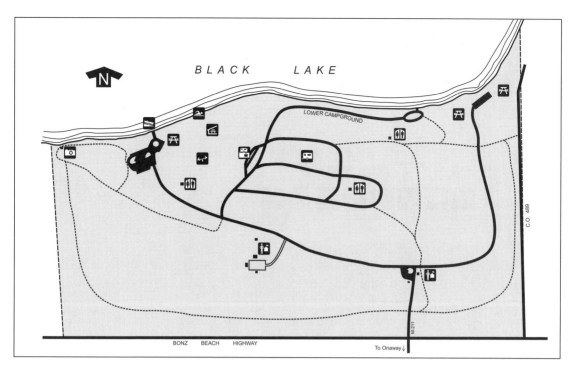

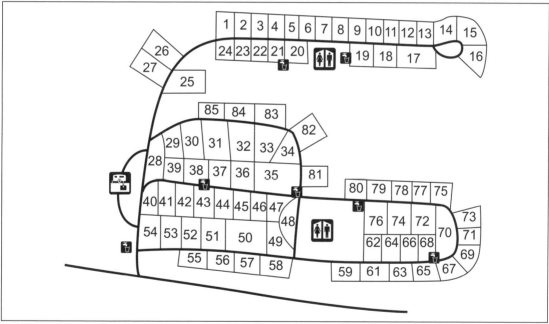

way, 10 miles east of the village of Onaway on highway M-68. There, in addition to 3-, 4-, and 6.5-mile loops through a beautiful forest, you can also soak you feet in the rumbling waters of the Lower Peninsula's only "major" waterfall.

COUNTY: PRESQUE ISLE
CAMPING SITES: 85, ALL MODERN.

SCHEDULE: THE PARK IS OPEN ALL YEAR, BUT THE CAMPGROUND IS CLOSED OCTOBER 15 TO MAY 15.
DIRECTIONS: GO 6 MILES NORTH OF ONAWAY ON M-211.
FURTHER INFORMATION: ONAWAY STATE PARK, 3622 NORTH M-211, ONAWAY, MI 49765; 989-733-8279.

Aloha

State Park

78

Overnight Accommodations:

Activities:

If you like water and water sports, there's plenty to do and plenty of room to do it at Aloha State Park. The 106-acre park stretches along the east shore of the 13-mile-long and up-to-5-mile-wide Mullett Lake, Michigan's fifth-largest. Mullett is also one of three lakes that, along with connecting rivers and two locks, make up the Inland Waterway, a 40-mile, scenic, navigable water route from Cheboygan on Lake Huron to Conway, only three miles from Lake Michigan. The locks limit boats to 60-feet in length and a 5-foot draft.

Mullett Lake consistently rates as one of the state's best walleye holes, and anglers also have good luck going after perch, pike, rock bass, small and largemouth bass, bluegills, muskies, smelt, and brook, brown, rainbow and lake trout. In 1974 the largest fish ever caught by a recreational fisherman in Michigan waters – a monstrous 193-pound, 87-inch-long sturgeon – was speared through Mullett's ice.

Fishermen and other boaters can launch from a wide concrete ramp in the park's large, well-protected boat basin that is sandwiched between two of the park's campground loops.

The camping area takes up most of the park's almost totally developed (with no room for natural areas or hiking trails) acreage. Campground use is heavy throughout the summer, filling to capacity nearly every weekend, making reservations a must. You won't find many shaded or private sites, but all are level, grassy, and spacious enough for the largest RV. All also have electrical hookups updated in 2003, of which a third offer 50 amp service, and access to modern restrooms. None of the sites are far from the water, and they have access to a sandy, gently-sloping, campers-only swimming beach. Two playgrounds lie within the campground loops.

A second sun-drenched beach at the day use-use area fronts a spacious, grass-covered picnic area, with tables and grills scattered among sheltering hardwoods and cedars with a large, grass-cushioned playground only steps away. Metal detectors are allowed in specific areas.

The park cozies up to the quiet little village of Aloha, but if you live to shop you have, at best, a 20-minute life expectancy here. Cheboygan is little more than a 5-minute drive to the north, and the Straits of Mackinac and its many tourist and historical attractions are a pretty, 30-minute ride away.

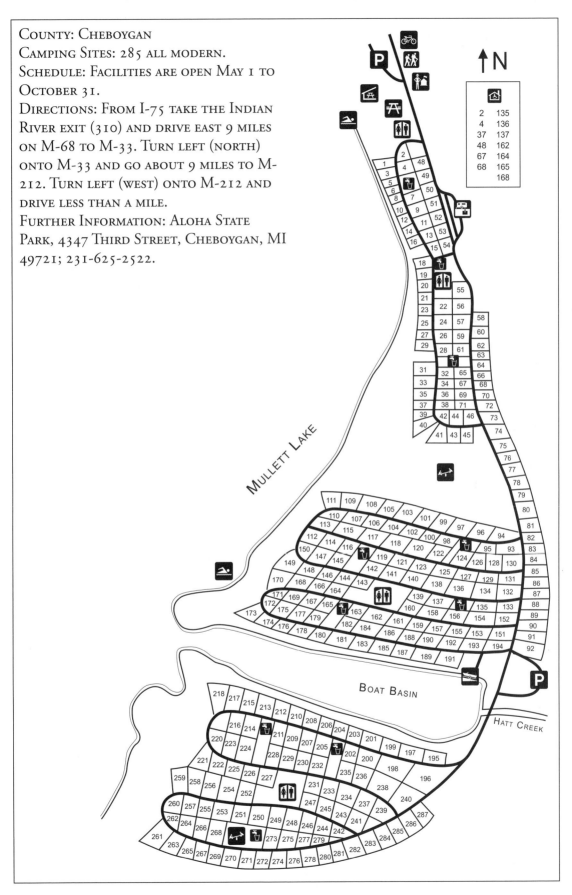

COUNTY: CHEBOYGAN
CAMPING SITES: 285 ALL MODERN.
SCHEDULE: FACILITIES ARE OPEN MAY 1 TO
OCTOBER 31.
DIRECTIONS: FROM I-75 TAKE THE INDIAN
RIVER EXIT (310) AND DRIVE EAST 9 MILES
ON M-68 TO M-33. TURN LEFT (NORTH)
ONTO M-33 AND GO ABOUT 9 MILES TO M-
212. TURN LEFT (WEST) ONTO M-212 AND
DRIVE LESS THAN A MILE.
FURTHER INFORMATION: ALOHA STATE
PARK, 4347 THIRD STREET, CHEBOYGAN, MI
49721; 231-625-2522.

2	135
4	136
37	137
48	162
67	164
68	165
	168

MULLETT LAKE

BOAT BASIN

HATT CREEK

Cheboygan State Park

79

OVERNIGHT ACCOMMODATIONS:

ACTIVITIES:

Plenty of rustic scenery; spacious, widely scattered facilities; and relatively few people to share them with are the draws to Cheboygan State Park. Its 1,240 largely undeveloped acres, five miles of Lake Huron beach, six miles of hiking trails, comfortable campground, isolated cabins, and sandy beaches attract only 60,000-plus people a year.

The park ranges over most of a narrow peninsula that is tipped by tiny Cheboygan and Lighthouse points. Near the peninsula's base on the west shore, the campground and day-use area are separated by the low, marshy backwaters of Little Billy Elliot Creek where it empties into shallow, protected Duncan Bay.

On the south side of the tree-ringed creek mouth, picnic tables and grills spread over an open area with fine views of a broad, sandy swimming beach, the bay, and its wooded shoreline. Other facilities at the day-use area include a picnic shelter, playground, and a bathhouse with modern restrooms and changing courts.

Roughly a half mile north across the impassable marsh, four miles away by road, lies the park's quiet, completely modern campground. All 75 lots are large and grassy with

better than average privacy. All overnighters are close to the beach and water, which are full of reeds and pebbles. Another overnight option is the campground's large canvas-and-pole tepee. Those who use the park for a base camp will find the Straits of Mackinac's many attractions an easy, 20-mile drive away.

Three secluded and widely separate, beach-side cabins offer overnighters a frontier-like experience. Each of the rustic (no electricity or indoor plumbing) one-room structures sleeps eight, in four double bunks, and comes with a wood stove, table, and chairs. You furnish the rest. Two of the cabins sit near the ruins of the historic Cheboygan Point

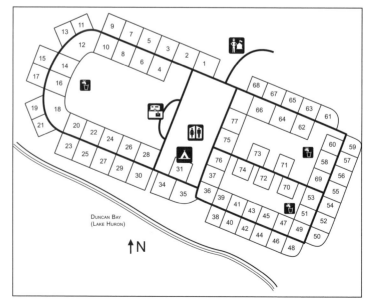

DUNCAN BAY
(LAKE HURON)

↑N

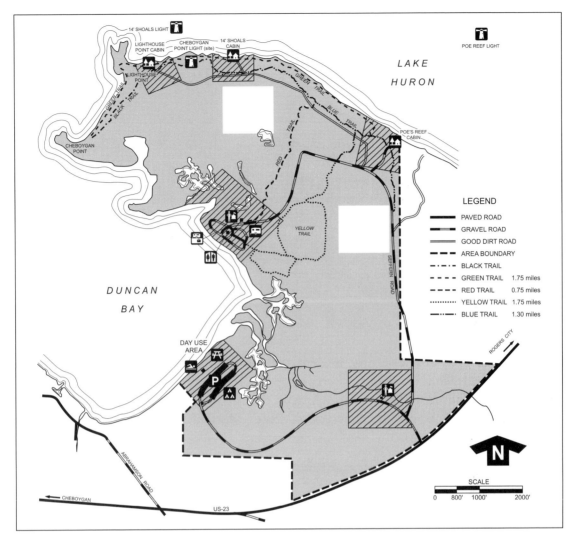

Lighthouse, built in 1851. The cabins rent for about $55 a night year round, but often the only access in winter is by cross-country skis. Contact the park ranger in advance for rental details and reservations at 231-627-9011.

More than six miles of trails, shared by hikers and bikers, web the park's undeveloped acreage, follow the coastline or cut inland and lead to low dunes, marshes, interdunal wetlands, and stretches of forests. The diverse habitat makes for good birding and an abundance of wildflowers including several varieties of lilies, many rare species found only in this region of the state, and carnivorous plants. The park is open for cross-country skiing in the winter.

The park's small, rustic boat launch handles only 14- to 16-foot craft, but fishermen with larger boats can float them at a public launch site less than four miles away in Cheboygan and go after northern pike, small and largemouth bass, and panfish in Duncan Bay. Little Billy Elliot Creek has a reputation for brook trout. Hunting is permitted in designated areas.

COUNTY: CHEBOYGAN
CAMPING SITES: 74, ALL MODERN, PLUS THREE RUSTIC CABINS AND ONE TEPEE.
DIRECTIONS: APPROXIMATELY 3.5 MILES SOUTH OF CHEBOYGAN ON US-23.
FURTHER INFORMATION: CHEBOYGAN STATE PARK, 4490 BEACH ROAD, CHEBOYGAN, MI 49721; 231-627-2811.

Mill Creek

MACKINAC STATE HISTORIC PARK

80

OVERNIGHT ACCOMMODATIONS: NONE

ACTIVITIES: 🐦 🥾 ☸ 🎣 🏕 V 🔭

In 1972 an amateur archaeologist discovered the remains of one of the first industrial complexes in the Great Lakes, a sawmill built by Robert Campbell in the 1780s. A bare 7 miles south of the Straits of Mackinac, the water-powered mill turned timber into planks for nearby Mackinac Island for over forty years before it fell into disuse.

Since its discovery scientists have meticulously excavated the area while historians pored over Revolutionary War-era books in a search for construction and operating secrets of water-powered sawmills. The result of the three decades of work and research is an authentically reconstructed, working replica of an 18th-century sawmill that is the centerpiece of Mill Creek State Historic Park.

The rough-hewn, picturesque structure nearly straddles a small creek at the exact spot of the original mill. Inside, every half hour an operator throws a lever to open a gate, water flows over the power wheel, and the jumble of monstrous wood gears and other arcane paraphernalia roars and clatters to life.

Park guides detail the intricacies and history of the mill as well as demonstrate shingle making and some of the other operations that took place here 200 years ago. You can get more history plus a capsule look at the reconstruction of the mill by watching a multi-image slide show, run throughout the day inside a museum at the park entrance. Also inside are showcases holding artifacts unearthed at the site during the archaeological excavations.

Building reconstruction with period tools and methods is an ongoing activity within the park. The most recently completed project is a millwright's house, opened to the public in 2005, which sits on the exact site of a house occupied by a millwright's family in the 1820s. The building contains exhibits, artifacts and the ruins of the home's original hearth.

Though the mill complex is the main draw, you can easily spend as much time enjoying the natural setting (popular with birdwatchers) as its living history. The 625-acre park is nestled high above and several hundred yards back from Lake Huron amidst low hills that seem to almost the cup the complex. Great views of the lake and the Straits area come from two scenic overlooks on either side of the mill pond, and 3.5 miles of self-guiding nature trails winding through the wildflower- and wildlife-filled hills. The longest trails lead to a series of beaver dams and ponds. Quiet, lucky, and keen-eyed hikers may not only spot a beaver but also find raccoon, waterfowl, hawks, owls, and a variety of other species. Naturalist programs are offered throughout the summer.

The park's small picnic area overlooks the sawmill and pond, and a nearby concession stand sells lunch, soft drinks, and snacks.

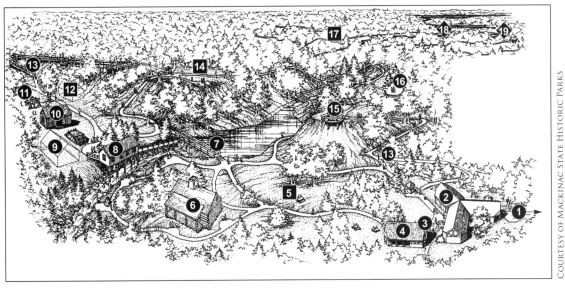

COURTESY OF MACKINAC STATE HISTORIC PARKS

Map Key:
1. Parking Area
2. Visitor's Center
   - Museum Store
   - Audio-Visual Program
3. Restrooms
4. Cookhouse: Lunches & Refreshments
5. Picnic Area
6. Millwright's House
7. Mill Dam and Bridge
8. Operating Water-Powered Sawmill
9. Site of Robert Campbell House
10. British Workshop
11. Sawpit Demonstration Area
12. Unexcavated Building Sites
13. Accessible Ramp to Trails
14. Scenic Overlook
15. Overview Telescope
16. Forest Clearing – Naturalist Programs
17. Nature Trails
18. Beaver Dam
19. Sugar Shack

COUNTY: CHEBOYGAN
CAMPING SITES: NONE.
SCHEDULE: OPEN MID-MAY THROUGH SEPTEMBER.
ADMISSION: ADULTS, $7.50; CHILDREN 6 – 17, $4.50; CHILDREN 5 AND UNDER, FREE.
DIRECTIONS: FOUR MILES SOUTHEAST OF MACKINAW, CITY ON US-23.
FURTHER INFORMATION: MILL CREEK HISTORIC PARK, c/o MACKINAC STATE HISTORIC PARKS, P.O. BOX 873, MACKINAW CITY, MI 49701; 231-436-4100.

Father Marquette
National Memorial

OVERNIGHT ACCOMMODATIONS: NONE

ACTIVITIES:

Sitting on a bluff overlooking the Straits of Mackinac on the St. Ignace side of the great, watery crossroads is a simple stone-and-wood structure dedicated to a Jesuit priest who, in nine short years, made a lasting impact on Michigan and America – Father Jacques Marquette.

In 1666 the Catholic Church sent the 29-year-old priest to New France, as Canada was then called, to bring Christianity to North American Indians. Considering that most of the continent was uncharted wilderness at the time, Father Marquette was as much an explorer as soul saver. He blazed his way from Canada to the rapids of the St. Mary's River, where in 1668 he established an Indian mission and Michigan's first permanent settlement, Sault Ste. Marie. Three years later he made his way to the north side of the Straits, where he founded St. Ignace. In May 1673 he, another Jesuit, and several voyageurs headed west from St. Ignace in bark canoes. They crossed northern Lake Michigan, then paddled and portaged across Wisconsin until they reached their goal – the legendary "Great River" that flowed north and south. Marquette and his group had discovered the Mississippi. Just two years later, Father Marquette died of an illness near the present site of Ludington.

Appropriately, the park that commemorates the remarkable priest provides a stunning view of the Straits he paddled so often when setting out and returning from his many expeditions. A paved path leads from a parking lot, which is bordered by a small, tree-shaded picnic area, to the modest, circular open-air building that looks out over the meeting place between lakes Huron and Michigan and the mighty bridge that spans it. An easily walked, 15-station interpretive nature trail loops across the bluff and offers more spectacular views of the Straits. A museum that was located a few yards from the memorial was destroyed by fire in March 2000. Plans call for reconstruction, but a schedule has not been set.

COUNTY: MACKINAC

CAMPING SITES: NONE

SCHEDULE: OPEN MEMORIAL DAY THROUGH SEPTEMBER FROM 9 A.M. TO DUSK.

DIRECTIONS: FROM THE INTERSECTION OF US-2 AND I-75 GO LESS THAN A HALF-MILE WEST ON US-2 TO MARLY STREET. TURN LEFT ON MARLY AND DRIVE 3 BLOCKS.

FURTHER INFORMATION: FATHER MARQUETTE NATIONAL MEMORIAL, C/O STRAITS STATE PARK, 720 CHURCH STREET, ST. IGNACE, MI 49781; 906-643-8620.

S traits State Park

Overnight Accommodations:

Activities:

A DNR brochure once described Straits State Park as a "convenient campover on a high bluff overlooking the Mackinac Bridge." Yeah, and Las Vegas is a convenient place to gamble in the desert. Both statements leave a lot unsaid.

The park's campground is a great place to stay, and you get a magnificent view of the bridge, especially at night. In fact, on a dark summer evening with the colored lights of the bridge reflecting off the waters of the Straits of Mackinac and the headlamps of the north and south bound traffic making like neon lights playing across a huge marquee, the view from the beach is an 8 to 5 favorite over any view from a hotel on the "Vegas Strip."

Perhaps even more importantly, the park makes an excellent base from which to explore the entire Straits area. Less than two miles away at St. Ignace you can board a ferry to Mackinac Island; the Father Marquette National Memorial is just across I-75; and Fort Michilimackinac and Mackinaw City's excess of tacky to tasteful souvenir and gift shops are five miles south across the Big Mac. Farther afield, the Seney National Wildlife Refuge, Tahquamenon Falls and the Soo Locks are each about an hour's drive away.

Most campers, evidently, opt for the one-night stand, because daily turnover is high. As a result, even though the campground is heavily used, you can almost always find an empty spot.

The 255 modern campsites are divided into two distinctly different units. Camping sites in the park's original campground are closest to the beach and are shaded by a stand of cedar, birch, and mixed hardwoods so thick that the trees screen not only views of your

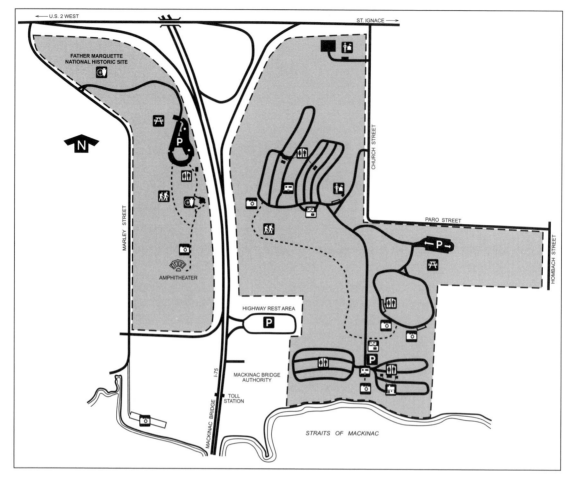

neighbors but often of the bridge and Straits. There's plenty of room on the beach, however, to plant a chair and take in the view. This lower campground used to hold 117 sites until the winter of 2006 when 15 highly desirable sites were added that hug the Lake Huron shoreline. But there's a tradeoff. The new sites lack electrical service. The park's two mini-cabins are in the east wing of this campground.

The 145 lots in the upper campground feature large, open, sunny sites located on high ground well back from the beach. Campers with big rigs will favor the 20 pull-through sites here. In the summer of 2004 the park's electrical system was upgraded by making 50-amp service available on nearly 100 sites. The 181-acre park's only trail descends from the west side of the camping area about a half-mile to a scenic overlook of the bridge and Straits.

A paved road also loops to the overlook, and the picture-perfect perspective of the bridge and Straits make the park a great place to take a break from driving and have lunch. A few tables are scattered around the overlook area with even larger picnic grounds set among the woods just north of the scenic-loop drive.

During the day, the beach provides a front-row seat for all the Straits boat traffic and a place to watch the kids skip stones. The beach is also good for walking and beachcombing or stretching out in the sun, but swimming is generally poor because of the rocky lake bottom.

COUNTY: MACKINAC
CAMPING SITES: 270 (255 MODERN, 15 SEMI-MODERN), PLUS TWO MINI-CABINS.
DIRECTIONS: FROM THE INTERSECTION OF I-75 AND US-2 GO LESS THAN A HALF MILE

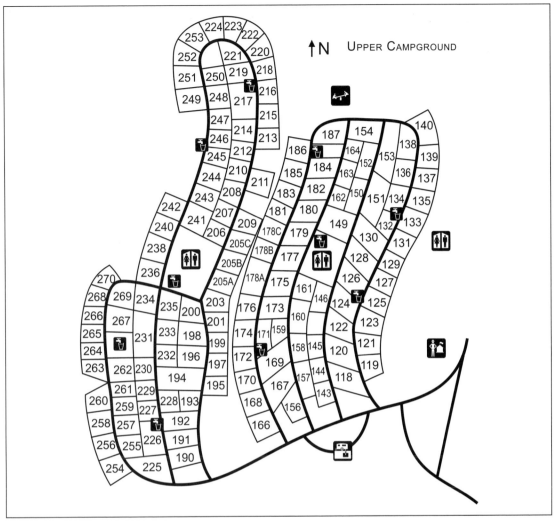

Upper Campground

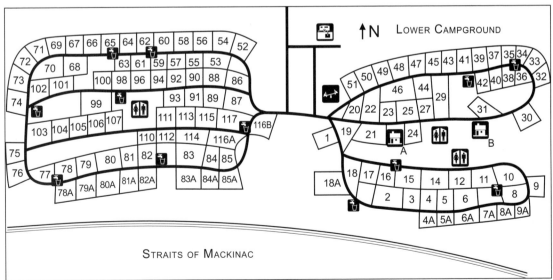

Lower Campground

Straits of Mackinac

east on US-2 to Church Street. Turn right (south) onto Church and go about three blocks.

Further Information: Straits State Park, 720 Church Street, St. Ignace, MI 49781; 906-643-8620.

Mackinac Island
State Park

OVERNIGHT ACCOMMODATIONS: NONE

ACTIVITIES: V

Mackinac Island State Park is one of the world's most unique and popular vacation spots and has been for more than 125 years. After just one visit you'll know why, and even after 20 visits you'll still want to come back for more of the crisp air, scenic beauty, vivid history, and cheerfully crass commercialism, all time-warped into a quaint Victorian atmosphere.

The state park takes up about 80 percent of the 2-mile-wide, 3-mile-long island, but you really can't separate what is and isn't park. There's no reason to try. Everybody who boards a ferry from the mainland gets the whole package.

When you step ashore, a short walk down the pier takes you right into another century. Huron Street, which parallels the harbor, seems – except for its asphalt – to have been lifted totally intact out of the late 1800s and deposited on the island. A steady stream of bicycles, horse-drawn carriages, dray wagons, and taxis passes in front of clap-board-sided Victorian buildings that line both sides of the street. Motorized vehicles are prohib-

ited on the island. The only traffic noise here is the clip-clop of hooves and the creak of harnesses, and the only polluting emissions are the odiferous leavings of the horses.

Many of the grand, old buildings are hotels that have been in business for over a hundred years and shops at which tourists for the past century, plus or minus a decade or two, have been buying everything from fine art, gifts, and clothes to tacky souvenirs and that well-known Mackinac Island institution: fudge. If you love to shop, you may never see more of the island than the few square blocks that border the harbor.

You should explore the island, especially if you like history, scenery, or, more often than

not, both combined.

Like a time traveler, wherever you go you pass in and out of segments of four centuries, your journey marked by ubiquitous green historical markers. Just a block north of Huron, the island's "Main Street," for instance, are warehouses, offices, and shops along Market Street, once the nerve center for a North American fur-trading empire.

At the street's east end is the site of a shooting that made medical history. In 1822 Dr. William Beaumont was summoned to the American Fur Trade Co. store to treat a young trapper who had suffered a severe gunshot wound to his abdomen. The man recovered, but the outside of the wound never healed. As a result Dr. Beaumont was able to peer inside the man's body and study the process of human digestion firsthand.

Around the corner from where the fur-trapper became an unwilling participant in medical history, on Fort Street, is the McGulpin house, the oldest known residence in Michigan.

Up the hill on Fort Street, you can take in one of the most beautiful panoramas in the state – a bird's-eye-view of the Straits, the island's harbor, and the downtown area from atop the ramparts of Fort Mackinac. It's easy to see why the British chose the commanding, easily defensible site to construct the 2 ½-to 8-foot thick, white stone walls into and on the high bluff in 1780. Today, you can walk through the restored barracks, officers' quarters, and 12 other buildings while, outside, authentically costumed guides perform rifle drills, fire cannon, and otherwise act out military life as it was lived during the 1880s.

At the base of the fort across Huron Street is a state park visitor center, which is a good place to get an overall orientation to the island as well as purchase combination tickets to many of the major historical attractions.

After the military and fur-trading significance of the island faded, its importance as a summer vacation destination began to grow. When railroad money built the Grand Hotel in 1886-87, Mackinac Island was already firmly established as a premier summer retreat of the world's wealthy. The pinnacle of high society also built enormous summer homes, leaving what today, on the south third of the island, must be one of the highest concentrations of Victorian buildings anywhere in the United States. Most still serve as palatial summer getaways for today's wealthy and powerful, including the gov-

and gravel roads that thickly web the hilly interior. The most traveled route is the 8-mile, nearly perfectly flat tour around the island's perimeter on M-185, the only Michigan state highway that bans automobile traffic.

You can also hop aboard a horse-drawn-carriage group tour, or rent a two-person horse and buggy and take the reins yourself. If you have the time and energy, you can walk any or all of the island's 70 miles of roads, trails and paths, including several remote interpretive nature trails.

Most people come just for the day, but those who stay overnight at one of the many fine hotels or bed-and-breakfast inns see the island take on a whole new character. After all the "fudgies," as day visitors are called, have departed, what was busy and crowded becomes eerily quiet as the streets empty and the lights of Mackinac Bridge and passing freighters reflect and dance across the waters.

ernor's summer residence which is open for tours from 9:30 to 11:30 a.m. Some of these grand Victorian masterpieces, however, have been turned into restaurants, businesses, living quarters for summer help, resort hotels, and bed-and-breakfast inns. The Grand itself, of course, is still one of the world's bastions of elegant, gracious, and expensive 19th-century hospitality. You can get within yards of the Grand's 700-foot-long pillared porch by walking up Cabotte Street, but to look inside you have to pay an admission fee.

Some people are surprised to find that half of the island's 2,200 acres are essentially undeveloped, quiet woods edged by sand and rock beach. The quickest and most popular way to take in a lot of scenery – including arch rock, a unique geological formation on the east side, plus nearly infinite perspectives of Lake Huron, the Mackinac Bridge and the Straits area – is on a bike. You can bring your own on the ferry or rent one near the island ferry docks then pedal on any of the paved

COUNTY: MACKINAC

CAMPING SITES: NONE

SCHEDULE: THE PARK IS OPEN MAY 6 – OCTOBER 9.

ENTRANCE RATES TO FORT MACKINAC: ADULTS $9.50; CHILDREN (6-17) $6.00; 5 AND UNDER FREE (INCLUDES 5 HISTORIC DOWNTOWN BUILDINGS).

DIRECTIONS: FERRY SERVICE DEPARTS FROM EITHER MACKINAW CITY OR ST. IGNACE APPROXIMATELY EVERY 30 MINUTES DURING PEAK SUMMER HOURS.

FURTHER INFORMATION: MACKINAC ISLAND STATE PARK, P.O. BOX 370, MACKINAC ISLAND, MI 49757; 906-847-3328.

Brimley State Park

84

OVERNIGHT ACCOMMODATIONS:

ACTIVITIES:

To enjoy Lake Superior, there's no better Michigan state park than Brimley. Oh, granted, if you just want to look at the world's largest freshwater lake you can probably get more scenic perspectives from other parks. The views from Brimley, however, sure aren't bad. Across Whitefish Bay, the Canadian highlands darken the horizon, and a continuously passing show of ore carriers and ocean-going freighters head into and out of nearby Soo Locks. If you want to get onto Lake Superior, Brimley's boat-launching ramp (large enough to handle only small boats) gives access to some of the most sheltered waters along its entire shoreline.

Best of all, from the shore here you can jump into the warmest waters – by Superior standards – anywhere on the lake. A wide strip of sand fronts the entire park, and the water is fairly shallow many yards out into the bay, which makes for about as fine a beach as you can find anywhere on this deep, rocky Great Lake.

Back from the beach on the park's east side, a modern campground is laid out like a small subdivision, in regularly spaced loops that parallel the shoreline. Most sites are level, grass covered, and roomy, and that was true before the park reduced camping sites from 270 to 237. The new configuration includes 23 pull-through sites, 50 amp service on many sites, and overall less crowding. Lowest-numbered lots are farthest from the lake and least shaded. The parks sole mini-cabin rests on the eastern end of the campground. Park officials report the campground is heavily used during the summer and recommend reservations if you plan to arrive on the weekend.

At the west-side day-use area, a wide grassy lawn separates a narrow strip of sand from a bathhouse and picnic shelter. Behind the rough wood structures, a large open, grassy picnic area extends well inland. At the extreme west edge of the beach, fishermen launch at the park's boat ramp and go after Whitefish Bay's pike, perch, bass, trout, and walleye. There are a number of trout streams within a few minutes' drive of the park.

There are no hiking or cross-country ski trails within the park, but an old railroad right-of-way edges the park and accommodates both skiers and walkers. Hobbyists with metal detectors are allowed to pursue their sport in certain areas of the park.

The many attractions of both the Canadian and American Soo Locks are little more than a half-hour from the campground by car. Both Tahquamenon Falls and Whitefish Point can be reached in an easy drive around the bay to the west.

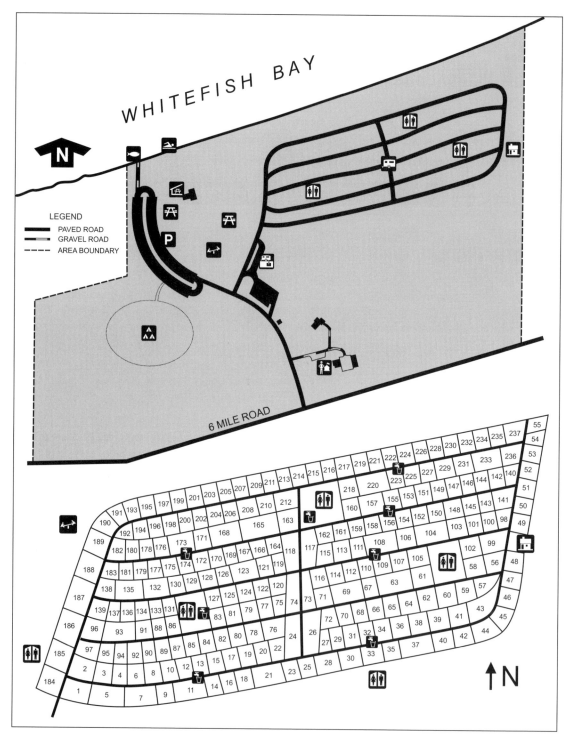

County: Chippewa

Camping Sites: 237, all modern and a mini-cabin.

Directions: From I-75 about 8 miles south of Sault Ste. Marie, exit onto M-28 and drive west 7 miles to M-221. Turn right (north) onto M-221 and go 2 miles to 6 Mile Road in Brimley. Turn (right) east and go less than a mile.

Further Information: Brimley State Park, 9200 West 6 Mile Road, Brimley, MI 49715; 906-248-3422.

Tahquamenon Falls
State Park

85

Overnight Accommodations:

Activities:

Nineteen miles from where it empties into Lake Superior, the Tahquamenon River is abruptly, momentarily, and dramatically freed from its rocky 200-foot-wide streambed. With a thunderous roar, 50,000 gallons a second of the tea-colored water plunges 50 feet over a sharp ledge into a foam-flecked pool. The spectacle, Upper Tahquamenon Falls, is the largest waterfall in Michigan and the second largest east of the Mississippi.

Four miles downstream the river presents an encore, this time splitting and dropping 23 feet around both sides of a large midstream island. The water here doesn't become airborne long. Rather, in tumultuous cascades it crashes and bangs into rocks and boulders as it hurdles over a succession of small, closely spaced ledges and steps.

The upper and lower falls are the heart of Tahquamenon Falls State Park. Each year, nearly half a million visitors from around the country come to watch the bottom drop out of the Tahquamenon River. Not only are the falls stunningly beautiful, they're also easy to get to. The quarter-mile-long, paved path to the Upper Falls cuts through a beautiful stand of hardwoods to the lip of the canyon through which the river flows. From there, one asphalt trail heads about 200 yards upstream, another about the same distance downstream. The upstream path borders the edge of the gorge, with several fine views of the falls coming along the way. The route ends by descending nearly 100 wood stairs to a platform that hangs – seemingly almost within touching distance – out over the top of the falls. An even-longer series of steps at the end of the downstream path drops to

sweeping river-level views through the canyon back to the falls.

A head-on panorama of the Lower Falls is even easier to get to. A 100-yard paved path from the Lower Falls parking lot gently rises to a prime viewing area above where the two channels rejoin at the base of the falls. To get to within inches of the white water that drops through the north channel, take a 15-minute walk along a trail that follows the riverbank from the main overlook. Or for unique close-up views of both channels' cascades, rent a boat at a concession below the overlook, row a few hundred yards to the midstream island, and walk the trails that circle its shoreline.

Facilities at both upper and lower falls day-use areas include large parking lots, tree-shaded picnic grounds, souvenir shops and food-concession areas.

Though a day visit to the falls is the main draw, there are also good reasons to stay overnight at the park. The park's three campgrounds, with a total of 277 sites, are heavily used. There are occasional vacancies, even on weekends, but if the park is your vacation destination, it's best to make a reservation.

The Lower Falls Campground is made up of two widely separated loops. The Overlook

Loop rests well back from the river on a high bluff while the Riverbend Loop lies close to the river and just downstream from the lower falls. All sites are worn, shaded, have electrical hookups, and provide access to modern restroom facilities. Recent improvements to the campground include 15 pull-through sites; eight sites rated as handicapped accessible and two-dozen sites with 50-amp service. Privacy is only fair at either loop. Bring plenty of insect repellent to ward off the reason why the park's staff sometimes works with netting over their heads here – hordes of mosquitoes.

Miles away, either by river or road, the park's other two campgrounds are tucked into the last long, lazy loops the Tahquamenon makes just before emptying into Lake Superior's Whitefish Bay. The Rivermouth Campground's modern unit occupies a narrow peninsula formed by the river, and many of the camping sites are hardly more than a stone's throw from the Tahquamenon. There are five pull-through sites, four handicapped accessible sites, and better than a dozen sites have had electrical upgrades and provide 50-amp service. The 36-site, semi-modern (electricity but no modern restroom facilities) Rivermouth Unit lies farther from M-123 and hugs the south side of the river.

Across M-123 from the Rivermouth Campground, a picnic area lines the bay north of the river's outlet. Canoers put in here, as do fishermen and boaters at the park's only boat ramp, then set out to fish or explore 17 miles of river, plus the open, sometimes treacherous waters of Lake Superior.

More than 35 miles of foot trails cut through the heart of the 42,500-acre state park, Michigan's second largest. Much of that mileage is along a portion of the North Country Trail – which ultimately will connect the Appalachian Trail in Maine to the Lewis and Clark Trail in North Dakota – that runs from border to border in the park. One popular section is the 15 miles between the

Lower Falls campgrounds to Lake Superior. The North Country Trail also makes up portions of three loops that begin at the Upper Falls parking lot. Those circuits, which range from 3.7 to 13 miles long, head over old Indian trails and logging railroad grades into a backcountry world of pine, muskeg and picturesque bog lakes. Backcountry camping is not permitted.

Moose are sometimes seen in the park feeding in wet areas with the best chances coming along M-123 from the village of Paradise to the Lower Falls. You will also want to be on the lookout for a glimpse of coyotes, otter, deer, beaver, porcupine, black bear and mink. Bird watching can also be good in the park with its wide variety of resident waterfowl and songbirds. Nature programs are offered everyday of the week throughout the summer in a variety of locations within the park.

Hunting is allowed on much of the park acreage, with deer, grouse, and woodcock the most-abundant game. The Tahquamenon River yields brown trout, walleye, northern muskie, northern pike, yellow perch, and smallmouth bass. Handicapped accessible shore fishing is available at the Rivermouth Campground.

Though not many do it, winter is an especially good time to visit Tahquamenon Falls State Park. Blue-tinted ice sculptures frame the falls then, and cross-country skiers have four miles and snowmobilers 16 miles of trails to set tracks on. Winter camping is available at the Lower Falls.

COUNTY: CHIPPEWA

CAMPING SITES: 277 (241 MODERN, 36 SEMI-MODERN).

SCHEDULE: THE PARK AND CAMPGROUNDS ARE OPEN YEAR ROUND, BUT MODERN RESTROOM FACILITIES ARE CLOSED FROM OCTOBER 16 TO MAY 19.

DIRECTIONS: THE ENTRANCE TO THE LOWER FALLS AREA IS 10 MILES WEST OF PARADISE

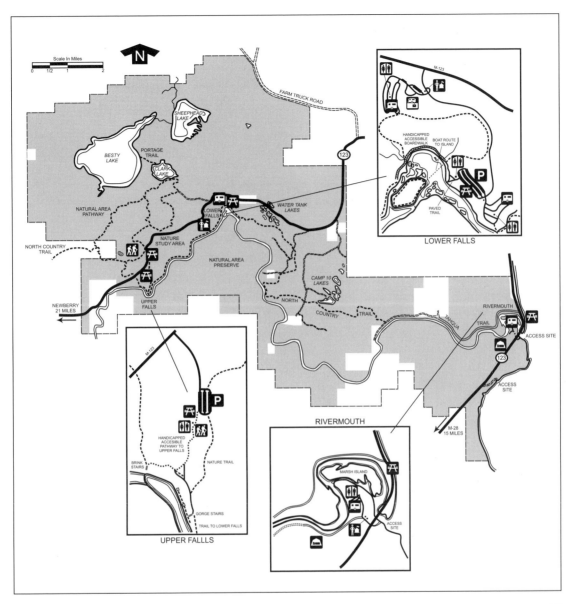

LOWER FALLS

UPPER FALLLS

RIVERMOUTH

ON M-123. THE UPPER FALLS IS 4 MILES FARTHER WEST. THE RIVERMOUTH UNIT IS 5 MILES SOUTH OF PARADISE ON M-123. FURTHER INFORMATION: TAHQUAMENON FALLS STATE PARK, 41382 WEST M-123, PARADISE, MI 49768; 906-492-3415.

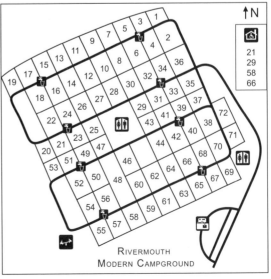

RIVERMOUTH
MODERN CAMPGROUND

Muskallonge Lake
State Park

OVERNIGHT ACCOMMODATIONS:

ACTIVITIES:

Most state parks are near someplace or on the way to somewhere. Not so with Muskallonge Lake State Park. About the only reason to drive 20-some miles up County Road H-37 from Newberry is to visit the narrow strip of state-owned property that separates Lake Superior from Muskallonge Lake. More than 60,000 people a year think it's worth the trip.

At the north edge of the more-than-mile-long park, you can spend hours searching for the odd-shaped pieces of driftwood or colorful stones and agates on rocky portions of the Lake Superior shore. On the alternating patches of sand, you can spend the same amount of time stretched out, hypnotized by the pounding surf and beautiful view. Many visitors make annual trips here in July and August to pick the plentiful blueberries and strawberries found in the area.

Only a thousand to 2,000 yards away from the Great Lake, the park's developed facilities line a section of the north shore of Muskallonge Lake. Centering the area is a modern campground with 159 sites arranged in seven short loops whose tips all point at the water. All lots are large, level, grass covered and close to the water and a sandy, campers-only swimming beach at the end of the eastern-most loop. Easy and quick set up for even the biggest rigs is possible at the campground's 6 pull-through sites. Lofty hardwoods shade and partially hide lots 1-130. For the most privacy try lots 131-159. Park officials recommend reservations from July 1st through late August.

At a shaded, grassy day-use area east of the campground one is hard put to find any foot prints marking the beach sand that gradually slides into the water. Few people come to this out-of-the-way park just for a day visit.

A boat ramp west of the campground is well used, however, almost totally by fishermen. Unlike at many downstate park lakes, anglers here don't have to worry much about speedboats interrupting their quiet sport. In 1987

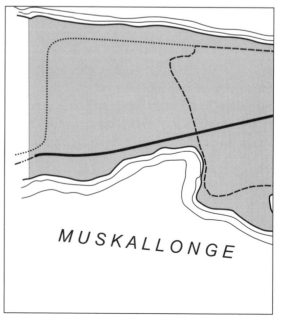

walleyes were introduced in Muskallonge Lake, already known for its fine northern-pike and perch fishing, and smallmouth bass and a remnant muskie population also bend more than a few fishing rods. Rental fishing boats are available at two stores near the park. Many excellent trout-fishing streams, including the legendary Two Hearted River, flow through the area and another 70 lakes are within a 20-mile radius of the park.

Hikers have the opportunity to wear down plenty of boot leather here. The park itself has only a single 1.5-mile trail, which closely follows the Superior shoreline. It connects with the North Country Trail, which when completed will cross the entire Upper Peninsula as part of a system that will connect the Appalachian Trail in Maine to the Lewis and Clark Trail in North Dakota. Today, from Muskallonge Lake State Park you can hike west approximately 20 miles to, then through, the Pictured Rocks National Lakeshore, but you don't have to go that far. A Lake Superior State Forest campground just five miles west along the route makes for a pleasant day-long round trip along the Superior shoreline. To the east on the North Country Trail, you can walk 40 miles to the mouth of the Tahquamenon River on White-fish Bay. Many backpackers, however, opt for a shorter, but still-strenuous, two-day, 20-mile round trip to a state forest campground at the mouth of the Two Hearted River.

In the winter the park attracts snowmobilers, cross-country skiers and snowshoers while Muskallonge Lake has proven popular with ice fishermen.

County: Luce
Camping Sites: 159
Schedule: The campground is open May 1 through November 1 but modern restrooms are not available the first and last months.
Directions: Drive 28 miles north of Newberry on County Road H-37.
Further Information: Muskallonge Lake State Park, 30042 County Road 407, Newberry, MI 49868; 906-658-3338.

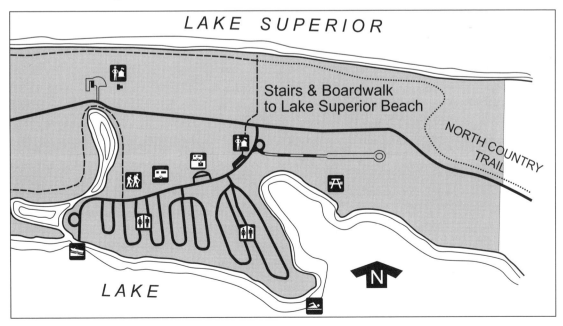

LAKE SUPERIOR

Stairs & Boardwalk to Lake Superior Beach

NORTH COUNTRY TRAIL

N

LAKE

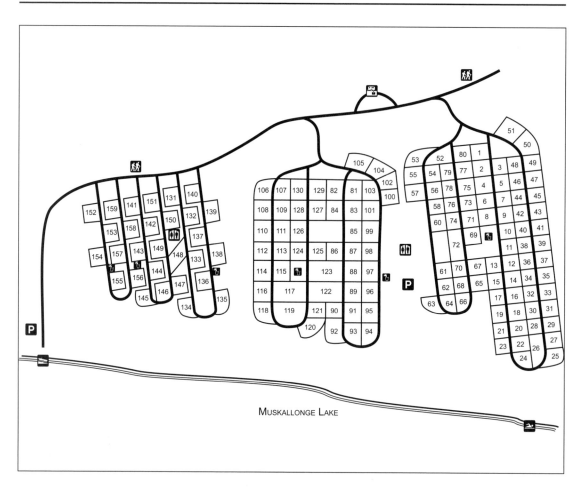

MUSKALLONGE LAKE

Wagner Falls

Scenic Site

OVERNIGHT ACCOMMODATIONS: NONE

ACTIVITIES:

It's easy to pass it by, but, come on, stop. You'll be glad you spent the few minutes it takes to explore this small, boisterous little waterfall that resembles a spirited colt that's been let out of the barn on the first day of spring.

An 800-foot-long trail climbs alongside Wagner Creek, and you only have to take a couple of steps up the path and away from your car before hearing the falls barreling downhill. A few feet farther and the exuberant cascade comes into view. Frothy, white water tumbles over several rocky ledges, its path obstructed by a jumble of large boulders and tree trunks that look like they've been tossed in a game of pick-up sticks by giants. Downstream, trees, flowers, and shrubs crowd the small, sharp-sided valley.

Only 22 acres of state land surround the falls, making this site one of Michigan's smallest state parks. It's also one of the least developed. The only "facilities" are a small roadside parking area, an identifying sign, and a gravel trail and boardwalk to the falls.

COUNTY: ALGER

CAMPING SITES: NONE

DIRECTIONS: FROM THE INTERSECTION OF M-94 AND M-28, ONE MILE SOUTH OF MUNISING, DRIVE WEST ON M-94 APPROXIMATELY 0.5 MILES TO THE PARKING AREA, ON THE SOUTH SIDE OF THE ROAD.

FURTHER INFORMATION: WAGNER FALLS SCENIC SITE, C/O INDIAN LAKE STATE PARK, 8970 WEST COUNTY ROAD 442, MANISTIQUE, MI 49854; 906-341-2355.

Pictured Rocks

National Lakeshore

OVERNIGHT ACCOMMODATIONS:

ACTIVITIES:

Even if you can only spend a couple of hours in the Pictured Rocks National Lakeshore, do it. Though you'll barely get a peek at this varied, spectacularly beautiful stretch of Lake Superior coastline, you'll take home unforgettable memories.

The next-best way to sample the waterfalls, inland lakes, streams, 300-foot-high Grand Sable Banks, mountainous sand dunes, vast beaches and near-vertical cliffs is to spend an entire day driving and walking. Even better, stay a night or two at one of the park's three secluded campgrounds.

And the ultimate? Dive into the heart of the park on a week-long backpacking expedition.

Nature has divided the 5-mile-wide, 42-mile-long park into three distinct sections. Dominating the west end are 15 miles of sheer cliffs that rise 50-200 feet directly from the lapping waves. Wind and water have carved the rock into pillars, arches, caves and other formations with such distinct character that they have acquired names such as Grand Portal Point, Miners Castle, Chapel Rock, and Indianhead. The faint, earthy pastels of a variety of minerals color the cliffs, and as sunlight plays across their face, the delicate greens, reds, and browns continuously shift in shade and mood.

There's only one road in the park that goes out to the shoreline in this section, Miners Castle Road, which leads to viewing decks near the top of the turret-shaped sandstone pillar known as Miners Castle. If the views

from here are spectacular and free, they are also limited. The best way to view the entire wall of rock and fully appreciate both the size and beauty of the stretch of coastline that gives the park its name is from a privately operated boat tour that runs out of Munising. Yes, you can use your own boat, canoe, or sea kayak to explore Pictured Rocks, but Lake Superior can be rough and unforgiving, and when danger threatens, the lee shore offers vertical rocks instead of sandy beaches and sheltered inlets.

The middle section of the lakeshore is a broad, seemingly endless straight stretch of sand and pebbles known as Twelvemile Beach. Beachcombers love the unbroken expanse, and indecisive sunbathers may spend an entire day wandering from perfect spot to perfect spot. To take a dip here, however, nearly requires membership in the Polar Bear Club. Warmer swimming comes at Grand Sable Lake.

That lake is cut off from Superior by acres of sand in the park's third and easternmost section, from Au Sable Point to near Grand Marais. The main attraction in that five miles of park coastline is the Grand Sable Banks, monstrous piles of gravelly debris left by receding glaciers. The banks rise from

Lake Superior at an angle of 35 degrees to a height of 275 feet in some places. Atop the eastern edge of the banks, four square miles of constantly shifting white sand known as the Grand Sable Dunes reach another 80 feet into the sky.

Eight waterfalls add exclamation marks along the park's entire length. Spray Falls plummets from the lip of the cliff directly into Superior, while Bridal Veil Falls cascades down the rocky face of the cliff into the big lake. Two of the most beautiful falls, Munising and Sable, are also the most accessible, almost serving as official greeters at the park entrances. From the west visitors center, a less-than-five-minute walk along a paved path ends with a head-on look at where Munising Falls drops like a plumb line for 50 feet from a large, rocky overhang.

At the opposite end of the park, tucked into a secluded, wooded setting just inside the Grand Marais entrance point, is Sable Falls. Sable Creek, in its last rush to the world's largest freshwater lake, tumbles through a narrow, steep-sided gorge over a series of rock ledges. To get to the top of the falls, take an easy-to-walk quarter-mile path from a parking area off H-58 just north of the visitors center. At the falls itself, great views and photos come from a long series of steps that parallel the stream. At the bottom, another path ends at one of the best agate beaches in Michigan.

Other short to moderate walks, many self-guided by interpretive brochures, provide visitors with a wide variety of experiences. Many end at still more waterfalls while the fully accessible 0.5-mile Sand Point Marsh Trail wanders through swamps, marshes, an active beaver colony, and old beach ridges. A 1.5-mile jaunt will take you along the lakeshore from Hurricane River Campground to the historic and picturesque Au Sable Light Station. The restored lighthouse overlooks one of the most historically treacherous sections of shoreline in the park. Lighthouse interpretive programs are scheduled here seasonally. Other trails lead past shipwrecks and circle inland lakes.

A 42.8-mile segment of the North Country Trail follows the Lake Superior coastline the park's entire length and serves as the backbone of the national lakeshore's 90-mile network of trails. Hiking all or even part of the route is well worth the effort, and you'll take in a variety of stunning scenes available nowhere else in the state or even the country. There are several access points for day hikes along County Road H-58, which runs the length of the park. In years past visitors knew the dirt road as the longest washboard in the state. From visitor centers on either end of the park, the dirt road, which in places gave motorists the impression they were riding a paint shaker, led tourists to unforgettable views and vistas and a variety of day hikes and picnic grounds. Old visitors and new will

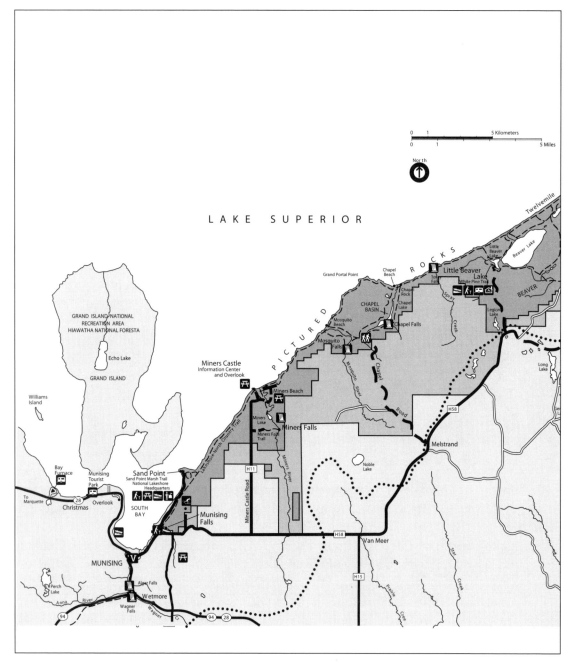

be happy to hear more than half the length of H-58 through the park has been paved.

Backpackers who make the several-day trek along the entire trail stay at 13 small, walk-in camping areas scattered at 2- to 5-mile intervals. You must get a permit at one of the visitors centers to backcountry camp or have advance reservations. Demand is heavy in July and August for the three to 10 sites at each area. A privately operated shuttle bus service relieves hikers of the necessity of either making a round trip or hitchhiking back to their car after an extended trek. The shuttle bus makes pick-ups at the visitor center and drops off at either the other end of the park or at a point down the trail where you can then hike back to your car.

If you want to drive up and park at your campsite, you have three areas within the park to choose from. Twenty-two sites at the Hurricane River unit are nestled in deep woods bordering the lakeshore. Not far down

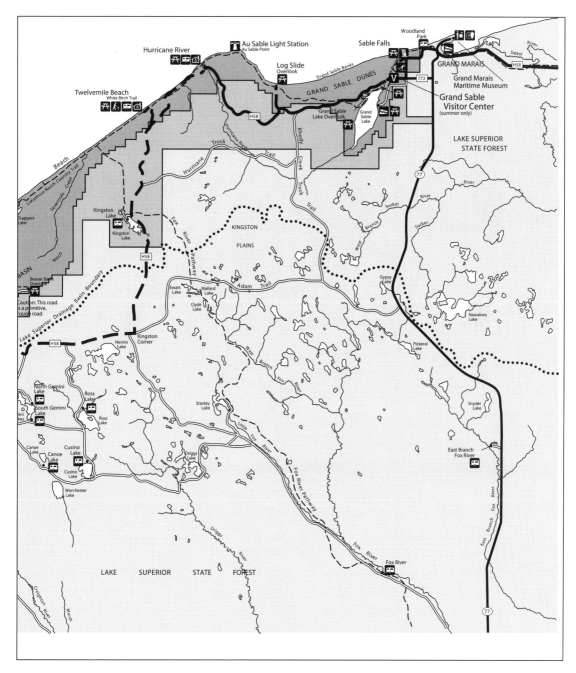

the coast, strung along a bluff overlooking Twelvemile Beach are 36 more lots, and near the center of the park an eight-site unit rests along the heavily wooded shoreline of Little Beaver Lake. With the grand total of only 66 sites, none reservable, "choose from" becomes "try your luck getting a spot at," especially in July and August.

All three campgrounds offer handicapped accessible sites, are secluded, scenic, and rustic, with water, picnic tables, and pit toilets but no electricity.

Sea kayaking is a popular pastime here, and several campgrounds are readily accessible via kayak. Intimate views of the beautiful sandstone cliffs are great from a sea kayak, but one should always keep in mind that storms brew up quickly on Lake Superior, and for a 15-mile stretch of lakeshore kayakers face nothing but sheer rock walls that provide no shelter from either wind or waves.

Hunting is allowed in the park and a Mich-

igan hunting license is required. Bear, white-tail deer, hare, grouse, ducks, and geese are pursued by hunters. Fishermen pull northern pike, smallmouth bass, walleye, brook and lake trout, whitefish, steelhead, and coho salmon from Munising Bay and several small inland lakes. For small boats, access to Munising Bay and the open waters comes from a ramp at Sand Point. Larger boats can be floated from the City of Munising ramp. There is also a ramp that gives boaters access to Grand Sable Lake. A Michigan fishing license is required to fish anywhere within the park. Ice fishermen spud holes and drop lines on Munising Bay and the park's inland lakes in the winter.

When the annual 150-inch-plus snowfall blankets the park, cross-country skiers glide over 16 miles of groomed trails or set out on more off-trail opportunities than you can shake a ski pole at. The entire park is open to backcountry skiing and snowshoeing, and several unplowed roads may be used by snowmobiles.

Rangers conduct a variety of interpretive programs throughout the park in July and August.

COUNTY: ALGER

CAMPING SITES: 67 PRIMITIVE DRIVE TO SITES AND 60-PLUS BACKCOUNTRY CAMPSITES DIVIDED AMONG THIRTEEN HIKE-IN CAMP-GROUNDS.

SCHEDULE: THE PARK IS OPEN ALL YEAR, BUT THE CAMPGROUNDS ARE CLOSED FROM NOVEMBER 1 TO MAY 9.

FEES: NO DAILY ENTRY FEE. BACKCOUNTRY CAMPING FEES ARE $4 A DAY AND DRIVE TO CAMPING FEES ARE $12 A DAY.

DIRECTIONS: TAKE COUNTY ROAD H-58 EAST FROM MUNISING OR WEST FROM GRAND MARAIS.

FURTHER INFORMATION: PICTURED ROCKS NATIONAL LAKESHORE, P.O. BOX 40, MU-NISING, MI 49862; 906-387-2607.

*L*aughing Whitefish Falls

Scenic Site

OVERNIGHT ACCOMMODATIONS: NONE

ACTIVITIES:

Near Sundell, a three-quarter-mile woodchip-covered path tunnels through a hardwood forest to one of the few official Scenic Sites in the state park system – Laughing Whitefish Falls. The designation is well deserved. The falls, which drop almost 100 feet into a deep, steep-sided gorge, is both spectacular and delicately beautiful.

From the top of a high, layered limestone wall, a small stream free-falls in thin ribbons for about 10 feet before splashing onto a bulging dome of rock that curves out and down to the bottom of the gorge. In a beautiful counterpoint to its reckless start, the water finishes its descent to a small pool by spreading into a thin, glistening film that barely dampens the rock dome. It's hard, in fact, to detect any movement of water over the shimmering, sparkling rock. The mood can change dramatically in the spring and other times when the volume of water passing over the falls markedly increases.

The best view comes at about the midpoint of a very long flight of stairs that drops alongside the falls and sheer rock wall to the bottom of the gorge. At the top of the stairs, a wood observation deck overlooks the lip of the falls.

With any luck at all, the walk to the falls will be a cool 15-minute stroll rather than a much-shorter vigorous aerobic hike when black flies are out in force. Even if you douse yourself with an entire bottle of insect repellant, you could still end up frantically windmilling your arms and swatting right and left to keep the pesky buggers at a respectful distance.

Minimal facilities include pit toilets and a couple of picnic tables, all located near the gravel parking lot. Except for the 330 acres designated as a scenic site, hunting is permitted the in park. When the snow flies, cross-country skiers and snowshoers are welcome, but they will not find any groomed trails.

COUNTY: ALGER

CAMPING SITES: NONE

DIRECTIONS: FROM SUNDELL IN ALGER COUNTY ON M-94 DRIVE APPROXIMATELY 2 MILES NORTH, CONTINUING STRAIGHT WHEN THE ROAD TURNS TO GRAVEL.

FURTHER INFORMATION: LAUGHING WHITEFISH FALLS SCENIC SITE, C/O INDIAN LAKE STATE PARK, 8970 WEST COUNTY ROAD 442, MANISTIQUE, MI 49854; 906-341-2355.

V*an Riper*

STATE PARK

OVERNIGHT ACCOMMODATIONS:

ACTIVITIES:

Located in the heart of the western Upper Peninsula, Van Riper State Park is surrounded by almost-limitless forest and near-trackless wilderness. This is a very special region, as you will discover when you see the first of many signs that read, "Moose Crossing Area." Only nine miles north of the park is the release point where the majestic animals were reintroduced into the Upper Peninsula. A slow drive on the surrounding gravel roads – especially the ones that cut through the wilderness to the north of the park – in search of moose is a must for overnight park visitors. Chances of spotting a moose are small, but for the lucky few who do, the rest of the trip could be a vacation from hell and still remembered with fondness.

You can also use Van Riper as a base from which to head off into the wilderness in a four-wheel adventure down faint two-tracks, in your car or RV along miles of good dirt roads, or you can stick close to Lake Michigamme and stroll the sandy beach, swim, fish, or just relax and enjoy the grand view.

US-41/M-28 bisects the park, and most of the developed facilities are south of the highway in a parcel that wraps around the eastern end of Lake Michigamme. Punctuating the eastern tip of the lake is a long, wide beach, backed by a modern bathhouse/restroom. There's plenty of room to spread blankets and beach towels on the open, sunny strip of sand, and you can take lengthy strolls along the shore in either direction. Spread over a low hill in a grove of large white pines back from the water are grills, tables and a picnic shelter. From almost anywhere in this section of the park, you get sweeping views of the lake and the green, tree-clad hills that ring it.

Just south of the picnic area, the stand of mature white pine shelters a 150-site modern campground. The lots are exceptionally clean and well kept, and the imposing trees and low shrubs combine to shade and screen many sites. None of the lots are directly on the water, but the lake and its swimming beach are only a short walk away. In the campground there are two each of handicapped accessible sites, mini-cabins, and pull-through sites. You can almost always find a vacant spot here during the week, but it's best to call ahead or make reservations for summer weekends.

An even quieter, more secluded overnight alternative is the park's 40-site rustic campground, on the banks of a creek and the shore of Lake Michigamme in the southwest corner of the park. The campground is accessible via a separate paved road.

Pleasure boaters and fishermen also use the road to launch from a ramp near the rustic campground. Walleye, bass, muskellunge, and perch are the fish most often pulled from the nearly 8-mile-long lake.

The park's north section is nearly undeveloped. There, the Peshekee River, in its last rush to Lake Michigamme cuts through the rolling, forested hills that make up the majority of the park's 1,044 acres. Four miles of hiking trails, ranging in length from the 0.25 to 1.5 miles, lead to abandoned mine shafts, pass through deep woods and along the banks of the river, and rise to high, panoramic overlooks. The trails are open to cross-country skiers in the winter, and snowmobilers are welcome. The park's single rustic cabin sits on the banks of the Peshekee River just north of the highway. Hunting is allowed in certain areas of the park as is the use of metal detectors.

County: Marquette
Camping Sites: 190 (150 modern, 40 rustic), including two mini-cabins and a rustic cabin.
Schedule: The park is open all year, but the campground is closed from October 15 to May 15.
Directions: Drive 1.5 miles west of Champion on US-41/M-28.
Further Information: Van Riper State Park, 851 County Road AKE, P.O. Box 88, Champion, MI 49814; 906-339-4461.

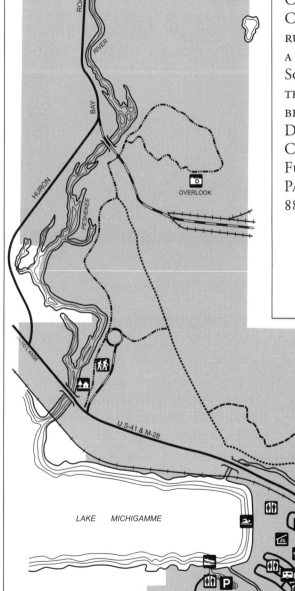

Craig Lake
STATE PARK

91

OVERNIGHT ACCOMMODATIONS:

ACTIVITIES:

Craig Lake State Park is about as primitive and off-the-beaten-track a park as you can find in Michigan's state-run system. Not only do most maps of the state omit the road leading to the park, many don't even show the park itself. When you do pinpoint its location, you quickly see that Craig Lake is at the edge of the largest roadless area in the state.

At one time, even calling the route into the park a road was debatable. Only recently have park personnel sharply reduced the "chances of an oil pan ding" by removing a great number of boulders and rocks from the roadway. It's still a good idea to make the trip in a vehicle with good ground clearance. Always check road conditions with officials at Van Riper State Park before starting your adventure.

Craig Lake is the doorway to some of the most rugged, primitive, and wild country in the entire state, and backpackers, hikers, and fishermen who enjoy roughing it can do so here with little if any company. The only developed facilities are two rustic frontier rental cabins, and the only marked hiking trails are eight-plus miles that circle Craig Lake, an uncompleted spur that will eventually reach Clair Lake and a 7.5-mile section of the North Country Trail that passes through the park. There's almost unlimited room for off-trail bushwhacking, and you can low-impact backcountry camp anywhere in the park except within 150 feet of water.

Teddy and Craig lakes are only short walks from roadside parking lots. With Keeway-din Lake Road ending at a parking lot/boat-launching area on Keewaydin Lake, it wins the award for being the most easily reached body of water in the park. It is also the only lake where motors are allowed. In recent years the route was improved to a gravel road that is maintained by the county, so you can actually get a car, boat trailer, and boat to the launch area without loosing all three to bad roads as could happen in the past. Three lakes – Clair, Craig, and Crooked – are linked by short portages.

Canoeists, shore fishermen, and sportsmen who carry in small boats on their shoulders all toss lures into Craig Lake, the park's best for angling. The response is excellent from bass, muskellunge, and northern pike and good from walleyes and perch. Special regulations, such as catch-and-release fishing (except for walleye and panfish) are in effect throughout the park. You can get a copy of the rules at either Van Riper State Park or directly from the DNR in Lansing.

Craig Lake State Park's 6,983 acres make up part of the area where moose were recently reintroduced in the Upper Peninsula, and several of the great animals have been spot-

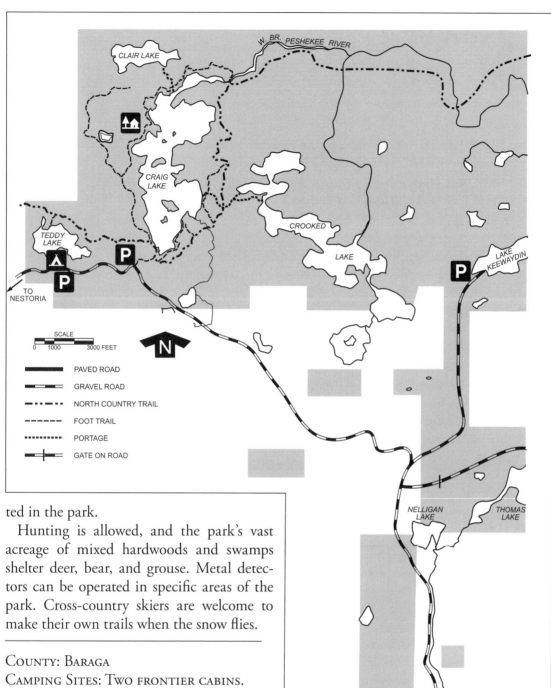

ted in the park.

Hunting is allowed, and the park's vast acreage of mixed hardwoods and swamps shelter deer, bear, and grouse. Metal detectors can be operated in specific areas of the park. Cross-country skiers are welcome to make their own trails when the snow flies.

COUNTY: BARAGA
CAMPING SITES: TWO FRONTIER CABINS. BACKCOUNTRY CAMPING IS PERMITTED FROM MAY 15 TO OCTOBER 15.
DIRECTIONS: FROM US-41/M-28 APPROXIMATELY 8 MILES WEST OF CHAMPION, TURN NORTH ONTO KEEWAYDIN LAKE ROAD. TO GET TO CRAIG LAKE, GO 8 MILES, TAKING THE LEFT FORK AT ABOUT 3 MILES.
FURTHER INFORMATION: CRAIG LAKE STATE PARK, c/o VAN RIPER STATE PARK, P.O. BOX 88, CHAMPION, MI 49814; 906-339-4461.

Baraga State Park

92

OVERNIGHT ACCOMMODATIONS:

ACTIVITIES:

Rising from the shoreline almost at the very tip of Keweenaw Bay, Baraga State Park makes either a convenient base camp or a welcome stopover during Keweenaw Peninsula or western U.P. vacations.

US-41 separates the park's day-use area from the campground, which usually has vacancies even on summer weekends if you arrive early in the day. All 116 camping spots, including the mini-cabin's site, are shaded, grass covered, exceptionally clean, and all have magnificent views of the bay. There's minimal privacy, and highway noise can be intrusive, but those are small tradeoffs. Recently, minor reconfiguring within the campground made it possible to add five pull-through sites and a tepee. All campers have access to modern restrooms with showers, but 10 sites at the north end of the campground have no electrical hookups.

It's just a short walk across US-41 to the open, grassy picnic area and small, sandy beach that are squeezed between the highway and Keweenaw Bay. The water here, at the foot of the bay, is as warm as any spot on Lake Superior, but that's still a long way from what most people would consider comfortable.

Fishermen, who launch onto the bay's sheltered waters from a ramp at the south end of the beach, go angling for the big lake's salmon, pike, and herring. Others drop hooks for largemouth bass, walleye, pike, perch, and bluegill in several nearby lakes.

There's not a lot of room to roam in the 56-acre park, but the lone trail that does loop from the back of the campground is first class. The ¾-mile self-guided (brochure available at park headquarters) route circles the top of glacial deposits and includes good looks at examples of area flora, several interesting natural features, and the bay and surrounding area. Park personnel also lead nature hikes and interpretive programs.

Metal detectors may be operated in certain areas of the park.

COUNTY: BARAGA
CAMPING SITES: 116 (10 WITHOUT ELEC-TRICAL HOOKUPS), ONE MINI-CABIN, AND A TEPEE.
SCHEDULE: THE PARK AND CAMPGROUND ARE OPEN ALL YEAR, BUT THE MODERN REST-ROOM FACILITIES ARE CLOSED FROM DECEM-BER 1 TO MAY 10.
DIRECTIONS: ONE MILE SOUTH OF BARAGA ON US-41.
FURTHER INFORMATION: BARAGA STATE PARK, 1300 US-41 SOUTH, BARAGA, MI 49908; 906-353-6558.

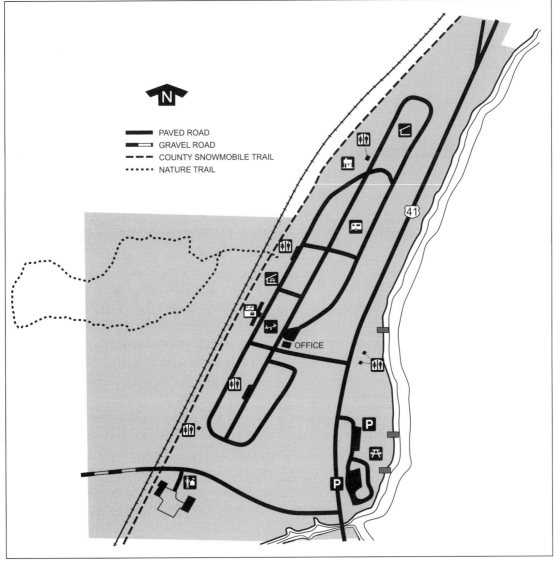

Twin Lakes
STATE PARK

93

OVERNIGHT ACCOMMODATIONS:

ACTIVITIES:

Conspired against by location, Twin Lakes is the least-visited state park in Michigan for which the DNR keeps records. While vacationers pass through most state-park entrances by the hundreds of thousands each year, this 175-acre parcel, hidden away at the base of the Keweenaw Peninsula, is all but ignored. Only 30,000 visitors each year bother to search it out.

Many of those who visit return again, and for good reason – quiet, uncrowded camping and near-ideal boating, water skiing, and swimming at one of the Upper Peninsula's warmest inland lakes. In addition, Twin Lakes State Park makes an excellent base camp for exploring surrounding Copper Country attractions.

M-26 splits the park into developed and undeveloped sections. To the east, between the blacktop and the shores of Lake Roland, is one of the Upper Peninsula's smallest, most-pleasant campgrounds. Twenty of the 62 spacious, grass-covered lots nearly touch the lake, but even the farthest from shore is only an Al Kaline toss from the water. A mini-cabin sits on the southern end of the campground. Reservations are recommended in July and the first three weeks in August.

A short walk north from the campground ends at the park's 500-foot-long swimming beach. The sand strip, only a few feet wide at its broadest, gently slopes into the clear, warm water. Stately, mature hardwoods shade much of the area, which includes a change court, two picnic shelters, tables, grills, and playground equipment scattered over a large expanse of grass back from the beach.

Near the park boundary at the north end of the beach is a launch ramp with its own access road, used by pleasure boaters, water skiers, and fishermen, who toss lures for tiger muskies, bluegills, perch, bass, and rainbow trout.

On the west side of M-26, a 1.5-mile hiking trail tunnels through the almost totally undeveloped woodland that makes up the vast majority of park property. On a clear day from two scenic overlooks along the loop, you can see Lake Superior shimmering on the horizon nearly 10 miles away. The forest and lakeshore both shelter a wide variety of birds and wildflowers.

In the winter, five miles of cross-country ski trails lace the park. Snowmobiles are welcome when four inches of snow have fallen. The park is traversed by the 37-mile-long, multi-use Bill Nicholls Trail that runs from Mass City to Houghton. Snowmobilers run the trail in the winter and hikers and mountain bikes do likewise in the summer.

Metal detectors can be operated in specific areas of the park.

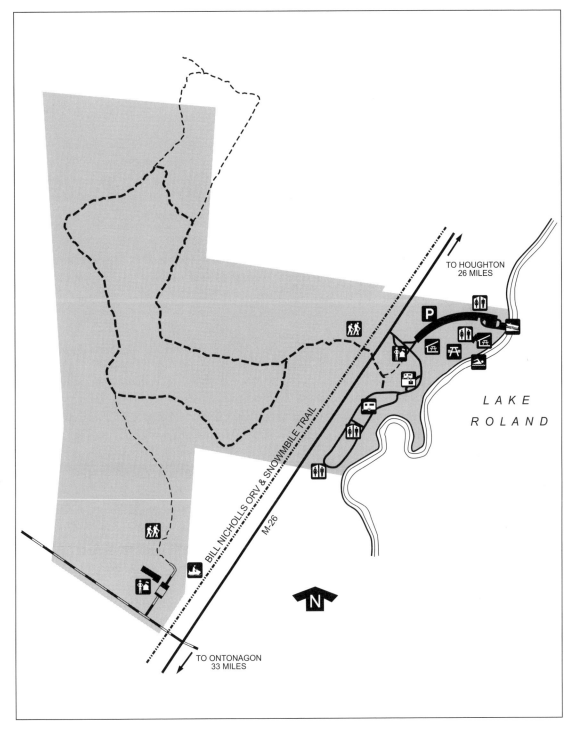

TO HOUGHTON
26 MILES

BILL NICHOLLS ORV & SNOWMBILE TRAIL

M-26

LAKE ROLAND

N

TO ONTONAGON
33 MILES

County: Houghton
Camping Sites: 62, all modern including a mini-cabin.
Schedule: Modern restrooms are closed from October 15 to May 15, and the entire park is closed November 1 to April 30.

Directions: Twenty-eight miles south of Houghton on M-26.
Further Information: Twin Lakes State Park, 6204 East Poyhonen Road, Box 234, Toivola, MI 49965; 906-288-3321.

OVERNIGHT ACCOMMODATIONS:

ACTIVITIES:

Rangers and other employees at McLain State Park like to boast that they work at one of the prettiest state parks in Michigan. They don't often get an argument.

The scenic magnet here is two miles of magnificent Lake Superior coastline, which varies from wave-eroded ledges that drop straight into the lake to wide expanses of water-lapped sand to steep-side dunes. Back from shore, large, open areas carpeted with lush grass interrupt a densely packed, mixed hardwood/pine forest.

One broad sweep of lawn, which runs down to the water's edge from a parking lot near the entrance, makes up the park's large picnic grounds. Tables and grills are generously scattered around the spacious area, and scenic views of the world's largest freshwater lake come from almost any spot. Playground equipment is set up near the water, and on the west side, huge old birches provide some shade as well as shelter from cool onshore breezes. The park has three picnic shelters, two of which have fireplaces and grills for cooking.

A wide strip of sand edges the water from the picnic grounds more than a half-mile down shore to the park's extreme southwest corner. There, one arm of a seawall that forms the mouth of the Portage Lake Ship Canal protects a large "swimming" beach. Well back from shore on top of a low, wooded dune is a combination bathhouse, concession stand, pavilion, and restroom building.

The open, sandy shore is great for sunbathing on hot days, and you can roll up your pant legs and wade the fringes until your feet go numb. You have to be hardy or foolhardy to take more than a brief dip in the frigid water. The seawall also serves as a fishing pier.

Back from and paralleling the sandy shore in this section of the park are low, wooded dunes. Several unmarked paths wind through the area, and a posted hiking trail connects the swimming beach and the main picnic area. The pleasant walk will have hikers both searching the forest floor for wildflowers and lifting their gaze for memorable views of Lake Superior. For a more intimate look

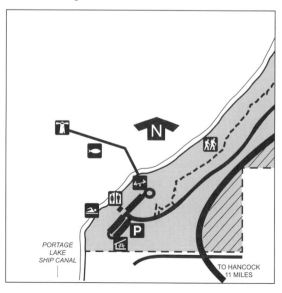

PORTAGE LAKE SHIP CANAL

TO HANCOCK 11 MILES

at the park's natural resources and heritage, you can join a nature hike or an interpretive program led by park personnel.

The only other marked path in the 417-acre park is the Bear Lake Trail. The mile-plus loop begins across M-203 from the park entrance, cuts east through deep woods to follow a section of Bear Lake shoreline, crosses the highway, and returns along Lake Superior to the campground. This trail is open in the winter for cross-country skiing, and the entire park is popular with snowshoers.

McLain State Park's 103 modern campsites are heavily used throughout the summer, filling daily in July and August, so reservations are a must. The spacious, grass-covered lots spread out in three loops that border the Lake Superior shoreline. The water is only steps away from any lot, and every evening campers congregate along the low dunes and bluffs to watch the sun set over Lake Superior. Numbered among the campsites are six mini-cabins that sleep four on bunks with mattresses. The cabins are equipped with electric lights, heaters, a hot plate, table and

chairs, and a picnic table and fire circle outside. Pets are not allowed, and reservations should be made in advance. The park's rustic cabin sits off by itself on the western end of the campground.

Hunting is allowed in the park, with deer, bear, rabbit, squirrel, and ruffed grouse the most sought after game.

The park makes an excellent base for exploring the uniquely beautiful Keweenaw Peninsula, the Houghton-Hancock area, and the Keweenaw National Historical Park.

County: Houghton
Camping Sites: 103 modern sites including 6 mini-cabins plus one rustic cabin.
Schedule: The park is open all year, but the restroom buildings are closed from mid October to mid May.
Directions: Drive 8 miles north of Hancock on M-203.
Further Information: McLain State Park, 18350 Highway M-203, Hancock, MI 49930; 906-482-0278.

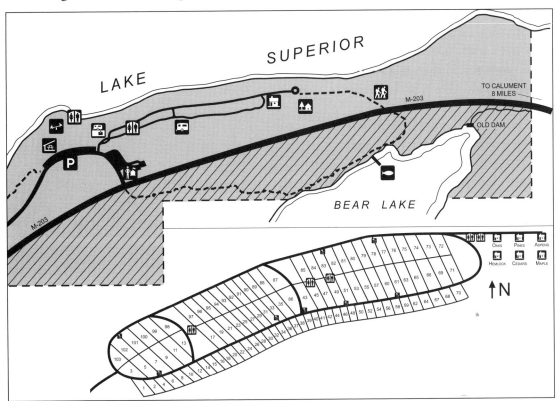

Keweenaw
National Historical Park

OVERNIGHT ACCOMMODATIONS: NONE

ACTIVITIES:

The site of one of America's first mining rushes has been designated as Michigan's newest national park. In the 1840s the Keweenaw Peninsula's rich copper-bearing rock drew thousands of miners, prospectors, con artists, dance hall girls, soldiers, and even the likes of Horace Greeley (of "Go west, young man" fame) to this rock-bound finger of land jutting into the icy waters of Lake Superior. Most who came here never got rich, but many ended up clawing a living out of the world's richest copper deposits. Eventually, more than 400 mines honeycombed the peninsula, and by 1920 Calumet, the queen of the copper towns, supported a population of 30,000.

By the end of World War I, however, all the petals on the copper rose had fallen and the area's mines closed one by one. Today, only 7,000 people call Calumet home, and the Keweenaw economy has limped along mining the tourist trade.

The potential for increased tourism got an immense boost on October 27, 1992, when the Keweenaw National Historical Park was established "to commemorate the heritage of copper mining on the Keweenaw Peninsula – its mines, its machinery, and its people." Historic buildings will be preserved, and museums and exhibits will help tell the dramatic and colorful history of the area.

Fittingly, the entire village of Calumet will be included in one of the park's two units. The boundaries of the second unit will encompass the Quincy Mine, near Houghton-Hancock. Development will not begin soon however. It will be several years, at best, before extensive visitor services operated by the National Park Service are built.

You don't have to wait to sample the unique atmosphere and history of the area. Many of the historical attractions slated for inclusion in the park are currently either governmentally or privately owned and are open to the public. Better yet, some of the most striking attractions are the small villages and towns of the Keweenaw Peninsula that are, in themselves, living museums of the copper area.

Calumet's downtown business district is already a virtual time capsule holding the glory of the old boomtown. Red brick and sandstone buildings line main street and wow visitors with their ornate cornices, bays, terra-cotta reliefs, and stone trim. The jewel of the city is the Calumet Theater, built in 1900 and now listed as a National Historic Monument. Counter-pointing the historic business district of Calumet is the residential district of Laurium, just a few miles east. Think of Laurium as Calumet's Grosse Point. It was here that the men who made small fortunes from the mines built grand Victorian homes in which to relax after a hard day at the bank or mine office. Many of the magnificent old homes have been beautifully restored, and a walk through the area takes you back to the turn of the 20th century. Detailed brochures of walking tours for both areas are available.

Another leading attraction is the Quincy Mine, which has been designated a National Historic Landmark District. Perched on a high hill overlooking Houghton-Hancock, the mine boasts the world's largest steam hoist, which during boom times raised 10 tons of copper at a time from depths of 9,000 feet. During guided tours you can stand next to the huge machine, but the high point of the visit is actually the low point – when you're taken down into the mine to experience, first-hand, the world of a Keweenaw copper miner. Farther to the north on the Keweenaw Peninsula, you can also take an underground tour of the Delaware Copper Mine, one of the oldest copper mines on the peninsula.

Other historical attractions in the area include several fascinating museums and the community of Old Victoria, which preserves small, log homes that housed miners. Numerous ghost towns and abandoned mines haunt the peninsula.

The Keweenaw Tourism Council, on the corner of US-41 and M-26, has a wealth of guides and pamphlets directing you to and explaining all the attractions. You can also pick up most of the same literature in virtually any business in Calumet or by mail from the addresses below.

COUNTY: KEWEENAW

CAMPING SITES: NONE

FEES: THE NATIONAL HISTORICAL PARK FACILITIES ARE FREE BUT MANY OF THE COMMUNITY HISTORICAL SITES ASSOCIATED WITH THE PARK HAVE VARYING ENTRANCE FEES.

DIRECTIONS: BEGIN BY WRITING OR PHONING AHEAD OR PICKING UP GUIDES IN CALUMET.

FURTHER INFORMATION: KEWEENAW TOURISM COUNCIL, P.O. BOX 336, HOUGHTON, MI 49931; 906-337-4579 AND KEWEENAW NATIONAL HISTORICAL PARK, 25970 RED JACKET ROAD, CALUMET, MI 49913; 906-337-3168.

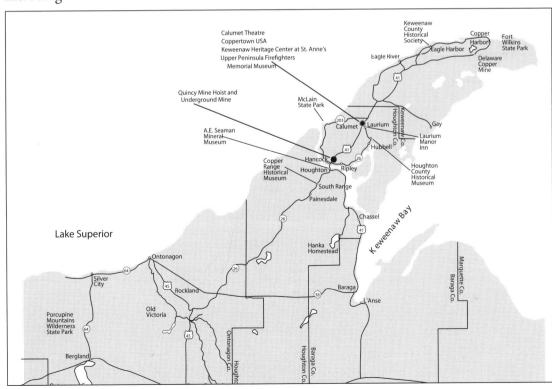

Fort Wilkins

Historic State Park

96

OVERNIGHT ACCOMMODATIONS:

ACTIVITIES:

Dark, mysterious Lake Fanny Hooe; rugged, rock-bound Lake Superior coast; a picturesque, historic lighthouse; and a superbly restored 160-year-old fort make Michigan's northernmost state park easy to enjoy and hard to forget.

The long, narrow park is squeezed between Lake Superior and Lake Fanny Hooe just a mile east of Copper Harbor, near the tip of the Keweenaw Peninsula. The Lake Superior coastline here is as scenic as any stretch of shoreline in the state. Looking north, a string of islands and a peninsula tipped by an antique lighthouse mark the boundary between deep-blue Copper Harbor and the open waters of the Great Lake. Huge rock slabs and boulders litter the harbor shore, and here and there stunted evergreens cling for life to fissures in the stone. Back from the edge of the exposed bedrock, mature pines carpet the ground with their needles and permeate the air with their thick scent.

Just a few hundred yards inland the pines, now mixed with cedars, spread to the dark, still waters of Lake Fanny Hooe. The trees ring the lake, growing right to the water's edge and even lean precariously out over it. Opposite the park, steep, tree-covered hills rise from the south shore. When summer fog shrouds the scene, as it often does, it's easy to feel like you're looking at a fjord half a world away.

Facing Lake Fanny Hooe from its north shore is the park's picturesque centerpiece – Fort Wilkins. Built at the beginning of the

copper rush in 1844 to guard miners from the Indians, it ended up guarding the Indians from the miners and the miners from each other. When the Mexican War broke out two years later, the troops were sent south, and the fort did not hold a garrison again until after the Civil War, when it was only briefly occupied. Since it was only used a grand total of about five years, there were very few additions or alterations to its original construction. As a result, the complex is one of the few classic examples of the wood forts that sprouted up along the American frontier during the mid-1800s. Many of the buildings have been completely and meticulously restored, and costumed interpreters explain and act out what mid-19th century military and family life was like at this remote outpost.

Just east of the fort, picnic tables and playground equipment are scattered over the grass in a grove of stately, old pines. From this day-use area, you can catch glimpses of Lake Fanny Hooe through the trees, but there is no swimming beach here or elsewhere in the park.

The park's 160 modern camping sites are divided between two wings, one west across Fanny Hooe Creek from the fort and the

222

other just east of the day-use area. Both wings have seen major improvements in recent years. The most privacy and seclusion come from the west unit's lots, most of which are screened by brush and trees. Old campsites on the water have been eliminated, and the wing has been extended westward adding nine paved pull-through sites with 50-amp power and 12 back-in sites featuring 30 amp outlets. A new boat ramp has also been added to the west wing. The park's lone mini-cabin is found in this wing.

Sites at the east unit, the older of the two wings, also overlook the lake but from a low hill. Mature evergreens shelter the small, worn lots, but the trees don't create much privacy. The east unit boasts a new toilet building and newly paved roads and parking lots. Campers here are also closest to the park's gift shop that sells clothing, books, souvenirs, pop, and ice cream. All proceeds go to fund activities and special events in the park. Near the gift shop you can peer down into the open pits of an early copper mine.

Reservations are recommended during July and August, and all 160 lots are a short walk from the shore of both lakes as well as the main attraction. Twilight is an especially appealing time to wander through the fort, and campers pretty much have the proud, old buildings to themselves. Nights are always cool; daytime temperatures rarely exceed the 70s, and the campground is heavily shaded, so bring sweaters and jackets. Since bears frequently wander through the park, don't cook or keep food in your tent, if that's what you're camping in.

Exhibits inside several of the fort buildings list all of the area's wildlife as well as give some good instruction on the 700-acre park's natural setting and geography. To apply what you've learned, walk the two miles of park trails that cut through forest and follow the shores of both Lake Superior and Fanny Hooe. Wildflowers abound in the area, as do thimbleberries, blueberries, and square-twin bilberries, a remnant species in Michigan found only in this area. The Keweenaw Peninsula is well known to birdwatchers, who come during spring migrations to watch great numbers of birds of prey funnel up to its tip.

Bicyclists will find a 2-mile, hard-packed gravel trail running from the park to Copper Harbor and several other opportunities for mountain biking on the peninsula.

If you like to fish, you can get plenty of action, too. You can launch from the west

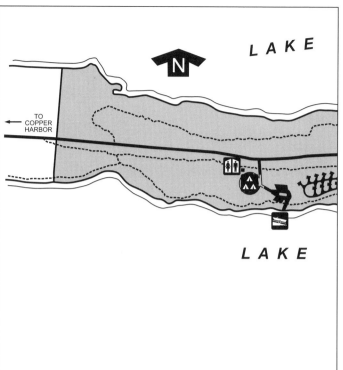

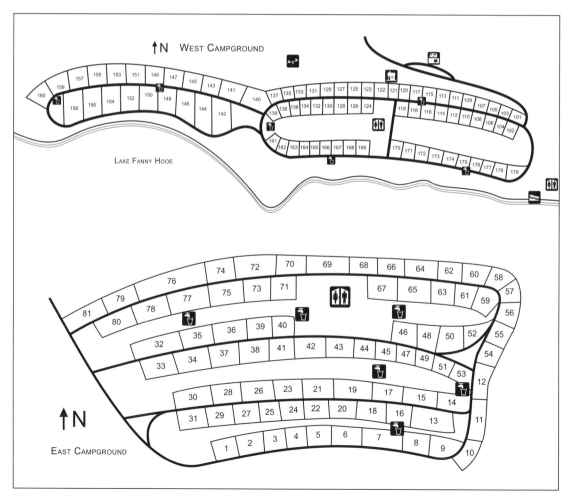

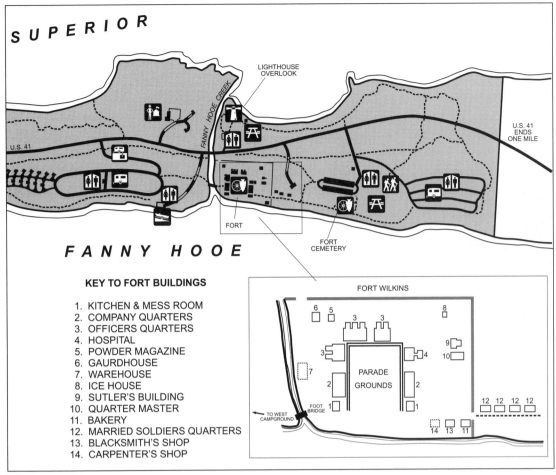

KEY TO FORT BUILDINGS

1. KITCHEN & MESS ROOM
2. COMPANY QUARTERS
3. OFFICERS QUARTERS
4. HOSPITAL
5. POWDER MAGAZINE
6. GAURDHOUSE
7. WAREHOUSE
8. ICE HOUSE
9. SUTLER'S BUILDING
10. QUARTER MASTER
11. BAKERY
12. MARRIED SOLDIERS QUARTERS
13. BLACKSMITH'S SHOP
14. CARPENTER'S SHOP

campground onto Lake Fanny Hooe and go after rainbow trout, smallmouth bass, perch, and walleye. From the Copper Harbor Marina you can float your boat on the big lake and drop lures for lake trout, splake, and coho.

At the state-owned and –operated marina, you can hop aboard a tour boat, which leaves several times a day in the summer, for a ride across the water to a small peninsula tipped by the Copper Harbor Lighthouse. A beacon has guided ships into the shelter of the harbor from the site, now park property, since 1848. The current structure, almost fully restored and filled with displays, replaced the original lighthouse during the 1860s.

During the winter, cross-country skiers can use four miles of trails in the park plus several more miles at nearby Copper Harbor Pathway.

Fort Wilkins State Park makes an excellent base from which to explore the Keweenaw Peninsula's abandoned copper mines, ghost towns, waterfalls, beautiful coastline, and small, quaint villages. Not to be missed and only a couple of miles from the park are Estivant Pines, a stand of virgin white pine, and Brockway Mountain Drive, the highest above-sea-level road between the Alleghenies and the Rockies.

County: Keweenaw

Camping Sites: 160, all modern plus 1 mini-cabin.

Schedule: The park is open mid-May to mid-October. The fort buildings are open daily from 8 a.m. to dusk.

Directions: Go one mile west of Copper Harbor on US-41.

Further Information: Fort Wilkins Historic State Park, P.O. Box 71, Copper Harbor, MI 49918; 906-289-4215.

Porcupine Mountains

WILDERNESS STATE PARK

OVERNIGHT ACCOMMODATIONS:

ACTIVITIES:

Peace and solitude are not only just about guaranteed in Michigan's largest state park, they're almost hard to avoid. Its 60,000 acres of untamed rivers, spectacular waterfalls, crystal-clear lakes, miles of rugged Lake Superior coastline, ancient mountains, and the Midwest's largest virgin hemlock/northern hardwood forest seem to swallow up anyone who ventures from the few developed areas.

Since there's so much to see, begin your trip to the Porkies at the visitor center, near the junction of South Boundary Road and M-107. A multi-media show, exhibits, and displays tell the story of the Porcupine Mountains, you can pick up the latest maps, and there is always a park ranger on duty to answer questions. A variety of interpretive programs and activities are offered here throughout the year.

Then, set out to see the Porkies the one best and basic way – on foot. Easy walks to breathtaking scenery, rugged multi-day backpacks deep into one of the last large wilderness areas in the Midwest, and just about every kind of hiking experience in between are all available along the 90 miles of trails that network Michigan's premier state park.

A short, paved path from a parking lot at the end of M-107, for instance, gently rises to the rim of a vertical cliff and the park's easiest-to-reach, most-famous attraction: a bird's-eye view of Lake of the Clouds. From the overlook you can take a strenuous one-hour hike down a steep trail to the lake and back up. Or, you can just stay atop your perch near the park's center and enjoy the

views of white clouds mirrored on the glassy, blue water and the miles of pristine wilderness that stretch out from it. It's tempting to imagine it was the view from here that inspired early Indians to give the area its name. In fact, it was the birch-bark canoeist's view of the high, thickly forested hills from Union Bay that reminded then of crouching porcupines.

The Summit Peak Tower Trail, accessible from the South Boundary Road, may soon rival Lake of the Clouds in popularity. From the parking lot, a half-mile route rises to Summit Peak, at 1,958 feet, the highest point in the park. Crowning the peak is a 40-foot-tall observation tower. The gasps from those who climb the tower are not only the result of slogging up the trail and climbing the structure but also from the stunning view that encompasses the park and distant views of Wisconsin, Minnesota, and the Apostle Islands. A memorable view of the Little Carp River Valley comes from a deck on the trail to the summit.

At the east end of the park, the Union Mine Trail meanders through second-growth pine/hardwood forest and alongside the Little Union River on its way to the ruins of the area's first copper mine, dug in 1845. Access to the one-mile path comes two miles south of M-107 on South Boundary Road.

At the opposite end of the park is one of the most memorable one-mile stretches of river anywhere in the Midwest. During its final rush to join Lake Superior, the Presque Isle River drops 125 feet through a gorge in a roar of rapids and three stunning waterfalls. You can get good views from a boardwalk and trail that lead upstream from the river-mouth picnic area.

The elaborate network of interconnecting longer trails that lace Porcupine Mountains makes it the finest hiking and backpacking state park in Michigan. You can step into the wilderness from any of several access points and hike the rugged, wild interior for several days without retracing your steps. Before heading into the backcountry, however, you must register at the visitor center. You can also pick up a detailed map there, which is absolutely essential to finding your way through the miles and multitude of footpaths. Most trails are rugged, with many unbridged stream crossings and very little level walking. When you carry a fully loaded backpack, figure on covering about a mile an hour.

You can backcountry camp anywhere in the park except within a quarter mile of roads, designated scenic campsites, shelters or cabins. Several small campsites are scattered throughout the backcountry. A few, usually those near trail intersections, are furnished with dry tent pads, campfire rings, and pit toilets. Others are slated to be equipped with "bear poles" and simple box-style toilets. The rustic camping areas are available on a first-come, first-served basis. This is black-bear country, so hang all food and scented items, such as toothpaste and deodorant, at least 10 feet off the ground, 150 feet from any campsite.

The ultimate in rustic living comes at 19 one-room cabins set amid some of the park's most secluded, scenic beauty. Each is furnished with a cupboard, table, benches, wash basin, pots and pans, tableware, coffee pot, broom, mop and bucket, an axe, saw, and two to eight bunks with mattresses. Outside are pit toilets and downed wood, which you can pick up and cut to size if you want a fire in the stove. Anything else you consider essential you have to haul in on your back from one to four miles. The unique accommodations are very popular, so if you want to give pioneer living a whirl, make reservations with the park well in advance.

Still rustic, but a little closer to civilization are three designated camping areas strung out along the South Boundary Road and the Presque Isle Campground on the west end of the park. The latter overlooks Lake Superior from a high bluff and has 50 sites spread over a grassy clearing. Trees shade most of the lots, but they also obstruct views of the lake. The Presque Isle River and its beautiful waterfalls are just a short walk away. The campground features pit toilets and hand pumps for water. You can often find a vacancy, even on summer weekends.

The modern Union Bay Campground lies on the park's eastern edge and is conveniently close to grocery stores, the visitors center, Lake of the Clouds, and numerous trailheads. One hundred large sites are laid out on an open grassy shelf overlooking Lake Superior. Views of great slabs of bedrock that line the shore, plus the vast expanse of the greatest of the Great Lakes come from almost every lot. Campers here have access to electrical hookups and modern restrooms with showers. The campground fills almost every night from July through mid-August so reservations are a must. Both Union Bay and Presque Isle Campground sites are reservable by phone or online. Campers can register for a site in one of the three primitive campgrounds along the South Boundary Road at the visitor center or Union Bay Campground.

Nights can be cool with an offshore breeze, so bring a jacket and long pants. In late May and early June, you may want to bring a "bug-net" hat and carry a supply of industrial-strength insect repellent. There are often enough black flies to carry off a small dog.

Since there is a steady offshore breeze, the flies probably won't interrupt your lunch at any of several picnic areas scattered throughout the park, but the views might. You can't go wrong hauling coolers to the tables right at the edge of Union Bay near the campground or alongside the Presque Isle River on the west side. And the panoramas from two small areas on M-107 just before you reach the Lake of the Clouds overlook are just about guaranteed to make you miss your mouth with your sandwich. From tables there, you look down upon a green blanket of treetops that rolls away to the shoreline, sometimes a half-mile distant, where water then spreads to merge with the sky.

Not surprisingly, this vast, undeveloped tract shelters a long list of wildlife. Coyotes have been sighted within a 100 yards of the visitors center, and you can practically wear out your binoculars and the pages of your bird books here – 194 species have been spotted in the park. Additionally, wildflowers, including several species found in few other areas in the Midwest, carpet the forest floor.

Most of the park's vast acreage is open to

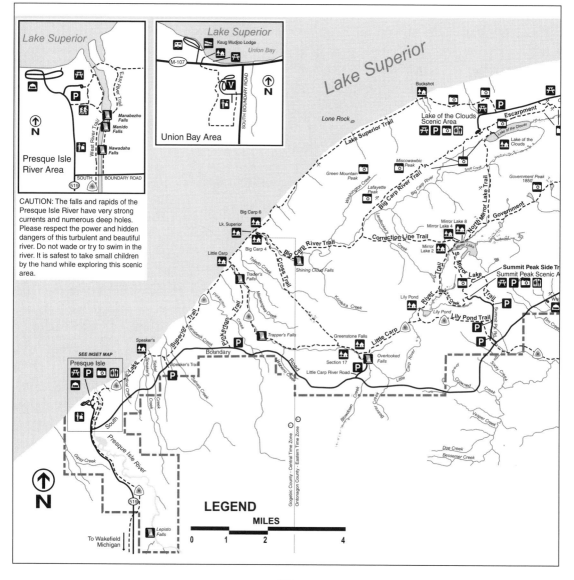

hunters in season. Bear is near the top of the list of popular game, and during the past few years, bird hunting has also been good, particularly for ruffed grouse. Every deer-hunting season, the trailside cabins are in such demand that reservations are often filled up to two years in advance on a first-come, first-served basis.

The same is true during the first week of brook-trout season, when fly fishermen go after "brookies" in the park's several inland streams, some only yards from the cabins. Fishermen with boats launch them down a ramp near Union Bay Campground and then troll for lake trout in the bay and surrounding Superior waters. Park rangers report, "a notable steelhead run in spring and salmon runs in the fall."

Swimmers who can suck up the courage can stick a toe in the decidedly chilly waters of Union Bay and wish they had a wet suit like the wind surfers ripping across the water. Miles of mountain bike trails honeycomb the eastern end of the park and lead to several backcountry cabins. Many of the trails boast challenging changes in elevation. Metal detectors can be operated in some areas of the park.

When the snow flies, Porcupine Mountains is transformed into a major winter recreation area that includes the largest ski complex in any Michigan state park. A triple chairlift, a double chairlift, a T-bar, and a handle-tow transport downhill skiers to 11 miles of Alpine trails that drop 641 vertical feet.

Cross-country skiers can also ride to the top then head off on 42 kilometers of power-tilled, double-track-set trails. Snowmobilers can make tracks on their own 25 miles of trails, which interconnect with hundreds of miles of other trails throughout the Upper Peninsula.

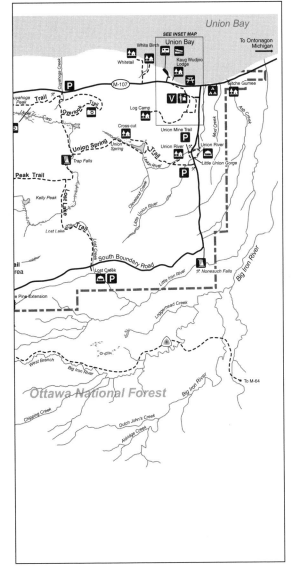

COUNTY: ONTONAGON

CAMPING SITES: 150 (100 MODERN, 50 RUSTIC) AND 3 YURTS.

NINETEEN TRAILSIDE CABINS ARE AVAILABLE FOR RENT FROM APRIL 1 THROUGH NOVEMBER 30, PLUS THREE OF THEM ARE OPEN ALL YEAR. RESERVATIONS ARE ACCEPTED ON A CALENDAR-YEAR-PLUS ONE BASIS.

SCHEDULE: THE PARK IS OPEN YEAR ROUND, BUT THE CAMPGROUNDS ARE CLOSED FROM DECEMBER 1 THROUGH APRIL 30.

DIRECTIONS: DRIVE 17 MILES WEST OF ONTONAGON ON M-107.

FURTHER INFORMATION: PORCUPINE MOUNTAINS WILDERNESS STATE PARK, 33303 HEADQUARTERS ROAD, ONTONAGON, MI 49953; 906-885-5275.

Lake Gogebic State Park

98

OVERNIGHT ACCOMMODATIONS:

ACTIVITIES:

Great walleye fishing, swimming, a fine campground, and 361 beautiful acres with frontage on the western shore of the Upper Peninsula's largest lake are the draws at Lake Gogebic State Park. You won't have much company either. If, by UP standards, the park is busy from July 1 to August 15, only 50,000-plus campers and day-use visitors go out of their way to come here each year.

The park's focal point is long, narrow and shallow Lake Gogebic, which spreads out in front of the developed facilities like a giant front porch. The campground and day-use area are strung along a thin strip of land squeezed between the lake and M-64. One hundred twenty-seven spacious, grass-covered, fairly shaded campsites are arranged in several rows paralleling the lake. Almost a fourth of the lots directly front the shore, but you're within sight of and a short walk to the lake from any campsite. Twenty-two of the lots (the entire row farthest from the lake) have no electrical hookups, but all campers have access to modern restrooms with showers. The campground has three pull-through sites. As you would expect from the park's annual attendance figures, camping sites are almost always available.

On the south end of the developed area is a boat-launch ramp that is heavily used by walleye fishermen. Daily limits are the rule rather than the exception here. Bass, perch, and northern pike are also hooked, but it's the walleyes that bring fishermen back year after year. Rental boats are available at nearby private liveries.

North of the boat ramp, a sandy swimming beach lines a small cove. Lake Gogebic's shallow water (maximum depth 37 feet) warms by early summer, so swimming is excellent. A picnic shelter, with change courts and restrooms, a large playground area back from the beach, and nearby, state-owned trees shade and shelter a large, grass-covered picnic area that overlooks the lake.

A two-mile-long nature trail begins at the day-use parking lot (or at the north end of the campground), crosses M-64, and then circles through the wild undisturbed back-country that makes up the vast majority of park land.

Cross-country skiers set tracks on the trail during the winter. You can't snowmobile within the park boundaries, but hundreds of miles of trails crisscross the vast wilderness areas surrounding the park.

Hunting is not allowed in the park, but adjacent parcels of the Ottawa State Forest yield deer, partridge, rabbit, and bear. Metal detectors may be used in certain areas of the park.

COUNTY: GOGEBIC

CAMPING SITES: 127 (105 MODERN, 22 LACK ELECTRICAL HOOKUPS).

SCHEDULE: THE PARK AND CAMPGROUND ARE OPEN MAY 1 THROUGH OCTOBER 30, BUT THE MODERN RESTROOMS ARE ONLY OPEN FROM MAY TO THE SECOND WEEK OF OCTOBER.

DIRECTIONS: GO 10 MILES NORTH ON M-64 FROM THE INTERSECTION OF US-2, OR DRIVE 8 MILES SOUTH ON M-64 FROM THE INTERSECTION OF M-28.

FURTHER INFORMATION: LAKE GOGEBIC STATE PARK, N 9995 STATE HIGHWAY M-64, MARENISCO, MI 49947; 906-842-3341.

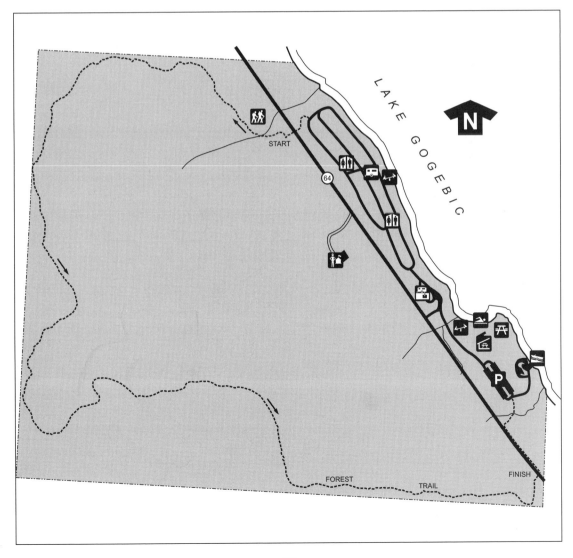

 # Agate Falls

SCENIC SITE

OVERNIGHT ACCOMMODATIONS: NONE

ACTIVITIES:

At Agate Falls Scenic Site the middle branch of the Ontonagon River cascades 40 feet down a series of staggered, sandstone benches producing a waterfall that, at times, looks like a glistening, multi-tiered layer cake. Long considered one of the most picturesque waterfalls in the Upper Peninsula, it is now one of the state's newest scenic sites.

The new designation includes an updated, handicapped accessible foot trail to the falls and picnic tables, toilets, and water at the parking lot on M-28.

COUNTY: ONTONAGON
CAMPING SITES: NONE
DIRECTIONS: ON M-28 FOUR MILES WEST OF TROUT CREEK.
FURTHER INFORMATION: AGATE FALLS SCENIC SITE, c/o BARAGA STATE PARK, 1300 US-41 SOUTH, BARAGA, MI 49908; 906-353-6558.

Bond Falls
Scenic Site

OVERNIGHT ACCOMMODATIONS: NONE

ACTIVITIES:

Bond Falls, on the middle branch of the Ontonagon River, takes a 50-foot tumble over a series of irregular steps and ledges that whips the water into a frothy confection that sometimes almost passes for meringue. The beautiful and dramatic watery drop has drawn waterfall aficionados for decades and is one of the most recent additions to the state park system.

Roadside parking and a picnic area lie adjacent to the top of the falls. Visitors will find a handicapped accessible boardwalk that leads to a variety of memorable overlooks.

COUNTY: ONTONAGON
CAMPING SITES: NONE
DIRECTIONS: FROM US-45 NORTH IN SPAULDING TURN EAST ON TO BOND FALLS ROAD AND DRIVE 4 MILES TO THE PARKING AREA.
FURTHER INFORMATION: BOND FALLS SCENIC SITE, c/o BARAGA STATE PARK, 1300 US-41 SOUTH, BARAGA, MI 49908; 906-353-6558.

OVERNIGHT ACCOMMODATIONS:

ACTIVITIES:

If you're looking for trendy tourist shops, chain restaurants, and the usual northern Michigan tourist attractions, you won't want anything to do with Bewabic State Park. If, however, you like the feeling of camping, swimming, and fishing in the middle of nowhere, it's worth the drive, a long drive, from anywhere south of Big Mac. All that interrupts the unspoiled scenery for hundreds of miles in just about any direction is an occasional turn-of-the-century mining town. The surrounding sharply rising hills and thousands of acres of dense forest seem more appropriate to West Virginia than western Michigan.

Yet almost surrealistically plunked down in the middle of the park are two tennis courts. Bewabic, about as remote from any population center as you can get, is the only state park in Michigan where you can play tennis.

Carved out of the dense forest that covers most of the park's 315 hilly acres is a modern campground with 135 sites widely dispersed over three large loops. Stands of trees and heavy undergrowth surround and separate most lots to the point you feel like you're camping alone in the vast northern forest. Only lots 120-137, in an open, nearly treeless meadow, and a few other scattered sites get full sun. Recent improvements include several pull-through sites and 50-amp service. There are four semi-modern walk-in campsites on the southern edge of the campground. You can usually find a vacant site any day of the week.

Just a few minutes' walk from the campground's northern loop lies the park's day-use area where towering pines and hardwoods canopy a large, grassy knoll doted with picnic tables and grills. A large picnic pavilion, the tennis courts, and a bathhouse overlook a small strip of sandy beach that takes up just a tiny fraction of the park's forest-fringed shoreline along the first in a string of four interconnected lakes imaginatively named Fortune 1, 2, 3, and 4.

For some scenic views of the lake and park, walk a little north of the beach and cross a footbridge to a short trail that circles a small, tree-clad island. Another path cuts a two-mile arc through the park's undeveloped southern section and briefly touches Fortune 1's shore. Benches are scattered along the route, which is open in the winter to cross-country skiers although the park is officially closed.

Canoeists put in at the park and paddle south on day trips through the beautiful, relatively undisturbed chain of lakes. Fishermen, who launch at the park's ramp, go after walleyes, perch, northern pike, and bass. Rental boats are available at a nearby livery. The use of metal detectors is allowed in cer-

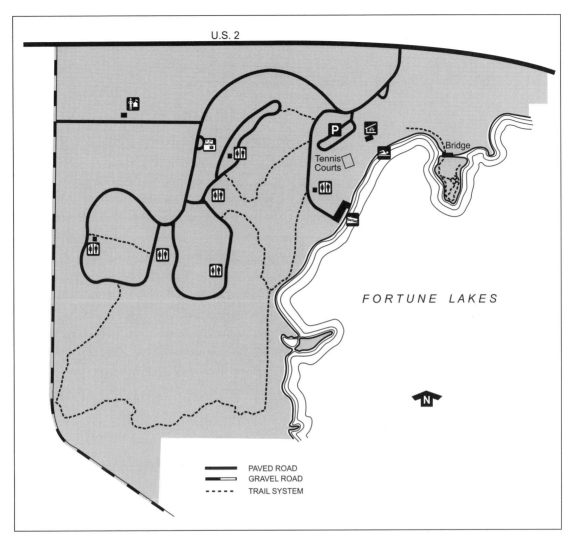

U.S. 2

Tennis
Courts

Bridge

FORTUNE LAKES

N

PAVED ROAD
GRAVEL ROAD
TRAIL SYSTEM

tain areas of the park. The area holds numerous waterfalls waiting to be explored as well as local museums that reveal the region's unique mining and lumbering history.

COUNTY: IRON
CAMPING SITES: 135, ALL MODERN.
SCHEDULE: THE PARK AND CAMPGROUND ARE OPEN APRIL 15 TO NOVEMBER 30, BUT THE MODERN RESTROOMS IN THE CAMPGROUND ARE ONLY OPEN MAY 15 TO OCTOBER 15.
DIRECTIONS: FOUR MILES WEST OF CRYSTAL FALLS ON US-2.
FURTHER INFORMATION: BEWABIC STATE PARK, 720 IDLEWILD ROAD, CRYSTAL FALLS, MI 49920; 906-875-3324.

J W *Wells* STATE PARK

102

OVERNIGHT ACCOMMODATIONS:

ACTIVITIES:

At J.W. Wells State Park, natural beauty comes at almost every turn. Like a long, green ribbon, quiet forest – carpeted with ferns and wildflowers – covers the park's developed area, a narrow 3-mile-long strip between M-35 and Green Bay. East across the blue water, Wisconsin's Door Peninsula and Washington Island smudge the distant horizon. Inland, across the highway, not even a trail penetrates a deer-filled, undeveloped tract of old-growth pine, maple, beech, cedar, spruce, and elm.

Three marked trails, ranging from 1.1 to 3 miles long, trace the shoreline, wind through peaceful woods, and probe the remote corners of the developed parcel. In winter, cross-country skiers ply the ungroomed trails. Three roofed trailside shelters are used more by skiers than hikers.

Skiers also make good winter use of the five rental cabins, which line the shore only yards from the bay at the north end of the park. The one-room cabins, located at the end of a gravel road that tunnels through dense woods, are secluded and rustic. Bunk beds, a propane stove for heat, and a table and chairs are the only standard furnishings. Pit toilets and drinking water are within a hundred-yard walk. You have to supply any other amenities.

Also hugging the rocky shore, but far removed from the cabins, is the park's 150-site modern campground. All lots are large, level, grassy, and open with some shade. Many of the lots directly edge the bay, and you get good looks at the water from most of the other sites. Six of the sites are handicapped accessible. You can usually find an empty

spot, except on summer weekends, if you arrive early in the day.

The park's large, sandy, swimming beach dips into the bay just south of the campground. A bathhouse overlooks the sand and water, and there's playground equipment for young children. Farther down shore, picnic tables and grills dot a grassy area under a dense canopy of stately, old hardwoods. A picnic shelter there, like the campground and most of the other park facilities, was built in the '30s and '40s by Civilian Conservation Corps workers.

Smallmouth bass fishing in the Cedar River is good all year, and just after ice-out, usually in early April, action for brown trout along the bay shore is as good as it gets anywhere in Michigan. Park rangers say that salmon, pike, perch, and walleyes are also caught in area waters. You can't launch from the park, but a ramp is available in Cedar River, less than a mile north.

Hunting is not allowed in the park, but the bordering Escanaba River State Forest is some of the finest deer-hunting country in the state. Sportsmen who go after grouse,

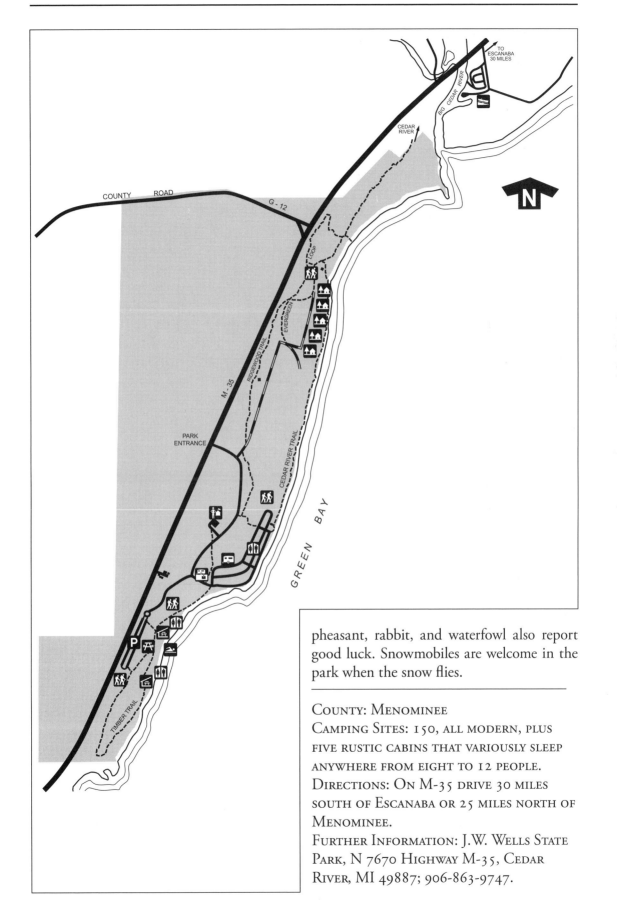

pheasant, rabbit, and waterfowl also report good luck. Snowmobiles are welcome in the park when the snow flies.

COUNTY: MENOMINEE

CAMPING SITES: 150, ALL MODERN, PLUS FIVE RUSTIC CABINS THAT VARIOUSLY SLEEP ANYWHERE FROM EIGHT TO 12 PEOPLE.

DIRECTIONS: ON M-35 DRIVE 30 MILES SOUTH OF ESCANABA OR 25 MILES NORTH OF MENOMINEE.

FURTHER INFORMATION: J.W. WELLS STATE PARK, N 7670 HIGHWAY M-35, CEDAR RIVER, MI 49887; 906-863-9747.

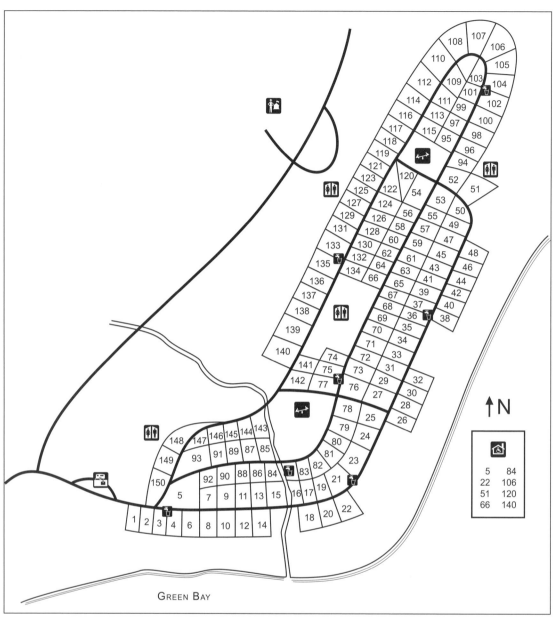

GREEN BAY

↑N

🏠	
5	84
22	106
51	120
66	140

ayette
HISTORIC STATE PARK

103

OVERNIGHT ACCOMMODATIONS:

ACTIVITIES:

Fayette's natural scenery rivals that found in almost any other Michigan state park. Part of its mile-plus of Garden Peninsula shoreline is made up of 90-foot-high limestone cliffs that wrap around one of Michigan's most photographic harbors. A magnificent white-sand swimming beach also lines the waters of Big Bay de Noc, and deep, lush hardwood forests cover nearly 700 inland acres.

But what draws most visitors to the park is the haunting beauty of its centerpiece – the almost-totally intact, carefully restored company town of Fayette. The village spreads over the fishhook-shaped finger of land that curls out into Big Bay de Noc to form Snail Shell Harbor. Perpendicular, white limestone walls, thick, green trees, the partially restored stacks of 100-year-old blast furnaces, and dozens of old, gray buildings almost totally enclose the small harbor's clear, blue water.

The setting, the scene, is near perfect. Fayette, without a doubt, is the most picturesque village, deserted or inhabited, in Michigan.

Fayette began life in the 1860s with only one purpose: to process Upper Peninsula ore into pig iron for the Jackson Iron Company. The plentiful hardwood forests in the area yielded all the charcoal needed, and the outcroppings that overlooked the company town provided the other essential ingredient, lime. At its peak during the 1880s, the bustling industrial village was home and workplace to nearly 500 people. Just 20 years later, new smelting processes in the East rendered Fayette's blast furnaces obsolete, and the entire town picked up and left. The shells of the

wood buildings and huge stone blast-furnace complex stood a lonely vigil over the picturesque harbor then began crumbling into ruin until 1959 when the spot was resurrected as a state park.

More than 20 of the original buildings – including the town hall, hotel, doctor's office, superintendent's home, and company office – today stand as they did over 100 years ago. Some have been fully restored and furnished to look exactly as they might have in the 1880s. Others serve as museums that illustrate daily life in the village as well as the history and industrial development of the town. Self-guided tour maps of the village are available at the visitor's center, and guided tours run regularly during the summer.

The museum village alone is definitely worth a day trip, but you should also consider staying at the park's campground and enjoying the other fine facilities and attractions in this off-the-beaten track area away from crowds, traffic, and tourist traps. A half mile south of the townsite, 61 fair-sized, semimodern (electrical hookups but no modern restrooms) sites are nestled in a stand of

hardwoods several hundred feet back from the water. The tall trees are good for both shade and privacy, but they also completely screen any view of the bay. Overnighters only use the area moderately, and you can almost always find a vacancy during the week. Reservations are recommended for summer weekends. Boat camping is allowed in Snail Shell Harbor, but there are few spaces and they are allotted on a first-come, first-served basis.

The park's 2,000-foot-long white-sand beach, backed by low dunes, is just a quarter-mile walk (or a two-mile-plus round-about drive) down the shore from the campground. Facilities include a large picnic area, vault toilets, a water fountain, and a picnic shelter.

Fishermen can launch at a ramp between the campground and beach then drop bait into some of the best perch, smallmouth bass, pike, and walleye waters in the entire Great Lakes. Among the many local fishing hot spots is Snail Shell Harbor.

There is more than fishing action in the little harbor. Scuba diving is allowed during certain times of the day. A fee and use permit are required, and divers must leave all submerged artifacts in place.

Much of the park is open to hunters, who take squirrel, ruffed grouse, deer, and bear both in and around the park.

Some of the best opportunities for spectacular photographs come along more than five miles of well-marked hiking trails that loop through the 711-acre park. One trail edges the limestone cliffs above Big Bay de Noc before heading into the deep woods while others make extensive jaunts through the backcountry. Cross-country skiers can use the trails in winter, and the park is open to snowmobilers.

County: Delta
Camping Sites: 61, semi modern and a few overnight boat berths.
Schedule: The park is open May 15 to October 15. Village hours are Spring and fall, 9 a.m. to 5 p.m.; Summer 9 a.m. to 8 p.m.
Directions: Approximately 15 miles west of Manistique on US-2 turn south on M-183 and drive 17 miles.
Further Information: Fayette Historic State Park, 13700 13.25 Lane, Garden, MI 49835; 906-644-2603.

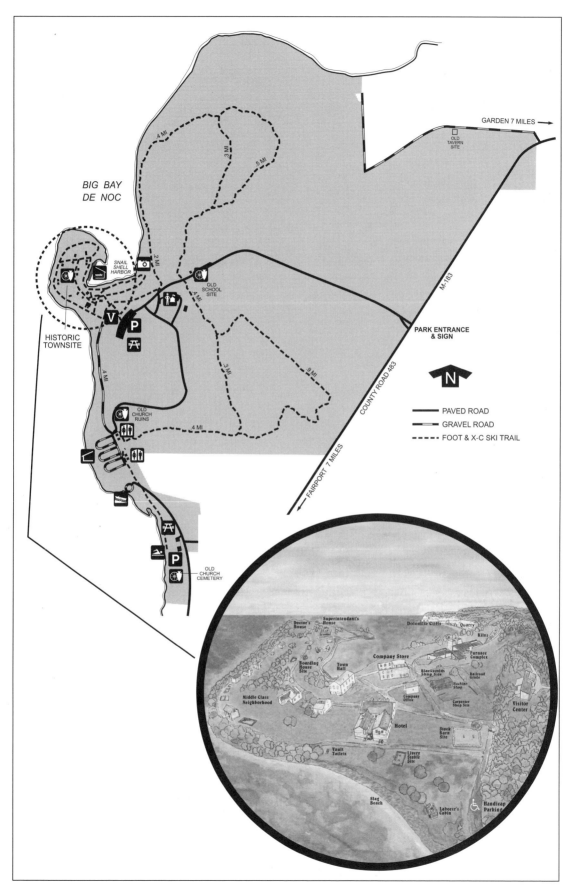

BIG BAY
DE NOC

GARDEN 7 MILES →

4 MI
3 MI
5 MI
2 MI

SNAIL
SHELL
HARBOR

OLD
SCHOOL
SITE

HISTORIC
TOWNSITE

V P

4 MI

3 MI

9 MI

OLD
CHURCH
RUINS

4 MI

M-183

PARK ENTRANCE
& SIGN

COUNTY ROAD 483

FAIRPORT 7 MILES ←

OLD TAVERN SITE

N

——— PAVED ROAD
=== GRAVEL ROAD
- - - FOOT & X-C SKI TRAIL

OLD
CHURCH
CEMETERY

Doctor's
House
Superintendant's
House
Dolomite Cliffs
Quarry
Kilns
Boarding
House Site
Town
Hall
Company Store
Furnace
Complex
Blacksmith
Shop Site
Railroad
Grade
Machine
Shop
Middle Class
Neighborhood
Company
Office
Carpenter
Shop Site
Visitor
Center
Hotel
Stock
Barn
Site
Vault
Toilets
Livery
Stable
Site
Slag
Beach
Laborer's
Cabin
Handicap
Parking

Palms Book
State Park

104

OVERNIGHT ACCOMMODATIONS: NONE

ACTIVITIES:

Sparkling like a precious jewel mounted in a Sherwood green setting of thick cedar and pine in Palms Book State Park is Kitch-iti-kipi, Indian for "big cold water" or "big spring." Kitch-iti-kipi is, in fact, the biggest freshwater spring in Michigan, and the deep, nearly round pool is one of the most unusual and strikingly beautiful sights in the state.

It isn't sheer size that impresses the visitor. Kitch-iti-kipi is definitely big – 200 feet across and 40 feet deep – for a spring, but even from its shore you can take it in with a single quick sweep of the eyes. What's so captivating is the almost unbelievable clarity of the water.

The best way to experience it is through a large viewing portal or over the side of a large raft that one (or more) of 30-40 passengers pull along a cable from shore to shore. The spring's old raft was recently replaced with a roofed model that improves viewing and is handicapped accessible. From the edges of the pond, submerged, mineral-encrusted fallen tree trunks seem to hang suspended in space, their tapered ends pointing to the magic taking place in the depths below. The bottom moves slowly by – colorful patterns of sand, moss, and algae are interrupted by several roiling inlets that pump in 10,000 gallons of water a minute. Even at the center, the deepest point, you get a near-perfect view down to the bubbling cauldron of gray-white sand 40 feet below. Slowly cruising in and out of the picture are large trout, magnified to look even larger by the water. The scene is one of few in Michigan where you become absorbed in, rather than overpowered by, the great natural beauty.

A 50-yard paved path connects the raft embarkation dock around the north edge of the spring to the parking lot. Facilities at the day-use-only park, all within a few yards of the parking area, include a small grassy, shaded picnic area, restrooms and a concession stand/gift shop.

COUNTY: SCHOOLCRAFT
CAMPING SITES: NONE
DIRECTIONS: FROM US-2 IN THOMPSON, ABOUT 5 MILES WEST OF MANISTIQUE, TURN NORTH ONTO M-149 AND FOLLOW IT 10 MILES TO THE PARK.
FURTHER INFORMATION: PALMS BOOK STATE PARK, C/O INDIAN LAKE STATE PARK, 8970 WEST COUNTY ROAD 442, MANISTIQUE, MI 49854; 906-341-2355

Indian Lake
State Park

105

OVERNIGHT ACCOMMODATIONS:

ACTIVITIES:

Two… no, actually three for one is what you get at Indian Lake. The popular park itself is composed of two distinctly different, widely separated units, both with frontage on the Upper Peninsula's fourth-largest lake. And while at either, you should make the very short trip to Palms Book State Park for a raft ride across Michigan's largest spring.

The 567 acres that make up Indian Lake's largest unit sprawl along and back from the lake's south shore. More than a mile of sandy beach fronts a large day-use area and a 145-site modern campground. You'll probably get tired of wading before you reach even waist-deep water, however, because the 4.5-mile-long, 3-mile-wide lake is an immense, shallow saucer. Ninety percent of the 8,000-plus acres is less than 15 feet deep, and its maximum depth is only 18 feet. When around water, children always need watching, but this lake ranks as one of the safest places in the state to turn small children loose for wading and playing along the shore.

In the eastern half of the unit, the grass-covered campground stretches along the shoreline in a long loop. All lots are generally roomy, and a tree or two on most provides some shade. Nearly forty of the lots are directly on the water, and the rest all have views of the lake and ready access to modern restrooms. Ten sites are designed for handicapped camping, and the campground boasts two mini-cabins.

West of the campground, picnic tables, grills, a couple of stately, old log-and-limestone pavilions, and a handicapped-acces-sible trail line the shore.

Pleasure boaters and fishermen all put in at a launch ramp, which marks the westernmost of the unit's developed facilities. Indian Lake is rated as one of the finest walleye holes in the state, but perch, pike, muskies, bass, and bluegills also provide plenty of action.

Two marked hiking trails loop through this south-shore unit. The longest, a mile circuit, follows the shore from the picnic area, cuts inland along a creek, then winds through dense forest to the entrance road. Another path, the Chippewa Trail, though only a few hundred feet long can take more than an hour to walk.

Numbered posts along the route, which loops from and to the day-use area's eastern-most parking lot, correspond to numbered paragraphs in a brochure, available at the trailhead. It's easy to get caught up in learning how early Indians used the variety of plants and trees that grow along the trail for medicine, food, and tools. Park rangers also conduct natural history and interpretive programs throughout the summer.

Nearly three miles up the beach from the south-shore unit is the park's much smaller west-shore unit. That area features a small

243

picnic area, a playground, and a campground completely different in layout and atmosphere from the south unit. The 72 semi-modern sites are clustered in small cul-de-sacs at the ends of short roads that radiate out, like the spokes of a wheel. Thick woods shade all lots, and from any site you can see only a few other lots through dense foliage. Each site has electricity, but there are no modern restroom facilities, only vault toilets. It's a quarter- to half-mile walk from the sites to a campers-only beach that, while nice, doesn't rival the shoreline at the south unit. You can often find a vacancy at the west unit, but if you want to camp in the south unit, make reservations, as it usually fills first.

Hunting is allowed in the fall at the west-shore unit, with partridge and other small game the most pursued. In addition to Indian Lake, anglers will find good fishing in other nearby small lakes. Just a few miles away on Lake Michigan, especially at the mouths of Thompson Creek and Manistique River, fishermen pull good catches of coho and steelhead in season. Metal detectors may be used in some areas of the park.

Pictured Rocks, Seney National Wildlife Refuge, and Fayette Historic State Park on the beautiful Garden Peninsula are all within about an hour's drive from Indian Lake.

County: Schoolcraft

Camping Sites: 217 (145 modern including 2 mini-cabins and 72 semi-modern).

Schedule: The park and campgrounds are open all year but the modern restrooms are closed from mid-October to mid-April.

Directions: Go 5 miles west of Manistique on County Road 442.

Further Information: Indian Lake State Park, 8970 West County Road 442, Manistique, MI 49854; 906-341-2355.

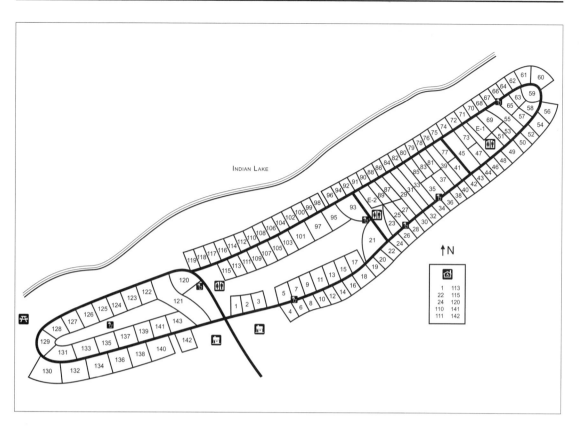

INDIAN LAKE

↑N

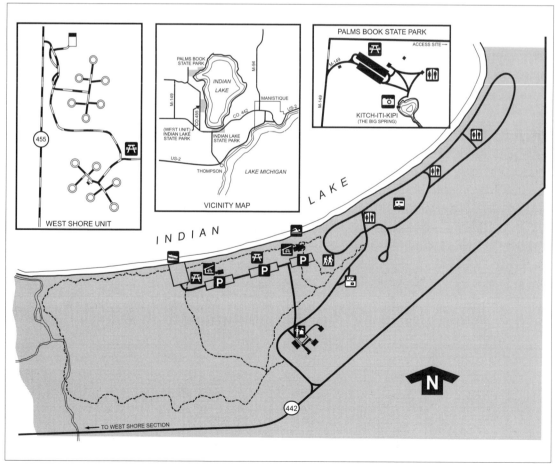

WEST SHORE UNIT

VICINITY MAP

PALMS BOOK STATE PARK

ACCESS SITE →

KITCH-ITI-KIPI
(THE BIG SPRING)

INDIAN LAKE

→ TO WEST SHORE SECTION

N

Isle Royale
NATIONAL PARK

106

OVERNIGHT ACCOMMODATIONS:

ACTIVITIES:

Isle Royale isn't a park. It's paradise. This remarkable 210-square-mile oasis, surrounded by the cold waters of Lake Superior, is uniquely wild and beautiful. The narrow, rocky inlets, sharp promontories and dozens of small offshore islands that form the coastline are more remindful of Maine than Michigan. Inland, 42 quiet lakes are etched into thick pine, spruce, and cedar forests pierced by long, rocky ridges. The sight and sounds of the island's wildlife, including the well-known moose and wolf populations, are a variety and mix like nowhere else in the world.

In addition, it's remote. The Michigan mainland is 56 miles away at its closest, and the only way in and out is by seaplane or boat. Even so, the park attendance averages roughly 18,000 visitors annually, and Isle Royale boasts one of the highest backcountry overnight stays per acre of any National Park. People come not only for the remoteness and spectacular beauty but also because no drive-through gawkers litter the place with fast-food containers and aluminum cans, no loud radios squawk, no human herds trample the trails into muddy goo, and you never have to shoulder your way through a pack of camcorder users and snapshot artists to get a glimpse of the scenery. Even at relatively developed Rock Harbor and the usually crowded backcountry campgrounds you can walk a few hundred yards from the boat dock, lodge, or campsite and enter as close to a primeval forest as you will find in Michigan and be lost to the sight and sound of civilization.

Few people come here on a whim. Experienced backpackers, canoeists, fishermen, and those who prefer the comforts of Rock Harbor's lodge complex almost all plan their Isle Royale trip in advance, sometimes years in advance. And they don't spend the time (average stay is 4 days), effort, and money it takes to get here for the opportunity just to see the staggering beauty. They come to be immersed in it.

The unique combination of geologic, ecologic, and environmental forces that have molded Isle Royale's character began eons ago when immense lava flows oozed over the region. During the following millenniums, the center of the huge lava plate settled into the earth creating a bowl that now holds Lake Superior. Today, pieces of the bowl's rim stick out of the water as the Keweenaw Peninsula and Isle Royale. The edge of this bowl is not smooth and polished. The distinct surface of Isle Royale, in fact, looks like someone stood parallel rows of gigantic rock slabs on end, then toppled them over like dominoes. The edges of those bedrock ridges are still wrinkled and cracked, but over the centuries, glaciers and erosion have deepened and rounded the valleys between.

Native Americans mined the island's cop-

versa is one of the longest running research projects of its kind in the world.

The moose and just about all other park wildlife share a striking characteristic: we humans don't intimidate them. They even appear to deliberately let us know that it's their island, not ours. Moose would just as soon walk through a campsite as around it, and if you meet one on a trail there is no question who will step aside for whom. The majestic but comical animals have even been known to peer into the lodge restaurant windows as if checking out what's for breakfast. Fox constantly prowl campsites waiting to dart in and nab some food, and around Rock Harbor Lodge they walk the paved paths, often passing within inches of incredulous visitors who have just stepped off the boat. Wolves are the only bashful animals and usually only make their presence known by isolated howls at night.

As a result of most animals' apparent tameness, visitors need to be reminded to neither feed nor crowd the wildlife. And never forget, advise park rangers, that the animals have the right-of-way.

There's plenty of action below the surface, too – of Isle Royale waters, that is. The island's many inland lakes and streams are only poor to average yielders of fish, but the waters of Lake Superior are another matter altogether. The rainbow trout and northern pike that move through the island's many Lake Superior inlets and harbors leave fishermen dreaming about a return visit and wetting a line on the big waters. Monster lake trout await offshore, and if you want to go after the "big lakers," you can hop aboard a fishing charter at Rock Harbor or bring your own craft over on the Ranger III. Due to overfishing and their popularity, brook trout have sharply declined in the past few years. In order to re-establish a viable population, a catch and release order is in effect for brook trout, and only artificial lures and barbless hooks can be used on all streams and Hidden Lake. A Michigan fish-

per long before Columbus sailed from Spain, and with the coming of Europeans to Lake Superior, trappers, miners, and fishermen soon worked the island. By the late 1800s a few families were staying here year-round. From the dawn of the 20th century until it became a national park in 1940, Isle Royale was an expensive and popular summer resort spot.

Isle Royale's most famous inhabitants, moose, arrived shortly after the start of the 20th century, probably by swimming from the Canadian mainland. In the near-ideal environment, their numbers rapidly increased to the point that the herd almost wiped out its food supply and itself during a period of mass starvation. When wolves arrived via an ice bridge from the mainland in the winter of 1948-49, they helped stabilize the herd's population. The subsequent study of how the wolves influence moose numbers and vice

ing license is required before dipping a line in Lake Superior, or transporting fish from the island to the mainland, but no license is needed on any of the park's inland lakes or streams.

There's an awful lot to see and do, and there are many ways to take it all in. The best is to settle a backpack on your shoulders, cinch up its waist strap and strike off on the 165-mile trail system. You can literally spend weeks on the trails, which range from a one-mile walk to the 45-mile-long Greenstone Ridge Trail, without ever crossing your own tracks. Most of the 36 campgrounds are conveniently spaced at about full-day walks along the routes. If you want to see a lot of the island without trudging every step of the way, you can become a commuter on either a water taxi or a small passenger ferry that regularly drops off and picks up hikers at stops around the island.

All of the trails are accessible from either of the park's two entry points – Windigo, on the island's west end, and Rock Harbor, on the east. All routes are beautiful, and all are rugged. Experienced backpackers say that they come here for the R & R – roots and rocks. Trails are literally laced with both kinds of toe-stubbers, and the only dead-level walking on the whole island comes on the sometimes-lengthy stretches of planks that cross marshy areas.

Don't take on Isle Royale without first-rate equipment that you've broken in, along with yourself, on training hikes on the mainland. Good sturdy hiking boots are a must, and you should carry rain gear, insect repellent, a first-aid kit, and a 0.4-micron water filter. Tapeworm eggs contaminate all surface water, so it must be boiled for at least two minutes or filtered before drinking.

Take your time to both enjoy the scenery and avoid becoming exhausted. An injured, sick, or sick-at-heart backpacker deep in the interior can be days away from help. Any time you do need a dose of civilization, you can come out of the woods at Rock Harbor. The campground there has showers, and at a nearby restaurant you can put something other than freeze-dried food between your bellybutton and backbone.

Camping areas at the heart of the island are usually just clearings in the forest, but many along the coastline are furnished with roofed, three-sided, 8- by 12-foot shelters. You can use them to get out of the elements and escape potentially murderous mosquitoes and black flies. Most of the 253 campsites have an occupancy limit of one to five days, and you must get a permit at one of the park's two entry points. Based on the park's growing popularity, it is almost a given that you will have to double up on camping sites from late June through late August. Bring a backpacker's stove (ground fires are prohibited at most areas), and plan to carry out everything you carried in, including garbage.

Both shelters and tent sites are limited to a maximum of 6 campers. There are a limited number of group campsites that can accommodate 7-10 people. Groups larger than 10 are not permitted.

Another great way to see the island – and it seems to be a well-kept secret – is by canoe or kayak. Paddlers, who rent canoes at Rock Harbor or bring their own on any of the ferryboats, are the ones who can reach campgrounds that are located on several small inland lakes. Portages that connect sheltered harbors and long, narrow inlets on opposite sides of the island via inland lakes make for an outstanding circle canoe tour of the northern half of the island. That expedition also includes the only intimate looks at the jumble of odd-shaped peninsulas, islands, and long, narrow bays that shape, like the pieces of an unfinished jigsaw puzzle, the exceptionally scenic northeast end.

Not everybody who comes to Isle Royale sleeps in a tent or shelter, or under the stars. Many stay at motel-like units that line the edge of Rock Harbor or, on the opposite side of the narrow peninsula, in cottages that overlook Tobin Harbor. All rooms at Rock Harbor are furnished with spectacular views of Lake Superior, and the one-room cottages on Tobin Harbor, while not in the lap of luxury, do come with bunk and roll-away beds, a kitchenette, and table. Backpackers who come out of the wilds join lodge and cottage residents at a sit-down restaurant that serves breakfast, lunch, and dinner, including their specialty, fresh-caught lake trout. You can also get hamburgers, ice cream, soft drinks, and other take-out foods at a concession area attached to the restaurant.

From Rock Harbor, you can set out on a number of half-day and day-long hikes. You can also rent canoes or small boats with motors and paddle or cruise for a few hours, an entire day, or even combine the craft with hikes for overnight excursions. The most popular boat trip is an organized twilight cruise aboard the 45-foot Sandy. The two-hour-plus group outing, guided by a park ranger, starts with a skip across Rock Harbor to Raspberry Island for a mile hike through a spruce bog, which is followed by a voyage around the northern tip of Isle Royale to watch the sun set over Lake Superior.

Other regularly scheduled, guided day trips combine lengthy cruises on the Sandy with brisk hikes to abandoned copper mines, old fisheries, and the Rock Harbor Lighthouse. Closer to the lodge, rangers conduct interpretive walks and nightly programs in an auditorium.

COUNTY: KEWEENAW
CAMPING SITES: 253, ALL PRIMITIVE. GROUPS OF 7-10 CAMPERS MUST MAKE ADVANCE RESERVATIONS BY CALLING 906-482-0984. ROCK HARBOR LODGE FEATURES BOTH ROOMS AND MODERN HOUSEKEEPING COTTAGES.
SCHEDULE: ISLE ROYALE IS OPEN APRIL 16 TO OCTOBER 31. FULL SERVICES — THAT IS, CONCESSIONS, LODGE, RESTAURANTS

AND WATER TAXI — ARE OFFERED MID-JUNE THROUGH LABOR DAY.
DIRECTIONS (FROM MICHIGAN DEPARTURE POINTS): THE 100-PASSENGER ISLE ROYALE QUEEN IV MAKES DAILY ROUND TRIPS IN AUGUST (3 HOURS ONE WAY) AND LESS-FREQUENT TRIPS THE REST OF THE SUMMER FROM COPPER HARBOR.
THE 165-FOOT GOVERNMENT OPERATED RANGER III CARRIES 128 PASSENGERS ON A 6-HOUR CROSSING. IT LEAVES HOUGHTON ON TUESDAYS AND FRIDAYS, OVERNIGHTS AT ROCK HARBOR AND RETURNS TO HOUGHTON THE FOLLOWING DAY.
A CHARTER SEAPLANE OUT OF HOUGHTON MAKES 30-MINUTE FLIGHTS TO THE ISLAND.
FURTHER INFORMATION: ISLE ROYALE NATIONAL PARK, 800 EAST LAKESHORE DRIVE, HOUGHTON, MI 49931; 906-482-0984. ROYAL AIR SERVICE, INC., P.O. BOX 15184, DULUTH, MN 55815; 877-359-4754. THE ISLE ROYALE LINE, INC. P.O. BOX 24, COPPER HARBOR, MI 49918; 906-4437.

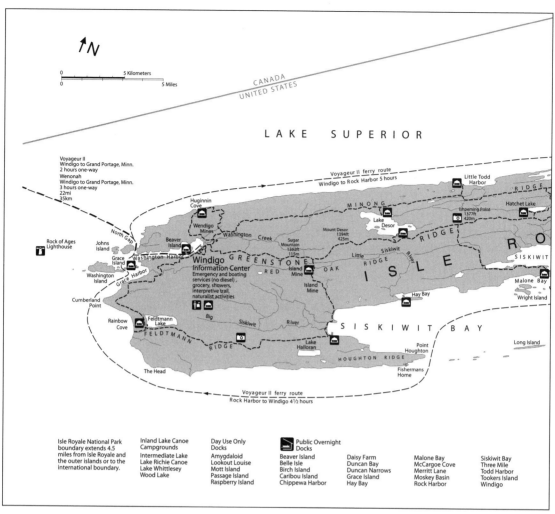

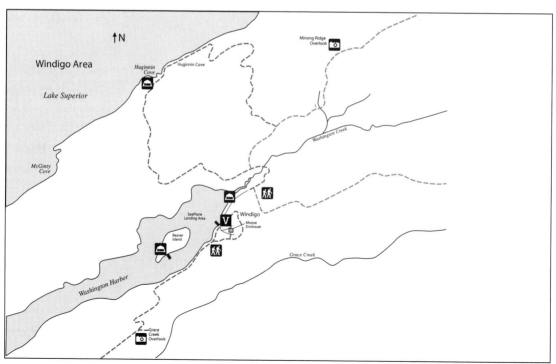

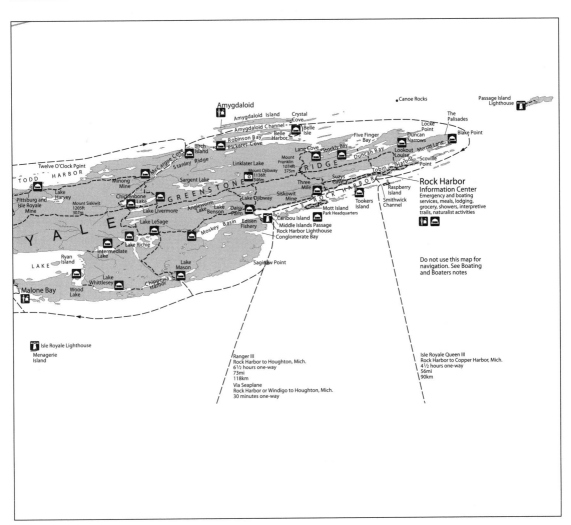

Canoe Rocks

Passage Island
Lighthouse

Amygdaloid

Amygdaloid Island
Crystal
Cove
Amygdaloid Channel
Belle
Robinson Bay
Belle Isle
Harbor
Pickerel Cove
Birch
Island
McCargoe Cove
Stanley Ridge
Twelve O'Clock Point
Linklater Lake
Lake Cove
Stockly Bay
Duncan Bay
Five Finger
Bay
Locke
Point
The
Palisades
Duncan
Narrows
Merritt Lane
Blake Point

TODD HARBOR
Minong
Mine
Sargent Lake
Mount Franklin
1074ft
375m
Mount Ojibway
1136ft
346m
GREENSTONE RIDGE
Lookout
Louise
Scoville
Point

Lake
Harvey
Pittsburg and
Isle Royale
Mine
Chickenbone
Lake
Mount Siskiwit
1205ft
307m
Lake Livermore
Lake LeSage
Angleworm
Lake
Lake
Benson
Siskiwit
Mine
Lake Ojibway
Daisy
Farm
Moskey Basin
Three
Mile
Suzys
Cave
Mott Island
Park Headquarters
Tookers
Island
ROCK HARBOR
Tobin
Harbor
Raspberry
Island
Smithwick
Channel

Rock Harbor
Information Center
Emergency and boating
services, meals, lodging,
grocery, showers, interpretive
trails, naturalist activities

YALE LAKE
Ryan
Island
Intermediate
Lake
Lake Richie
Edisen
Fishery
Caribou Island
Middle Islands Passage
Rock Harbor Lighthouse
Conglomerate Bay
Saginaw Point

Malone Bay
Wood
Lake
Lake
Whittlesey
Chippewa
Harbor
Lake
Mason

Isle Royale Lighthouse
Menagerie
Island

Do not use this map for
navigation. See Boating
and Boaters notes

Ranger III
Rock Harbor to Houghton, Mich.
6½ hours one-way
73mi
118km
Via Seaplane
Rock Harbor or Windigo to Houghton, Mich.
30 minutes one-way

Isle Royale Queen III
Rock Harbor to Copper Harbor, Mich.
4½ hours one-way
56mi
90km

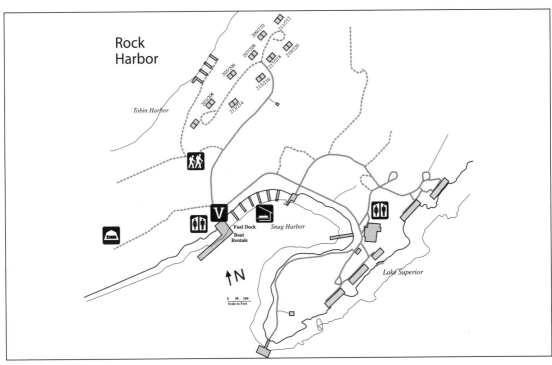

Rock
Harbor

Tobin Harbor

203/204
205/206
207/208
209/210
211/212
213/214
215/216
217/218
219/220

Fuel Dock
Boat
Rentals
Snug Harbor

Lake Superior

N

0   50   100
Scale in Feet

Appendix A
ACCOMMODATIONS & ACTIVITIES

Park by Alphabet	1	2	3	4	5	6	7	8	9	10	11	12	None
Agate Falls Scenic Site													•
Albert E. Sleeper	•		•									•	
Algonac State Park	•					•	•					•	
Aloha State Park	•					•							
Bald Mountain Recreation Area				•									
Baraga State Park	•		•			•	•						
Bay City Recreation Area	•		•									•	
Bewabic State Park	•						•						
Bond Falls Scenic Site													•
Brighton Recreation Area	•	•		•						•		•	
Brimley State Park	•		•									•	
Burt Lake State Park	•		•			•						•	
Cambridge Junction Historic State Park													•
Charles Mears State Park	•												
Cheboygan State Park	•			•			•					•	
Clear Lake State Park	•		•									•	
Coldwater State Park													•
Colonial Michilimackinac Historic State Park													•
Craig Lake State Park		•		•			•						
Dodge Brothers No. 4 State Park													•
Duck Lake State Park													•
F.J. McLain State Park	•		•	•	•								
Father Marquette National Memorial and Museum													•
Fayette Historic State Park						•					•		
Fisherman's Island Park		•											
Fort Custer Recreation Area	•		•	•	•							•	
Fort Wilkins Historic State Park	•		•									•	
Grand Haven State Park	•				•								
Grand Mere State Park													•
Harrisville State Park	•		•										
Hart-Montague Bicycle Trail State Park													•
Hartwick Pines State Park	•			•	•							•	
Highland Recreation Area				•						•		•	
Holland State Park	•				•								

Park by Alphabet	🚐	⛺	🏢	🏠	♿	◺	⛺	≈	⚠	🚤	▱	⛰	None
Holly Recreation Area	●		●	●	●	●						●	
Indian Lake State Park	●		●		●	●	●					●	
Interlochen State Park	●	●	●		●		●		●			●	
Ionia State Park	●		●		●					●		●	
Island Lake Recreation Area				●				●				●	
Isle Royale National Park		●											
J.W. Wells State Park	●			●	●								
Kal-Haven Trail State Park													●
Keweenaw National Historic Park													●
Lake Gogebic State Park	●					●							
Lake Hudson Recreation Area						●							
Lakelands Trail State Park													●
Lakeport State Park	●		●									●	
Laughing Whitefish Falls Scenic Site													●
Leelanau State Park		●	●									●	
Ludington State Park	●		●		●							●	
Mackinac Island State Park													●
Maybury State Park												●	
Metamora-Hadley Recreation Area	●		●										
Mill Creek Historic State Park													●
Mitchell State Park	●		●		●								
Muskallonge Lake State Park	●												
Muskegon State Park	●		●									●	
Negwegon State Park													●
Newaygo State Park		●											
North Higgins Lake State Park	●		●										
Old Mackinac Point Lighthouse													●
Onaway State Park	●												
Orchard Beach State Park	●		●										
Ortonville Recreation Area										●			
Otsego State Park	●		●		●								
P.H. Hoeft State Park	●		●									●	
P.J. Hoffmaster State Park	●											●	
Palms Book State Park													●
Petoskey State Park	●		●									●	
Pictured Rocks National Lakeshore		●			●								
Pinckney Recreation Area	●	●					●						
Pontiac Lake Recreation Area	●									●		●	
Porcupine Mountains Wilderness State Park	●	●		●			●					●	
Port Crescent State Park	●		●	●									

1	2	3	4	5	6	7	8	9	10	11	12	13	14	15	16	17	18	19	20	21	22	23	24
•	•	•		•	•		•	•		•	•		•	•	•	•		•		•			
		•					•	•		•	•		•	•	•	•	•		•	•			
		•		•			•	•		•			•	•	•	•		•					
•	•	•	•	•	•	•	•	•	•	•			•	•	•	•		•		•			
•	•			•	•		•	•		•			•	•	•	•	•	•	•	•			•
			•				•	•	•	•	•					•				•		•
				•			•	•		•			•	•	•	•	•		•				
•		•	•		•			•					•					•					•
							•		•							•							
		•			•		•	•		•			•	•	•	•	•		•				
		•			•		•			•			•	•	•		•		•				
•			•		•			•					•					•					
								•		•			•	•	•	•	•		•				
			•		•	•		•					•			•						•	•
	•			•		•	•	•		•		•	•	•	•	•		•					
•	•	•		•	•	•	•	•	•	•	•	•	•	•	•	•		•	•	•	•		•
•	•					•	•			•						•			•				
•			•		•		•	•					•	•	•	•			•				
	•	•		•	•		•			•			•	•	•	•	•		•		•		•
	•						•	•		•			•			•				•		•	•
		•		•			•	•		•			•	•	•	•	•	•	•	•	•		•
		•			•		•	•		•			•			•	•	•	•				
	•			•			•	•		•			•	•	•	•			•				
							•		•				•						•				•
	•	•		•			•						•			•	•		•				
•		•			•		•	•		•			•	•	•	•		•	•				
						•			•							•			•				
		•			•		•	•					•	•	•	•			•				
		•			•		•	•					•	•	•	•			•				
•		•	•		•		•	•		•			•	•	•	•		•	•				
		•			•		•	•					•	•	•	•			•				
•					•		•	•		•			•	•	•	•			•				
	•				•			•		•			•	•	•	•	•		•	•		•	
													•			•							
•					•			•					•			•	•		•				
•		•			•		•	•	•		•		•		•			•				•	•
•		•	•	•	•		•	•		•	•		•	•	•	•		•		•			•
•	•	•	•		•		•	•		•	•		•	•	•	•		•	•	•			•
•	•	•		•	•		•	•		•	•		•	•	•	•	•		•	•	•	•	•
	•				•		•	•		•	•		•	•	•	•			•				•

Park by Alphabet	🚐	🛏	🏠	⛺	🏡	⛵	⛺	🌊	⚠	🥾	🏚	ΛΛ	None
Proud Lake Recreation Area	●		●									●	
Rifle River Recreation Area	●	●		●								●	
Sanilac Historic Site													●
Saugatuck Dunes State Park													●
Seven Lakes State Park	●				●								
Silver Lake State Park	●				●								
Sleeping Bear Dunes National Lakeshore	●	●		●								●	
Sleepy Hollow State Park	●											●	
South Higgins Lake State Park	●		●										
Sterling State Park	●				●								
Straits State Park	●		●				●					●	
Sturgeon Point Scenic Site													●
Tahquamenon Falls State Park	●						●						
Tawas Point State Park	●		●		●								
Thompson's Harbor State Park													●
Traverse City State Park	●		●								●		
Tri-Centennial State Park										●			
Twin Lakes State Park	●		●										
Van Buren State Park	●											●	
Van Buren Trail State Park													●
Van Riper State Park	●	●	●	●	●								
Wagner Falls Scenic Site													●
Walter J. Hayes State Park	●		●		●								
Warren Dunes State Park	●	●	●									●	
Warren Woods State Park													●
Waterloo Recreation Area	●	●		●	●					●		●	
W.C. Wetzel State Park													●
White Pine Trail State Park													●
Wilderness State Park	●	●		●								●	
Wilson State Park	●		●			●						●	
Yankee Springs State Park	●	●			●					●			
Young State Park	●		●		●								

![ΛΛ] **Parks with Organizational Campgrounds**
Organizational campgrounds are available to organized youth groups, including schools, church groups or scouts and vary greatly in facilities and services. Descriptions of organized campgrounds do not appear in the text and lay outside the scope of this book. If your group is interested in booking an organizational campground you should contact the specific park and ask for details. If possible, a personal visit is recommended before booking.

🚲	🐦	🛶	🐴	🛶	⛷	🎿	🐟	🥾	⚙	🎯	🚶	🪂	🔍	🏕	⛺	🛝	📷	🚤	🏹	🏊	V	🌊	🔭
•	•	•	•	•	•		•	•		•	•		•	•	•	•			•		•		
•	•	•		•	•		•	•		•	•		•	•	•	•	•	•			•		•
					•		•	•															
					•			•					•	•	•		•				•		•
•	•	•		•	•		•	•		•			•	•	•	•			•		•		
	•						•	•	•	•	•	•	•		•						•		
•					•		•	•	•	•	•	•		•			•	•	•		•	•	
•	•	•	•	•	•		•	•		•	•		•	•	•	•			•		•		
		•			•		•	•		•			•	•	•	•	•				•		•
•	•	•			•		•	•			•		•	•	•	•	•				•		•
							•	•		•				•			•	•	•		•		•
					•		•	•			•						•				•		•
•		•			•		•			•	•		•	•	•	•	•	•			•		•
•	•				•		•	•	•		•	•	•	•			•				•		•
					•		•	•		•						•					•		•
•				•			•	•			•	•		•			•				•		
					•					•			•	•		•					•		
•		•		•			•	•					•	•	•	•	•	•			•		
							•	•			•	•	•	•	•	•					•		
•				•			•											•			•		
•	•	•		•			•	•		•	•		•	•	•	•	•				•		•
							•									•				•			
	•	•		•			•			•			•	•	•	•			•		•		
	•			•			•		•				•	•	•	•			•				•
	•			•			•						•			•							
•	•	•	•	•			•	•		•	•		•	•	•	•			•		•	•	•
				•			•		•										•				
•				•			•												•				
•	•	•		•			•	•		•	•		•	•		•	•	•	•		•		
				•			•			•	•	•	•	•		•	•		•				
•	•	•	•		•		•	•		•	•		•	•	•	•			•		•		•
	•	•		•			•	•		•			•	•		•	•		•				

L*odges*

Presently, there are lodges at seven state parks with more expected soon. Essentially, the lodges are remodeled, former homes of park managers. They are usually set off by themselves away from campgrounds and other park facilities.

All have modern kitchens with refrigerators, stoves, microwave ovens, pots and pans, and tableware. Towels and bed linen are provided. Most have generous, well-maintained yards with lawn furniture, grills, and a fire ring. There is no daily maid service, and guests are expected to clean and leave the lodge ready for the next occupants. No smoking or pets are allowed.

The lodges are open year round. The fluctuation in the daily rates reflects the difference in mid-week prices and those charged for weekend and holiday stays. Call the park to inquire about availability and renting.

Mears Lake Lodge sleeps eight in two sets of bunk beds, a queen, and one full bed. It features two bathrooms, a family room, and a washer and dryer. The house backs up to a sand dune and lies a short walk from the beach. Nightly rates: $162 – $195; weekly rate: $1,200. Call 231-869-2051.

Twin Lakes Lodge is nestled in the woods and gives immediately access to the Bill Nichols Multi-Use Trail that passes through the park. It sleeps eight in three bedrooms and has one-and-a-half baths and a family room. Nightly rates only: $135 – $170. Call 906-482-0278.

Grand Haven Lodge is a 1,600 square foot ranch with three bedrooms and two baths that sleeps eight. Downtown Grand Haven lies within easy walking distance. Nightly rates: $210 – $225; weekly rate: $1,500. Call 616-847-1309.

Bay Stone Lodge in J.W. Wells State Park was built in the 1940s by the Civilian Conservation Corp. The striking, two-story stone house features hand-hewn beams, hardwood floors, a great room, two full baths, screened porch, and a stone fireplace. It sleeps twelve. Nightly rates: $150 – $170; weekly rate: $1,090. Call 906-863-9747.

Fayette Cottage at Fayette Historic State Park is a neat, shipshape little home with one bath and a galley kitchen. It sleeps ten. It is tucked into the woods just off the park entrance road and within walking distance of the historic village. A two-night minimum stay is required on Friday and Saturday nights. Nightly rates: $100 – $125; weekly rate: $750. Call 906-644-2603.

Bear Lake Lodge, in Highland Recreation Area, comes with a rowboat and the home's large yard slopes down to the lake from which it takes its name. It sleeps six in two bedrooms. Nightly rates: $80 – $90; weekly rate: $580. Call 248-889-3760.

Porcupine Mountains Lodge was built in 1945. The log and stone home sleeps twelve and features cedar log beds in addition to other hand-crafted furniture, maple flooring, knotty pine paneling, a stone fireplace, and a view of Lake Superior through a 16-foot picture window. It also has one-and-a-half baths and a laundry room. Weekly rate only: $1,225. Call 906-885-5272.

Index

Reader's Log
Notes and Memories

About the Author

Tom Powers

I retired from the Flint Public Library in 1999, after 31 years of very rewarding work, in order to devote the appropriate amount of time that writing, reading, traveling, grandchildren, procrastination, nature, and hockey so richly deserve.

My previous books include, Natural Michigan, Michigan in Quotes, Audubon Guide to the National Wildlife Refuges: Northern Midwest, Great Birding in the Great Lakes, and Michigan Rogues, Desperados & Cutthroats.

Among my other stellar achievements is the creation of the world's first Mime Radio Show and the Julia A. Moore Poetry Festival, which honored America's worst poet. I steadfastly deny the Mime Radio Show was in anyway instrumental in the radio station's demise.

Barbara, my wife of 42 years; our two children and their spouses; and five grandchildren are a constant source of joy.

As always, once a book is published it is out of date. Camping and admission prices will change and new services will be added before a new edition finds its way to print. Keeping up with our state park system is like trying to roll an egg uphill with your nose, it needs constant attention. Until we meet again I'll be keeping my nose to the shell.